FITZROVIA
THE OTHER SIDE OF
OXFORD STREET

FITZROVIA

THE OTHER SIDE OF
OXFORD STREET
A SOCIAL HISTORY 1900–1950

ANN BASU

Front cover image: The Middlesex Infirmary in the 1930s, housed in the former Strand Union workhouse buildings in Cleveland Street (Reproduced with permission from UCLH arts and heritage, UCLH NHS Foundation Trust)

Front cover inset: Author's great-grandfather, Gershon Simkovitch (later Harris), with two of his daughters, Debbie and Mary. (Personal photograph reproduced by Erik Ros)

Back: A domestic tailoring workshop in the early twentieth century (Reproduced with kind permission of the Jewish Museum, London) First published 2019

The History Press
The Mill, Brimscombe Port
Stroud, Gloucestershire, GL5 2QG
www.thehistorypress.co.uk

British Library Cataloguing in Publication Data.
A catalogue record for this book is available from the British Library.

ISBN 978 0 7509 8790 5

Typesetting and origination by The History Press
Printed and bound in Great Britain by TJ International Ltd

Contents

Acknowledgements

I would like to express my warm thanks and gratitude to everyone who helped and supported me throughout the writing of this book. Many thanks to Nicholas Bailey who wrote the foreword, and to all who read and commented on the manuscript at various stages, especially Fiona May, Fiona Pettit, Louise Gallagher, Mike Pentelow and Portia Barnett-Herrin. A special thank you to Mike Pentelow for patiently replying to all my research enquiries and for sending me interesting relevant news items.

I'm very grateful to Dan Bates for all his support in launching the book. Grateful thanks also to Erik Ros for his vital help with photographing the book illustrations. And I greatly appreciate the contribution of Nicola Guy and the team at The History Press.

Thank you to all the archivists and librarians who helped in my research: Tudor Allen and his team at Camden Local Studies Library, Julie Tancell at the Carpenter's Company, and the staff at Westminster Archives Centre, London Metropolitan Archives, the National Archives at Kew, University College Hospital (UCLH) Archives, the John Lewis Heritage Centre, the Transport Museum Library, the Women's Library, the BBC Archive, Birkbeck College Library and the British Library.

I owe a big debt of love and gratitude to my mother, and my uncle and aunts: her twin brother, Abraham (Ubba) and her sisters, Cissie and Esther. Their experiences and anecdotes were the basis of my interest in the working lives of Fitzrovia, and in the place itself. I'm profoundly grateful to Henry Harris, my mother's cousin, with whom I have had many lively and rewarding conversations about his and my mother's childhood past.

My thanks to all present and former residents of Fitzrovia whose voices speak within the book. Special thanks to Simon John, who wrote to me in detail about his father's experiences as a policeman based at Tottenham Court Road.

Lastly, as always, my family's love and support has been indispensable. Dipak, Jay, Laura, Tamara, Erik, Alita and Asha: I dedicate this book to you.

Foreword

Take any neighbourhood in any major city and the chances are that a little research will reveal layers of history that help to define its character in the present day. Fitzrovia is one such area, which has developed over three centuries to have one of London's most varied and fascinating histories.

As historians such as Peter Ackroyd record, much of inner and central London evolved as a complex mixture of places of work, living and entertainment, and the interaction between these activities created neighbourhoods with a strong sense of place and their own unique identity. For London, it was only after the Blitz with its subsequent slum clearance and redevelopment, and the globalisation of production and consumption, that these close interrelationships began to unravel.

In the eighteenth century, urban development was largely carried out by the great estates owned by aristocratic landlords, and Fitzrovia was no exception to this. Yet, while the Bedford Estate to the east and the Cavendish-Harley Estate to the west managed to maintain substantial control over the use and repair of their properties, the Southampton (Fitzroy) Estate soon lost interest well before the first round of leases began to expire in the mid to late nineteenth century. It is not entirely clear why this happened, but it meant that the property around Fitzroy Square was sold off and soon became subdivided into cheap workshops and rooming houses.

Virginia Woolf and her brother Adrian were going against the social grain by taking rooms in Fitzroy Square in 1907, since families of wealth and influence were rapidly moving westwards into Marylebone and the new suburbs of the time such as Belgravia and Bayswater. Fitzrovia, therefore, became fertile ground for the manufacture of furniture and clothing, which involved many different crafts and trades often carried out by people working in their own homes. The availability of housing, albeit generally cramped and with few facilities, and work opportunities attracted refugees from Europe and a significant Jewish population. One of the main motivations for writing this book was because Ann's own ancestors were Jewish clothing workers who were living in Howland Street until 1938.

As this book makes clear, the name 'Fitzrovia' is a relatively recent invention generally ascribed to Tom Driberg, a *Daily Express* journalist, often to be found propping up the bar in the Fitzroy Tavern in the 1940s. It had always been the haunt of artists, writers and musicians because of the proximity to the Slade School of Art and the Queen's Hall and because of the availability of cheap lodgings and studio space. The 'bohemian' tendencies of many of the more celebrated residents led E. Beresford Chancellor to call it 'London's Old Latin Quarter' and this soon became the dominant image of the area. In fact, it was only in the 1970s that local community groups began to use 'Fitzrovia' in defining the locality and this was gradually adopted by the City of Westminster and the London Borough of Camden. But Fitzrovia as an artistic and cultural Bohemia is only part of the story.

Ann argues throughout the book that Fitzrovia has always had an 'edge-land quality' and is often defined as being on the 'other side' of Oxford Street that is clearly different from Soho. This theme runs throughout the book and is still apparent today. Fitzrovia is different from its neighbours, Soho, Marylebone and Bloomsbury, and is itself on the 'edge' of two very old parishes and divided between two newer London boroughs.

It is also different in that it became a major centre for the manufacture of furniture and clothing, not so much for the aristocracy but for the growing middle classes. Methods of production represented an early form of 'just-in-time delivery'. Pianos and furniture were assembled in the area for shops such as Maple's in Tottenham Court Road. For the major Oxford Street stores, ladies' clothing – the 'mantle and costume trade' – was made up in workshops and at home in order to deliver multiple stock so that the demand for ever-changing fashions could be satisfied with minimum delay. Long-term residents may remember the rails of the latest fashions being wheeled down the street to Peter Robinson or Bourne & Hollingsworth from the workshops around Mortimer Street and Eastcastle Street.

As Ann makes clear, the written sources on this vast workforce of skilled tradesmen and women are very limited. Amazingly, John Lewis' archive had never before been asked for information on the cutters and seamstresses who made up the garments in its store, and as Ann notes, this 'evokes invisibility and therefore also workers' powerlessness and voicelessness'.

While the garment and furniture industries have gone global, new industries and activities, such as design, media, advertising and digital services have moved into Fitzrovia.

Ann's book adds greatly to our knowledge about the ordinary lives of residents and their struggle against poverty and overcrowding. She also devotes several chapters to Fitzrovia's proud history at the vanguard of the growth of trade unions, and the growing interest in public health and political protest which extended well into the twentieth century. Thus, a combination of personal family history and in-depth research makes this book a fascinating read and an important contribution to the history of one of London's most characterful neighbourhoods.

Nick Bailey
Fitzrovia

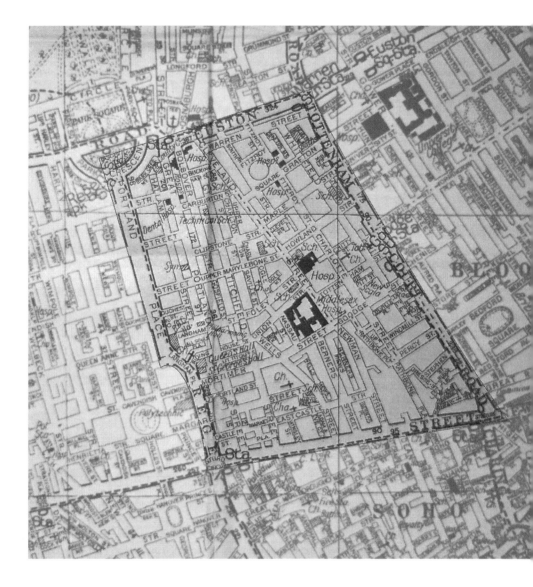

Map of the Borough of Saint Pancras dated 1934, highlighting the Fitzrovia area. (Camden Local Studies and Archives Centre: photograph by Erik Ros)

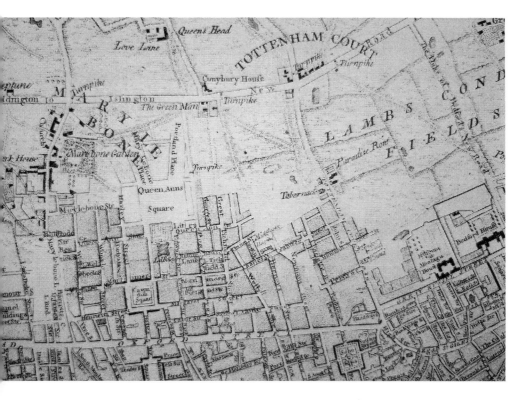

Roque's Map of London, 1769, detail showing the urban development of Fitzrovia. (Camden Local Studies and Archives Centre: photograph by Erik Ros)

Fitzrovia, the Other Side of Oxford Street

This book explores the distinctive place of Fitzrovia and its working people in the story of London, at a time of enormous change between 1900 and the end of the Second World War. It is the first work to be wholly focused on the daily activities and experiences of Fitzrovia's working population rather than on the select group of artists and writers known as the 'Fitzrovians' that famously included Dylan Thomas.

Fitzrovia, situated on the north side of Oxford Street – the other side of the street from Soho, to the south – was home to my mother's family of Jewish tailors before the Second World War. They were foreign immigrants, like many of Fitzrovia's working people who came from all over Europe and beyond. This is one important reason why Fitzrovia has always fascinated me.

Fitzrovia was, and is, many sided. In the nineteenth and twentieth centuries it was often publicly characterised by dark visions of an unruly nameless borderland contaminated with crime, deceit, poverty and sickness. However, other views have revealed its vigour and ability to harness change triumphantly and reinvent itself.

Fitzrovia never really fitted into the affluent West End, although this is perhaps now changing as it becomes ever more gentrified. At the same time it adjoins the West End in ways that make its exact boundaries hard to determine. Its edge-land quality, and the constant sense of movement conjured up by its changing populations and its fluid borders, has generated a sense of excitement in me from when I was a child.

Fitzrovia has always seemed, to some extent, unknown territory. It was connected to my feeling that my family's history was a bit mysterious, its origins being in places like Poland and Belarus, whose own boundaries, I discovered, had shifted over the years and centuries. From a young age I've been wondering and imagining what daily life in pre-war Fitzrovia was like, particularly for its many immigrant families, like my mother's family.

This family connection is one important reason why the book focuses on the period 1900–50. My matrilineal ties to Fitzrovia – 'around Tottenham Court Road', as my mother called it – began and ended within this timespan. But the other compelling reason for my interest in this historical period is that it brought major economic and social changes which affected Fitzrovia in numerous ways.

Transport and public health, work and leisure, and even food habits, were all transformed as underground trains came to central London; the car industry took root in and around Great Portland Street; the women's outerwear trade swept into the locality; the two local boroughs of St Pancras and St Marylebone became healthcare pioneers; new entertainments like cinema and radio came in, and cafe life, centred on Tottenham Court Road and Charlotte Street, became a leisure pastime for the working classes. Indeed, there's a good case for saying that the years 1900–50, momentous as they were for those who lived and worked on 'the other side' of Oxford Street, were the most interesting historically for Fitzrovia.

Why call the book *The Other Side of Oxford Street*? The reason is, I was intrigued by finding out that some West End Jews in Soho referred to Fitzrovia's Jews as coming from 'the Other Side' of Oxford Street. In fact, the idea that Oxford Street had an 'other side' in communal terms, began with local Jewish communities. It immediately begs the question, 'the other side of what?' There are several possible answers.

For those Jews who lived in Soho, south of Oxford Street, 'the Other Side' meant the area on the north side of Oxford Street: somewhere a little beyond their centrally located West End habitation. But the Jewish residents of Fitzrovia, in their turn, thought of Soho as 'the Other Side'. These groups of early twentieth-century Jews, separated by the barrier of Oxford Street, which was Fitzrovia's southern boundary, did in fact think of themselves as separate communities, and it was a matter of note when a member of one community married someone in the other community. Some of their comments about, and explanations of, this division between almost identical communities appear in the book.

This idiosyncratic sense of place also indicates a perception of separateness, shared by many other Londoners, between Fitzrovia and the West End. However, Oxford Street's Fitzrovia border hasn't always been fixed in people's minds, since the label 'Soho' has also embraced Fitzrovia at times in the past. These shifting relationships between Fitzrovia and Soho begin to illustrate the difficulty of firmly anchoring Fitzrovia within London, either geographically or imaginatively.

And there are yet more 'Other Sides' to Fitzrovia. Euston Road, lying at the opposite end of Tottenham Court Road, forms Fitzrovia's northern boundary. It is a formidable barrier that maintains Fitzrovia's place in Zone One of central London, but it is not an unchallengeable barrier. Euston Road was originally constructed in the mid-eighteenth century to define the northern edge of London itself; so, from here, the 'Other Side' takes on another meaning. To someone living north of the Euston Road, in Camden Town, Kings Cross or Kentish Town, which were all outlying districts of London in the nineteenth century, 'the Other Side' of the Euston Road would signify somewhere definitively belonging to the centre of the city, with all the changes in status that entailed. From this perspective, Fitzrovia, in the city centre but not central in the same way as the West End and Mayfair, still remained ambiguous.

This ambiguity about Fitzrovia's situation has persisted; so that, at one and the same time, Fitzrovia might be 'beyond the fringe' to a West Ender while being at the heart of London in the eyes of other Londoners. It is this constant wavering, and its oscillation between centre and margin, that has characterised Fitzrovia and is a source of fascination for me. And its western and eastern edges are even more fluid than its northern and southern boundaries, as we will discover.

In many-faceted Fitzrovia, 'the Other Side' can also mean the other side of the story: the voices of working-class people that have, relatively speaking, been unheard when narratives of Fitzrovia have been written. Just as the place name 'Fitzrovia' was a post-war invention of the 'Fitzrovians', obscuring previous names for this tiny but vital part of London, so has the story of the area's ordinary residents also been obscured by their fame. This book is an attempt at redressing the balance.

Family Ties and Fitzrovia

Until 1938, my mother, her parents and siblings occupied rooms in a house in Howland Street, before being rehoused by the council due to the planned demolition of their home in preparation for the building of the Museum telephone exchange. In 1965, the exchange itself was demolished and its site became part of the footprint of the Post Office Tower, today's British Telecom (BT) Tower. I was 13 years old when the Post Office Tower opened, and knowing that my family had this old connection to what almost immediately became one of London's best-known landmarks only heightened Fitzrovia's attraction for me. My lifelong preoccupation has matured into the commitment entailed in writing this book, when my mother, her parents, aunts and uncles, sisters, brother and all those family members who lived in and knew the area intimately are now sadly gone.

My mother's cousin, Henry Harris, aged 89, is my only living familial link with Fitzrovia as it existed in the first half of the twentieth century. Henry, as a child who lived in north London but frequently visited Fitzrovia, always thought of it with pleasure, associated as it was with family fun together with my mother, Becky, and her twin brother, 'Ubba'. He vividly remembers two venues constantly visited by local children: the Sphere and the Tatler news theatres, which both used to show an irresistible one-hour rolling programme of news and cartoons. He and his cousins used to entrench themselves at one of these cinemas for the day, until dug out by a paternal search party. To Henry, these cinemas were never thought of by their proper names but as the '*Sphera*' and the '*Tatteler*', the variants used by his Uncle Isaac, my mother's father. In Yiddish, '*Tatteler*' means 'little Daddy', a phrase whose context does much to sum up the indelible connections between persons and places.

This book is a social history of Fitzrovia's working people, not a history of my family. Yet, it's been inspired by family connections and this family story is in many ways a typical tale of its place and time, so it's worth a brief telling. My mother's family arrived on the Other Side of Oxford Street in 1895, so I've been told, in the years of peak migration before the passing of the Aliens Act of 1905. My great-grandparents, Gershon and Rebecca Simkovitch, and their six children, Debbie, Esther, Mary, my grandmother Annie, Maurice and Julius, all born between 1883 and 1894, originated from Schlov in Belarus. Before very long, they had changed their name from Simkovitch to Harris. The story is that Gershon, who worked – crossed-legged on a table in traditional tailor style – with English-born tailors who couldn't get their tongues around Gershon or Simkovitch and called him 'Harry', adapted this nickname to create a new surname.

The Simkovitches-turned-Harrises almost certainly began their British lives in Fitzrovia: neither official records nor the family memory store provides evidence of their having lived elsewhere in London beforehand. In the 1911 census year, Gershon's widow, Rebecca, after whom my mother was named, was residing at 1 Little Titchfield Street with her eldest daughter Debbie, my grandmother Annie, and her two sons. Mary, who was then married, lived close by at 162 Great Titchfield Street, while Esther lived with her husband at 17 Phoenix Street, off Charing Cross Road in Soho, across the gulf of Oxford Street.

In 1911, the unmarried daughters, Debbie and Annie, and Mary and Esther's husbands, Isaac Zalkin and Sussman Katchoff, were all making a living in the clothing trade. Isaac and Sussman were listed as ladies' tailors, while Debbie and Annie were 'tailoresses'. As we'll discover, Fitzrovia at that time played a key part in the women's clothing trade, so the family was in the right place. Like thousands of Russian and Polish Jews, they were escaping poverty and persecution to remake their lives, choosing their location to suit their skills, their pockets and perhaps their feeling for community.

Annie, my grandmother, married Isaac Coshever, also a tailor, in 1912. Isaac might have come from the East End, to judge from a postcard sent to family members by his brother, Sydney, made from a photograph taken in a Whitechapel studio. But, if Isaac came from East London, he probably made the move west by the time he married, or shortly afterwards.

When my mother and her twin brother Abraham were born in 1926, the Coshevers, with Rebecca Harris and her two sons, were living at 48–50 Howland Street. These two houses had the same owner, a landlady whom my mother dreaded as a child. My mother remembered her grandmother Rebecca as an elderly lady whom she called 'Bubbe'; she died when my mother was about 8 years old. Annie's sister Mary and her husband, Isaac, later opened a tailoring workshop across the road from them, at No. 41 Howland Street.

The Coshevers, with their four children – Cecelia, nicknamed Cissie, Esther, Abraham, called Ubba, and my mother, Becky – were to remain in Howland Street until they were rehoused in Anson Road, Tufnell Park in 1938, shortly before the Second World War began. In the 1950s and 1960s, we lived close to my aunts Cissie and Esther in Tufnell Park, and some of my happiest memories are of walking around the corner to visit them every Saturday afternoon in Anson Road, where a generously spread table, large helpings of affection and attention, and *Juke Box Jury* on the telly were waiting for me.

What's in a Name? The Multiple Identities of Fitzrovia and its People.

'Fitzrovia' as a district name had crystallised by the 1940s, through the agency of a small set of writers, intellectuals and well-educated, sometimes well-off, hangers-on circulating around certain pubs and cafes. The area became famed for its associations with Nina Hamnett, Dylan Thomas, Julian Maclaren-Ross and a number of others. The attractive qualities arising from its working-class, diverse and changing communities played an essential part in drawing the

'Fitzrovia' crowd into the area between the time of the First World War and the 1950s.

The 'Fitzrovia' label came from the Fitzroy Tavern, at the junction of Charlotte Street and Windmill Street. According to Sally Fiber, the granddaughter and daughter of the publicans, it originated with Tom Driberg, the politician and reporter who wrote the 'William Hickey' social column in the *Daily Express* and used to frequent her grandparents' pub.[1]

As I've explained, the aim of this book is not to attempt another recreation of this type of Fitzrovian life, as Hugh David's *The Fitzrovians* and Julian Maclaren-Ross' *Memoirs of the Forties* have already so memorably done. Rather, it's to celebrate and commemorate the unnoted working-class inhabitants who lived the first fifty years of the twentieth century in those same streets. Yet, I think it's well worth asking at this point – what caused the celebrated 'Fitzrovian' crowd to brush with the area's working population in its streets and pubs? Why was a certain group of writers, artists and intellectuals so fascinated by the locality of Tottenham Court Road at this historical juncture?

Part of the answer must lie in Fitzrovia's exciting remoteness to middle- and upper-class eyes: the sense that, if Soho was on the fringe of the fashionable West End, then the area north of Oxford Street was on the fringe of the fringe, if not quite in the wastelands of Camden Town and Kentish Town where only a very few outside the working classes had penetrated. It was Fitzrovia's in-betweenness, its liminality, that must have appealed: the feeling of being at, but not quite beyond, the boundaries of the known city that gave Fitzrovia its desired exclusiveness to those searching for something 'other'. In some ways, it was like the more familiar Soho; indeed, 'Fitzrovia' was a fluid concept to some Fitzrovians who regularly blurred Fitzrovia and Soho together as they crossed and re-crossed Oxford Street in search of another congenial cafe or pub.

Yet, north of Oxford Street, the air was perhaps that bit rougher, a little more 'edgy' – more working class, in fact. As Hugh David says, 'Bohemia had become Fitzrovia by throwing in its lot with the working classes for whom "laughing, talking and regaling themselves with beer" were far more important than luncheons in Belgrave Square'.[2] And Soho itself was already becoming passé to this Bohemian set, a haunt of the unfashionable: it was only there to 'feed the drab suburban population of London on the spree', according to Thomas Burke as early as 1915.[3]

Another major attraction must have been the 'exotic' atmosphere picked up on by Hugh David and praised in Nancy Cunard's poetic lines about the Eiffel Tower Restaurant in Charlotte Street, filled with 'strange-sounding languages of diverse men'.[4] As we'll see again and again, Fitzrovia's being home to numerous immigrant communities shaped its nature, helping to transform it in some contemporary minds into the 'Fitzrovia' of the 1920s, 1930s and 1940s. What David calls 'the true heart of Fitzrovia' was 'at about that point where Charlotte Street, Percy Street, Rathbone Street (originally Upper Rathbone Place) and Rathbone Place itself meet in what could almost be a corner of Montparnasse'.[5] This neighbourhood was, as we'll see in Chapter 1, densely inhabited by immigrants, not only, or even mainly, French, despite the 'Montparnasse' label, but also German, Austrian, Swiss, Italian and others. It was also home to many Jews from Russia and elsewhere.

The noted Eiffel Tower Restaurant was owned and run by Rudolf Stulik, a Viennese Jew who was the soul of the place and who created at the Eiffel Tower a 'liaison between power and art' by attracting members of the Establishment and intellectuals.[6] Stulik drew his visitors into a romantic intimacy that almost formed their circle for them and that made them, for a while, very loyal to the restaurant.

When, later in the 1920s, the Fitzroy Tavern started to become the favoured meeting place of wits and writers, they had been attracted by another Jewish-run enterprise. Judah Kleinfeld and his son-in-law, Charles Allchild, were the spirits behind the Fitzroy Tavern, transforming it from a moribund business during the First World War into perhaps *the* social and intellectual centre of the area between the 1930s and 1950s. Again, a great draw of the Fitzroy Tavern was its social variety, with local regulars drinking along with known names. It became their 'ultimate bolthole' away from upper-class 'tourists'.[7] It was joined by the Wheatsheaf and one or two other local hostelries which served the 'Fitzrovia Set'. At its extremes, this attraction became a love of what Dylan Thomas, perhaps self-referentially, called 'sordidness', possibly where the neighbourhood was linked with petty criminality and prostitution.

One material difference existed between the pubs of Fitzrovia and those of Soho: the Soho pubs closed half an hour later because they were across the borough boundary in Westminster and benefited from West End opening hours. So, 'late-night raiding parties' would cross Oxford Street in search of an extra half an hour's drinking to the south.[8] That was 'the only reason we ever crossed Oxford Street' away from Fitzrovia, according to Lord Killanin's foreword to *The Fitzroy*.

But, despite its allure to this set, Fitzrovia was not a place name that most contemporary residents would have known. Hugh David himself, one of the key chroniclers of Fitzrovia, states about the Bohemian group of Fitzrovians, 'It is wholly fanciful to imagine their having any real effect upon the economic life of the district'. In fact, David talks of their 'general invisibility' at the time.[9]

The writer Alan Ross wrote in the introduction to Julian Maclaren-Ross' *Memoirs of the Forties* that the Fitzrovia of the Fitzrovia Set was based just on 'a handful of pubs within a few hundred yards of each other just north of Oxford Street' and, at the time the Fitzrovians were active, their impact, and the impact of the 'Fitzrovia' brand, was limited.[10] My mother's family, for example, never spoke of 'Fitzrovia'. Their place of reference for their old neighbourhood was 'Tottenham Court Road', and my relative, Henry Harris, still thinks of it in these terms. Indeed, most people living around Tottenham Court Road at that time wouldn't have recognised the 'Fitzrovians' or a place called 'Fitzrovia', however powerful the allure of the label is today.

The mass of its inhabitants had settled in this neighbourhood not due to any fascination with Fitzrovia but because the locality offered them work. This included large amounts of casual work in catering and the small-scale production of goods, especially clothing and furniture: work eagerly sought after by recent arrivals to London, despite the low pay. The area also offered lower rents than surrounding areas and, crucially, an atmosphere accepting of foreigners in a locality where many different communities mingled.

Additionally, around the turn of the twentieth century and for several decades afterwards, the fast-paced economic and social changes washing through this locale meant huge new employment opportunities for those willing to grab them. And many did, especially among the first and second-generation immigrant communities. The Other Side of Oxford Street was the place to be for many of those who had new lives to build and chances to take, whether those opportunities came from the growth in the women's clothing industry which pushed the centre of women's outerwear production into the area, or the new media of film, radio and television that saw the locality becoming a home to a large cluster of cinemas and the BBC, or broadened options for the mass public in food and eating out that made Tottenham Court Road and Charlotte Street into growing hubs of cafe life.

Readers must have gathered by now that this patch of London – like some of its past inhabitants including the Simkovitch/Harrises of my family – had, and still has, multiple identities that have made it extremely difficult to capture its essence in one name. Sources on London, writing more than sixty or seventy years ago, not only go for 'Tottenham Court Road' but also describe it more vaguely as 'Marylebone' or 'St Pancras', reflecting how it was administratively split between these two parishes and, later, two separate boroughs. Additionally, another label, 'North Soho', seems to have come from the clothing trade, emerging when its nineteenth-century West End centre in Soho later expanded northwards across Oxford Street. In fact, as I have said, some older sources make little or no distinction between the areas directly north and south of Oxford Street, naming them both 'Soho'.

This confusion continued even into the 1940s when 'Fitzrovia' was gaining currency in some circles. Julian Maclaren-Ross, a key member of the Fitzrovia Set in the 1940s and 1950s, records that the poet and publisher Tambimuttu – a born chancer according to Maclaren-Ross – had introduced him to Fitzrovia and knew the area as 'Fitzrovia'. But, warning Maclaren-Ross not to spend too much time there for fear of its distractions, Tambimuttu surprisingly labels it 'Soho', saying, 'If you get Sohoitis … you will stay there always day and night and get no work done ever … You have been warned.'[11] Maclaren-Ross makes it clear that Tambimuttu is speaking of Fitzrovia, north of Oxford Street, when he mentions 'Sohoitis'. Even more confusingly, Maclaren-Ross reports this conversation as taking place, *not* in Fitzrovia, but in Old Compton Street, Soho – yet Tambimuttu believes Old Compton Street itself not to be a site of the Sohoitis disease! Their discussion leads on to even more possibilities where the place is concerned:

'Is this Fitzrovia?' [asks Maclaren-Ross]
'No, Old Compton Street, Soho. You are safer here.'
'Why won't I get Sohoitis in Soho? Or is Fitzrovia in Soho too?'
'Fitzrovia's really a part of Bloomsbury,' said a supporter called Steven. 'But the borough is St Pancras.'
'Sounds complicated,' I said, whereupon he asked me if I came from Streatham.[12]

I've faced the difficulties of naming this place with its many aliases – Fitzrovia, Tottenham Court Road, Soho, North Soho, Marylebone and St Pancras – by acceding to the popularisation of 'Fitzrovia' as the accepted place label and – most of the time – calling it Fitzrovia. Most Londoners, and many readers from outside London, now recognise the Fitzrovia place name and can visualise its position within the city, and reviving older usages seems bound to create confusion that might detract from what this book has to say about the place. At the same time, my arguments about the area's fluid, ambiguous, edge-land qualities make it permissible, I think, to summon up these qualities now and again in the alternative names that evoke its history, whether Tottenham Court Road, North Soho or 'the Other Side' of Oxford Street.

It is this multiple dose of 'other-sidedness' that has helped to make Fitzrovia a home for some of the varied, often marginal, activities that have given it its unique character. A major way of seeing otherness there was in terms of foreignness and immigration, and to progress through the chapters is to under-stand how important to the place are first and second-generation immigrants, economically, socially and politically. It is the continuous motion and flow of people and ideas across the boundaries of place that has kept Fitzrovia alive and continues to keep it alive in our imaginations.

Unruly Beginnings

The urban history of Fitzrovia has lasted around 250 years and, before moving on, this history needs to be summarised. It's important to understand that Fitzrovia's status as an area of ambiguity, diversity and constant flow within London was built into it from the time it first came into existence. This was largely due to the lack of planning in its development, which originated in its fragmented land ownership and the various leaseholders' handing over of development to small speculative builders.

Nick Bailey has given a comprehensive account of the ownership and the development process of the eastern side of Fitzrovia, between Cleveland Street and Tottenham Court Road, in his book *Fitzrovia* (1981). Even more detailed sources are available at the British History website.[13] I'm not attempting to replicate that detail here but will briefly describe the latter stages in the move-ment towards urbanisation north of Oxford Street.

At the beginning of the eighteenth century, Tottenham Court Road, little more than a trackway, was outside the city and was already a byword for unru-liness. The Tottenham Fair in the fields there irritated the authorities because of its licentiousness and was not suppressed until urbanisation was complete. As Bailey points out, there were no buildings in Tottenham Court Road in 1720, but London was growing rapidly at this time and in 1756 the New Road, renamed Euston Road in 1857, was approved.

Today, the Euston Road marks the northern boundary of Zone One, the centremost zone on the London Underground, and it also delimits the con-gestion zone of central London which drivers have to pay to enter. But it was originally created not only to facilitate transport from west to east across the city but also to establish a northern edge to the metropolis, past which no urban development should take place. The futility of this idea was shown in the speed with which building jumped this barrier, so that, by the beginning of the nineteenth century, construction – mostly of low quality – was stretching northwards into Somers Town and then to Camden and Kentish Towns. In the early decades of the nineteenth century, the road between the urban settlement of Camden Town and the hamlet of Kentish Town was seen as being 'the haunt of footpads'.[14]

The New Road, by 1800, could therefore be viewed as a barrier dividing the undesirable, mostly working-class and jerry-built northern outer localities from 'proper' London, where development had now filled up the inner limits of the highway. Late into the nineteenth century, the urban areas immediately to the north of the Euston Road barrier were home to numerous criminal gangs, though planned suburbs further away from the centre were respectable enough to attract the middle class and some of the more prosperous working class. By the last decades of the nineteenth century, the headlong expansion of the city with its concentrations of poorer inhabitants, both outside the centre and in central pockets just inside Euston Road, meant 'the prevailing imaginary landscape of London [had changed] from one that was geographically bounded to one whose boundaries were indiscriminately and dangerously transgressed'.[15] The 'danger' of Fitzrovia included its being a home for reformers and radicals of many persuasions from the time it first became urbanised in the eighteenth century.

To the political and legal authorities, and a public already concerned with immorality and criminality within the West End and its environs, fears of an additional criminal influx from the north gave force to views of the Euston Road as a hygienic barrier, separating what had become the central area of the city from possible contaminating influences outside of it. Fitzrovia, though mostly poor and undesirable, was firmly within this retaining barrier. It was situated on the Other (inner) Side of Euston Road just as it was located on the Other Side of Oxford Street and the centre of the West End.

Nonetheless, London's residents and its media retained memories of Tottenham Court Road's unsavoury past and feared that its old reputation for disorder would continue to prove true. And it did continue: in a feature on 19 November 1949, the *Picture Post* reporter, Hilde Marchant, would label Warren Street, with its used car market, as possessing 'a split personality'. The market's position at what she called 'the northernmost boundary of Soho' had, she says, led to the market attracting 'a fair amount of gutter garbage from the hinterland'. This vague 'hinterland' could have included both the rough stretches north of Euston Road and the seamy southern reaches of Soho, with the 'gutter garbage' flowing back and forth in a contaminating, boundary-obliterating stream, continuously polluting the streets of Fitzrovia.

Fitzrovia was therefore designated as an edge-land right from the start. This suspect in-between zone of London never, apart perhaps from the Fitzroy

Square development at the northern end, acquired the solid social status of the Bloomsbury developments just to its east. As Bailey explains:

> The gentry had already moved westwards, and it is quite likely that many leaseholders were subletting their houses soon after they were completed. By the middle of the nineteenth century large parts of Fitzrovia were densely occupied by the poor and immigrant families, while the ground floors were converted to shops and workrooms.[16]

As we'll see throughout the book, Fitzrovia's shifty reputation lingered well into the twentieth century, shaping its story in numerous ways.

The Growth of Fitzrovia

Firstly, a note about how I've defined Fitzrovia – reputationally and topologically one of the shiftiest of London localities – as a geographical space. Some sources have taken the western boundary of Fitzrovia to be Cleveland Street: these include Nick Bailey's *Fitzrovia* (1981) and the Camden History Society's *Streets of Bloomsbury and Fitzrovia* (1997). However, I've claimed a wider western reach for Fitzrovia, as some other authorities do.

The City of Westminster's 'Conservation Audit of East Marylebone' (No. 33), for example, places East Marylebone within Fitzrovia: East Marylebone being an area stretching from Cleveland Street and Newman Street in the east almost as far as Langham Place and Portland Place in the west. This book regards Portland Place and Langham Place as forming the western boundary of Fitzrovia, giving Great Titchfield Street, an important street that was the heart of the women's outerwear trade, its proper status within the locality and avoiding arbitrarily cutting the smaller cross-streets of Fitzrovia in two. And, unlike Bailey, but in line with recent official sources, I've treated Tottenham Court Road as being the eastern boundary of Fitzrovia (see the map of Fitzrovia on page 12).

Making the question of boundaries still more complicated and consequential, Fitzrovia was administratively split between the council authorities of St Pancras, which covered, roughly speaking, the eastern part of Fitzrovia, and that of St Marylebone, which covered the western portion. The administrative boundary ran, and still runs, down Cleveland Street for part of the way, then meanders to the south-east down to the bottom of Hanway Street and the junction of Oxford Street and Tottenham Court Road. Nowadays, Camden and Westminster are the relevant local boroughs. Local people sometimes felt powerful consequences from this split, as we'll see in the chapter on healthcare.

Urban development began from the 1720s at Fitzrovia's southern edge, near Oxford Street, where there was a little field of 2½ acres that straddled the parishes of St Marylebone and St Pancras. The field became the site of Hanway Street, Pettys Court, John's Court and Hanway Place. The street and place get their name from Thomas Hanway, a Commissioner of the Royal Navy. There was also a nearby strip of land that became the site of Rathbone Place and Rathbone Street, named after the Rathbones who owned this land from the seventeenth century up to the time it was built on. There was a waterworks covering the west side of Charlotte Street and most of Rathbone Street in the 1760s, consisting of the windmill which gave the name to Windmill Street.

The rest of the St Pancras portion of Fitzrovia, from Tottenham Court Road in the east stretching northwards to the Euston Road and westwards to the boundary of St Marylebone, was divided into four fields: Crab Tree Field, Walnut Tree Field, Culver Close and Home Field (see the historical map on page 12).

Crab Tree Field and Walnut Tree Field became the Hassell and Goodge estates. They belonged to the manor of Tottenhall and extended as far north as the present Chitty Street. In 1717 the landholder, John Dudley, leased part of it to John Hassell, a brewer of St Giles. Mr Hassell spent £1,000 over three years on developing the site, centred on what became Gresse Street.

The progress of building along Tottenham Court Road is indicated by the petition to the Commissioners of Sewers from John Hassell and others in 1720, to clear the common sewer that was choked with dirt. In 1752, with the south side of Gresse Street already having been built on, the Hassell estate was sold in lots. The planning of Gresse Street, Stephen Street and Tudor Place suggests that it was not developed uniformly with the Tottenham Court Road frontage: this piecemeal development was typical of most of the area except for Fitzroy Square.

The rest of Crab Tree and Walnut Tree Fields, comprising 16 acres, was leased by John Dudley for 111 years to William Beresford, a yeoman. The northern boundary of the estate ran westward from Tottenham Court Road just north of Whitfield's Tabernacle, through Chitty Street, to Cleveland Street on the south side of the old workhouse belonging to the parish of St Paul, Covent Garden, later to become the Strand Workhouse. At this time, the only buildings on this land were the Crab Tree Alehouse, just north of Percy Street, and one more house a bit further north still. William Beresford's widow, Ann, married

John Goodge, a carpenter, who started the development on this land. By the time he died in 1748, the pace of building had increased: economic times were favourable, and London's population was booming. He left his estate to his two nephews, Francis and William Goodge, who continued the building.

Fitzrovia was now rapidly becoming an urban area. Francis and William Goodge planned and developed Goodge Street as a major shopping street, more than half of which was completed by 1770. The building developments led to an Act of Parliament in 1768 under which commissioners were appointed to provide for paving and lighting, etc. Bailey notes, 'The first occupants of Goodge Street in the 1760s included carpenters, oil men, tallow chandlers, undertakers, soap and candle makers, ironmongers, tobacconists and a silk dyer – trades associated with Fitzrovia for at least 200 years.'[17]

This was not a development for aristocrats and the affluent professional classes, then, but for the artisans, small business people and workers who gave Tottenham Court Road and its western offshoots its energetic and industrious flavour, if not much glamour. By the 1770s, Fitzrovia up to Chitty Street was almost fully developed.

Immediately north of Crab Tree and Walnut Tree Fields was farmland: Culver Meadow, a field of 12 acres belonging to the Bedford Estate. Its northern boundary lay just south of Maple Street. The Duchess of Bedford granted Culver Meadow to Robert Palmer in 1776. This was obviously part of a plan to develop the land, as in 1777 the Duchess leased it for ninety-nine years to William Gowing, in Palmer's name. Building then started over the whole area comprising Howland Street, Russell Place (now part of Fitzroy Street), parts of Cleveland Street and Whitfield Street, and was completed by 1791.

Home Field, north of Culver Meadow, extended from the present Maple Street up to Euston Road, the northern edge of Fitzrovia. At this time, it belonged to Charles Fitzroy, who was created Lord Southampton in 1780. Fitzroy had to pay a perpetual rent charge to Dr Richard Browne, the holder of the Tottenhall prebend in St Paul's, and his successors. The payment allowed Lord Southampton to develop a valuable estate on Home Field – Fitzroy Square, partly designed by the famed architects, the Adam brothers. It was built in stages, with the eastern and southern sides of the square being begun in 1792 and 1794 and the other two sides completed at the beginning of the nineteenth century. Horwood's *Map of London* of 1799 shows that, apart from the missing two sides of the square plus sections of Cleveland and Conway Streets, the St Pancras part of Fitzrovia was completely built up.

The St Marylebone portion of Fitzrovia fell under different ownership: it was part of two separate estates, Cavendish and Berners. The first phase of its development was in the second half of the eighteenth century when St Marylebone was becoming part of the newly fashionable West End of London.

The Cavendish development started after Lady Henrietta Cavendish, who inherited the land from the Duke of Newcastle, married Edward Harley, Earl of Oxford and Mortimer. Harley decided to develop the estate in imitation of the great squares and streets south of Oxford Street. In 1717, John Prince, the earl's surveyor, began to lay out the Cavendish Estate, beginning with Cavendish Square – to the west of Fitzrovia – and the surrounding streets, some of which became part of Fitzrovia. It was a scheme intended to attract the wealthy noblemen of the period and, as with the eastern part of Fitzrovia, many of the area's current street names derive from these initial residents and investors.

The eastern side of the St Marylebone part of Fitzrovia belonged to the Berners family. The Berners Estate developments, begun in 1746, centred on Newman Street and Berners Street with a frontage along Oxford Street from Wells Street to Rathbone Place. The Middlesex Hospital was first built in Windmill Street in 1745 for sick and lame patients, moving north to Marylebone Fields, as the site was then called, in 1755. The land was leased from Charles Berners for ninety-nine years and subscriptions sought from the gentry, nobility and other influential people for the hospital's construction.

The area around Berners Street and Rathbone Street became part of London's new artistic quarter with many writers and musicians taking up residence in the area. Famous names include Thomas de Quincy, Henry Fuseli and Charles Wesley. The landmark of All Saints Church in Margaret Street, opposite BBC Broadcasting House, was built by William Butterfield in the mid-nineteenth century.

By the beginning of the nineteenth century the street pattern and development of East Marylebone was virtually complete and, as in the streets east of Cleveland Street, most of its occupants belonged to the working classes rather than the top drawer.

Fitzrovia's Story Continues

This book begins with an overview of how foreign immigration – which peaked at the beginning of our timespan, the 1900s – shaped Fitzrovia. Chapter 2 then explores how the movements of people around, and sometimes under, its streets were facilitated and controlled by new transport developments. It looks at some of the spaces that its inhabitants claimed for themselves within its urban fabric, such as the wartime shelters in Tottenham Court Road and Goodge Street Tube stations, and the Warren Street second-hand street car market.

Chapter 3, on public health and healthcare, will show how place, politics and public health became intertwined when Fitzrovia's two local councils were implementing major new public health regulations, and how changing concerns about public health affected residents' daily lives.

Chapters 4 and 5 will examine aspects of residents' daily work: how the area's long-established furniture industry weathered the first half of the twentieth century and changing contemporary tastes in design; and the rise of the women's clothing industry and its effects on workers, as the mass trade in women's outerwear swelled from its West End base in Soho to engulf the north side of Oxford Street.

In Chapter 6 we'll see how and why political protest manifested itself in local streets, workers' clubs and houses, and explore Fitzrovia's communist and anarchist traditions and their links with European migrants.

The last two chapters will explore working people's use of their leisure time, and how some of them found new work opportunities, in the dawning age of mass entertainment; and find out about residents' changing, often European-influenced, experiences of eating out, from buying goods on local market stalls to enjoying local cuisine in Charlotte Street and having tea at the magnificent Lyons' Corner House in Tottenham Court Road.

Each chapter will explore the qualities of otherness, in-betweenness and mutability that infused everyday life in Fitzrovia. I have explored Fitzrovia's changeful place within London with the help of works on urban spaces such as Richard Sennett's *Flesh and Stone* (1994) and Fran Tonkiss' *Space, the City and Social Theory* (2005). Jerry White's major works, *London in the Nineteenth Century* (2008) and *London in the Twentieth Century* (2002), were of great help to me in understanding the wider political and economic background, as were many others, from the writings of Henry Mayhew to Gareth Stedman Jones. Judith R. Walkowitz's substantial work on Soho, *Nights Out: Life in Cosmopolitan London* (2012), besides being a goldmine for sources in some areas of my research, has done much to help me clarify similarities and differences in perceptions of Fitzrovia and Soho – each distinct in character but twinned with each other across Oxford Street – and to appreciate the periodic formation and breaking down of the boundaries between the two neighbourhoods. My book is in the grain of writers such as Jerry White, Gillian Tindall, Gerry Black and Sarah Wise, who have chronicled the daily life and struggles of London's working-class citizens. I have also written out of admiration for the works of London chroniclers and mythmakers such as Peter Ackroyd and Iain Sinclair.

This book also aims to continue, and in places makes direct use of, the valuable work carried out on collecting oral recollections of Fitzrovia, such as Gerry Black's *Living Up West* (1994) based on interviews with Jewish people born in the West End before the Second World War, and Jacobsen & Leonard's *Ebb and Flow in Fitzrovia* (2010), consisting of interviews with old residents collected by the Fitzrovia Neighbourhood Association, as well as oral source material in the Jewish Museum and the British Library. My own recollected family stories and anecdotes add their own mite to this trove of memories, as do the very kindly offered and gratefully received recollections of a very few remaining pre-war residents of Fitzrovia who have personally contacted me.

Myths of place have shaped and shaded perceptions of Fitzrovia and its population. The modern name, 'Fitzrovia', has fixed the place's identity, but obscured other, older, sometimes contentious ones. This book aims to bring them into the light.

A Home for Outsiders:
Immigrants in Fitzrovia

Fitzrovia in the 1900s was crammed with outsiders. Few places in London accommodated so great and varied an immigrant population. In fact, the majority originated from outside Great Britain.

The number of immigrants to London as a whole had been rapidly growing since the 1880s. According to Jerry White, by 1911 there were 176,000 foreign-born Londoners and the city was at a peak of diversity.[1] Much of the increase, in Fitzrovia as elsewhere in London, was due to Jewish immigration from central and eastern Europe, spurred by intensifying hostility towards Jews in their home countries. But, as we'll see, Fitzrovia was also home to many different immigrant families like mine, from across Europe and elsewhere.

However, from 1905 the first national restrictions on immigration had been put in place with the Aliens Act. The new Act had a deterrent effect, even on those who weren't restricted by the new law, and numbers entering the country fell drastically by 1910. Then, from 1914, the First World War slashed London's big German population, which never recovered despite an influx of refugees from Nazi rule from 1933 on. By the mid-1920s, 'London [had] half closed her door to the foreigner'.[2] Finally, cultural assimilation had diluted London's ethnic mix by the 1920s. Yet Fitzrovia continued to be a welcoming home to strangers right through to the 1950s.

A Census Snapshot of Fitzrovia's Immigrant Families

The National Census provides some fascinating insights into who lived in Fitzrovia and where they came from. This chapter will begin by taking a snapshot view of who lived in one block of streets in the area, using the

1911 census. At this time, immigration had peaked. The block I chose to survey was the one that surrounded the infirmary in Cleveland Street, formerly the Strand Union Workhouse, located at the heart of Fitzrovia.

The workhouse infirmary was feared by many people. In 1911 it still catered for pauper inmates, although it later became part of the Middlesex Hospital. It inserted itself into the lives of the surrounding poor families in a way that was often harsh and unwelcome. The three-winged Cleveland Street Infirmary, as part of the workhouse system, could be viewed not only as caring for the destitute sick but also as a mechanism of social control; at the same time, it was central to the community.

Which families lived in the shadow of this rather bleak institution? I looked at all the census-listed households in the four streets that formed a block around the infirmary, only surveying the sections of those streets that directly encircled the building. The streets were: Howland Street on the infirmary's northern edge, where my mother was later to be born and grow up; Cleveland Street on its western side; Tottenham Street on its south side; and Charlotte Street to its east.

On this block, numerous foreign settlers from across western Europe and Russia were to be found. Americans, Scandinavians, Turks, Algerians and South Africans also lived here. This sample area contains sections of two of Fitzrovia's busier streets, Charlotte Street and Cleveland Street, as well as parts of quieter Howland Street and Tottenham Street. The block is also centrally placed within Fitzrovia. Consequently, we can perhaps assume that the evidence of high immigration figures we are about to see is typical of Fitzrovia as a whole and bears out the premise that directly north of Oxford Street there was a London hub of migration.

I was interested in finding out, from the total numbers of inhabitants listed in this block, who were first- and second-generation immigrants and where these settlers had been born. I also wanted information showing how they had moved around within the city to find a home. I tried to find out whether there was much intermarriage between immigrants and established residents. I looked at what types of work people did. And I compared the census with the *Post Office Directory* for 1911, to see how the people living at an address were involved with businesses or organisations listed as being at the same address, trying to show how immigrants might have contributed to the local economy.

The 1911 census showed the names of the heads and members of individual households; what the relationships were among them; their marital status, gender, age and year of birth; and occupations of those in employment. It was carried out on Sunday, 2 April, administered by census enumerators who were each responsible for about 200 households or as many as could be covered in a day. The enumerators collected forms that had been distributed to households a few days beforehand. They were usually filled in by heads of households (assumed for the most part to be male), sometimes with help from enumerators if residents were illiterate. The forms were supposed to state the details of everyone who would be sleeping at that address on that Sunday night, including night workers who were away working, and visitors. The enumerators checked the accuracy of returns.

There are many ways of analysing this information to produce vivid pictures of the local community, but at the same time these census portraits can never be completely accurate since the information is a snapshot of who was within doors at times that the census takers paid their visits. One finds gaps: sometimes household members are absent while sometimes visitors add greater numbers to a household.

There were occasionally momentous reasons for the missing information. In 1911, some Suffragettes boycotted the census and made sure they weren't recorded at home by staying out all night and avoiding census enumerators. Their slogan was, 'No vote, no census!'

Addresses also appear to be missing from the census record in our sample area around the infirmary, to judge by gaps in the house number sequence. Was no one in at the time, or was the building untenanted? For example, there should be eighteen separate addresses on the east side of Charlotte Street between Howland and Tottenham Streets, but only fourteen appear on the census record. Perhaps this is due to some of the many restaurants on Charlotte Street being closed on a Sunday night, but there is no way of filling the gaps for sure. Therefore, the record is necessarily incomplete, but it's more than substantial enough to represent how greatly Fitzrovia was made up of immigrant communities and to tell us some important things about how those communities lived together.

The houses around the infirmary were packed full of people. Most houses contained several households, of varying types: husbands and wives (sometimes widows or widowers) with their children; single residents; families with lodgers; and perhaps also servants or visitors. Fifteen residents per property was commonplace. In all, I counted 225 households lodged at ninety-two addresses directly around the infirmary. They sheltered a total of 766 adults and 246 children under 16. Then, as now, living space was in huge demand in central London and working people, recently arrived immigrants most of all, were probably in no position to be able to spread themselves. Whole families in one or two rooms were, it seems, the rule rather than the exception in this part of town, almost as much as in Whitechapel or Stepney.

Foreigners predominated among the 766 adults listed in our census sample. Only 268 inhabitants had been born in Britain, but it's worth noting that, of the British-born, roughly half (179) were born in London; in fact, the London-born made up the largest single grouping. About a third (fifty-eight) of these original Londoners could be called local as their birthplaces were in St Marylebone or St Pancras, the boroughs covering the western and eastern halves of Fitzrovia. Another thirty-one residents were born close by, across the divide of Oxford Street in Westminster. The exact locality of birth within London was often not specified, so these numbers may have been higher. So, we can see that there was still some continuity of presence in Fitzrovia along with an ever-changing flow of newcomers.

There was modest evidence of movement from East London to Fitzrovia, particularly of Jewish families. Eleven adults and twenty-three children had East End birthplaces such as Whitechapel or Shoreditch. Seventy-six residents came from elsewhere in England, while a few Scots (four), Irish (six) and Welsh (three) completed the British mix.

The rest were outsiders. German-born immigrants were the biggest category after Londoners, numbering 111. Russian or Russian-Polish incomers (eighty) were not far behind, trailed by the Swiss (sixty-nine). French and Austrians (fifty-three and forty-nine) were also a significant presence. A lesser number of Italians (eighteen) and a sprinkling of immigrants from nine other nations across Europe made up the rest of the community, joined by a few Americans, Danes, Swedes and Norwegians, two Algerians, a Maltese and a South African. It's a rich mixture, notable to our eyes for a complete absence of Asians and very few Africans – these would arrive in numbers in the great post-Second World War migrations.

It's clear that the adults living around the infirmary were mainly first-generation immigrants, but the children were different. Most of them were native born, while of second-generation immigrant heritage, so it seems that many immigrant parents had been living in this country for some time. Of the 246 children counted, 194 were London born. Of these, eighty-five were born in St Marylebone or St Pancras, while eighteen came from Westminster. As with the adults, the exact place of birth within London was frequently not recorded, so considerably more children could have been local. Another eight were born in England but not in London. Of the forty-four children born abroad, fifteen were listed as being born in Russia or Russian Poland and, given the history of migration at that time, were most probably from Jewish families. This was by far the largest category of the foreign-born children. Several others were German. Most of the rest were from France, Switzerland,

Belgium, Poland, Norway or South Africa. These birthplaces in most cases reflected their parents' place of birth. In five cases, no place of birth was recorded at all.

There weren't many signs of immigrant families living together exclusively with their own countrymen and women. The double house where my mother's family later lived, 48–50 Howland Street, is a good example of international mixing in 1911. It housed the Altman family from Russia, Carl Meyer from Germany and the Hartings, a German man married to a Norwegian woman with two Norwegian-born children, as well as several English residents, two of them born locally.

However, there were certain places where some nationalities did tend to cluster together. This is particularly true in Charlotte Street, where many of the houses contained mostly Swiss, German and Austrian residents. The reason was that they were mostly employees in Charlotte Street's hotels and numerous eating places: waiters, chefs and porters from the countries which dominated these occupations in Fitzrovia.

Mr and Mrs Harting were far from being the only mixed-nationality married couple here. I counted sixteen husbands and wives living around the infirmary where one party was foreign-born and one British-born. In virtually all these partnerships the wife was British. The only exception was Blanche Horner, a Frenchwoman married to the London-born Wecford Horner, and living with him at 70 Charlotte Street. The bulk of immigrants to London were men arriving on their own, so this finding is probably in line with the general trend. Where these men had families, they often came to join them later, but where the men were single, they were often much more likely to meet local British women rather than their countrywomen.

Making a Living

These immigrant communities had arrived to work in the city and make better lives for themselves and their families, their London-born children probably already becoming indistinguishable from the host population. So, what did the local immigrant population do for a living? What groups of workers called these full-to-bursting buildings home?

Tailoring, boot and shoemaking trades and the making of accessories were significantly the greatest lines of work, occupying 174 people in the block around the Cleveland Street Infirmary. These trades employed most of the eighty Russian and Russian-Polish residents who were mostly Jewish, along with some of the German and French, and of course English, population of the neighbourhood. This included a significant number of women and girls.

Some of these trades sound unusual today. Eva Crate, the 26-year-old daughter of a widow living at 43 Cleveland Street, was a pearl stringer. At 78 Charlotte Street, the St Pancras-born Eliza Lagne was an ostrich feather curler, presumably for the millinery trade. The English–French married couple, Wecford and Blanche Horner, were partners in making corsets. My mother, Rebecca Coshever, the daughter of Belorussian and Polish immigrants, was employed in millinery after she left school in 1940, until she decided that it wasn't for her and found a job at Boots, the chemist, instead.

A westward movement of Jewish families from the East End into Fitzrovia is detectable in this close-up local view of the 1911 census, probably due to developments in the clothing trades. The tailors' strike of 1889 was a stimulus to this move, with the destination first being Soho. The Reverend J.H. Cardwell, the vicar of St Anne's Parish in Soho, states:

> The tailors' strike was the cause of a considerable exodus of Israelites from Whitechapel to Soho. The increase in the number of Jewish residents may be gathered from the fact that whereas in 1891 there were very few Jewish children in St Anne's schools they now [in 1911] form 25 per cent of the scholars.[3]

The oral histories of former residents quoted below bear out this movement of Jewish families from east to west.

The rapid increase in clothing factories and workshops around Oxford Street by the turn of the twentieth century also spurred a move of businesses northwards from Soho to Fitzrovia in pursuit of space and cheaper rents. It pulled clothing workers with it and, again, this movement shows up in the 1911 census. The information from our sample block shows clear evidence of people moving from Westminster to Marylebone or St Pancras. Thirty-one adults born in Westminster, and their families, subsequently moved north of Oxford Street. At least some of these migrants across Oxford Street were tailors, such as the Simler family of 46 Cleveland Street: the father, Nathan Simler, was a tailor whose elder children also worked in the same trade or in the millinery trade. Census information like this is a testament to the attraction of the clothing trades for many new migrants to Fitzrovia.

Hotel and restaurant work such as cheffing and waitering was the second most common occupation, almost exclusively employing immigrants, who were usually from Germany, Switzerland, Austria, Italy or France. Charlotte

Street, where so much of the hotel and restaurant trade of the area was based, housed numerous such workers. Certain addresses there were obviously lodging houses for these staff, who presumably slept two or more to a room given the numbers of people listed. At 82 Charlotte Street, for example, Frau Lochinger kept apartments for at least twelve German and Italian waiters, all young single men in their twenties. Next door at 84 was the International Chefs' and Waiters' Society where many club and hotel staff are recorded as being present on census day. Down the road at 74 Charlotte Street, showing the strength of the Swiss presence, was the Schweitzerbund Swiss Club. The household here was headed by F. Bosshard, the steward and a licensed victual-ler from Zurich, while residents included Staneslas de Rotten, a fellow Swiss hotelier. We'll find out more about workers like these in Chapter 8.

After the tailoring and hospitality trades came various crafts and skilled trades apart from clothing, which I've grouped together for convenience. Fitzrovia's artisanal tradition is represented here by foreign woodworkers such as cabinetmakers. An Austrian, Frank Yellen, of 50 Tottenham Street, is a cabi-netmaker, while the Polish Isaac Bowman is, unusually, a boat maker, who lived along the street at No. 27.

But the rise of crafts and trades based on newer technologies is evident, too: Tottenham Street is also home to Frenchmen Maurice Levenson and Louis Barthelemy, who are both listed as mechanics. They probably worked in the emergent motor car trade that was soon to have a big impact on the area.

Another group of workers that stands out are cigarette makers: there are about a dozen of these on the block, including one of the few Turkish residents, Raphael Habif, of 24 Cleveland Street. At 30 Cleveland Street, the Warsaw-born cigarette maker, Henry Friede, was married to Mary, a tobacconist.

Domestics formed the next largest group of workers: cleaners, maids, cooks and general servants, often women. Where domestic staff served in a club or hotel there was a good chance they were immigrants, while some foreign-born women were also occupied in domestic service.

Labouring and manual trades made up the fifth grouping of occupations: carmen, porters, laundrywomen and general labourers, again with a contin-gent of foreign workers, some of whom were young, comparatively recently arrived and perhaps trying to work their way up, while others were older and possibly more settled in the work.

A smaller number of male and female residents did shop work, perhaps in the large shops and department stores nearby; but few first-generation foreign immigrants seemed to have made their living in this way. Most in our sample who worked as shop assistants were British-born, like Dolomars Gilchrist of

51 Howland Street, the 15-year-old Marylebone-born son of Russian-born parents, who was assistant to a hosier. This might have been because a high standard of spoken English was required by employers, and one can't rule out the possibility of discrimination in West End establishments with an affluent clientele where any obvious 'foreignness' could have been an unfavourable mark against a member of staff.

Some foreigners living around the infirmary opened their own small neighbourhood businesses, making an impact on the local economy. Comparing the 1911 census returns with the *Post Office Directory* at this time reveals a sprinkling of such enterprises, several concerned with the clothing trades and personal care. Most of these businesses were in Charlotte Street, one of Fitzrovia's busiest and most important streets. This is where Wecford and Blanche Horner had set up their corset shop, at No. 70. A couple of doors along at No. 66 was Solomon Herzfeld, a 'tailor, a gents outfitter' from Russia, while a Prague-born fellow tailor, Anthony Selix, had his home and workshop over the road at No. 77. More tailoring businesses set up by immigrants were close together in Howland Street: Israel Fisher's at No. 49 and A. Hartung's at No. 50. Another business concerned with personal appearance was that of Gustav W. Ruff, a German maker of hairdressers' sundries and manufacturer of razors at 97 Charlotte Street. Meanwhile, spouses F. and N. Zsinkovits ran a steam laundry, Madame Rose's Shirt and Collar Dressers, at 43 Howland Street.

Other businesses pursued by immigrants reflected the long local tradition of arts and artisanship. A Pole, Bolestas Raczynski of 79 Charlotte Street, gave lessons on the zither from home, while a French modeller and restorer, Jean Camboursin, lived – and also presumably worked – at Alfred A. Carpenter's decorative artists' shop at No. 64. At 56 Howland Street an Italian, Giovanni Delicata, had a wood carver's business, while his countryman, D. Arditti, ran an oriental goods and carpet shop at 24 Cleveland Street.

Hospitality and food businesses which, as we've seen, attracted many European workers, were also sometimes owned and run by foreign entrepreneurs. At 74 Charlotte Street, the Schweizerbund Swiss Club was the home of the Swiss hotelier, Staneslas de Rotten – perhaps an off-putting name for anyone intending to eat there! Not far away, at 32 Cleveland Street, was a confectioner, F. Santucci. Another popular food business, for German immigrants in particular, was butchery, although there are no examples in our sample census area. And, reflecting migration from within Britain, Fitzrovia had at least three Welsh dairies; we'll find out more about these later in the chapter.

Sometimes these small entrepreneurs Anglicised their names. A Bohemian tailor, listed in the 1910 *Post Office Directory* as Franz Germak, of 55 Cleveland

Street, had become Francis Sermak in the 1911 Census return. This might reflect a desire for integration, but it's also possible that, three years before the outbreak of the First World War, anti-German feeling may have been at least partly responsible for this change of a Germanic sounding name.

Professionals were few and far between in this crowded block around the infirmary, but those I found were mostly foreign born. The fragrantly named Hyacinth de Frettes, a French gentleman and Doctor of Medicine, resided at 43 Cleveland Street, while a German doctor, Adolph Hinz, lived at 33 Howland Street. We don't know whether they were practising their profession in the city, as the *Post Office Directory* for 1910 shows no sign of them working at those addresses. A few teachers were scattered in the locality as well. Besides the zither teacher, Mr Raczynski, there was a Hebrew teacher, Jacob Joseph Landau, of 54 Tottenham Street, and a teacher of art, Gilbert Cubitt, at 64 Charlotte Street. One or two residents were engaged in literary occupations: William Muller, listed as a writer, lodged at 46 Tottenham Street, and the German-born Paul Quosigk, of 45 Howland Street, was a journalist, one of two foreign correspondents who lived in the infirmary block. Only about a dozen professional people altogether lived on the block.

One last category of workers in this survey is of particular interest: stage performers and theatre workers, some of whom were probably employed at the Scala Theatre, located at the corner of Charlotte Street and Tottenham Street. Most of those listed in our sample block lived at 121 Charlotte Street at the Theatrical Mission & Home, which gave lodgings to women and girls to ensure that they didn't risk falling into disrespectability. A significant number of these performers were born outside England, in several cases in Ireland, like Katherine Mercer, a singer, or Scotland, like the actress Jean Hamilton. A very Scottish-sounding actress, Alice Mary Stuart, was in fact born in Paris. Elizabeth Kennedy, another actress, came from as far away as Natal, South Africa. In fact, almost all the theatrical performers at this address came from outside London, if not from outside Britain; this makes sense given that the mission must have concentrated on providing a home for women without family or connections in the capital.

It's worth emphasising once more that the degree of diversity in Fitzrovia evidenced in the block around the Cleveland Street Infirmary was unusual, even for cosmopolitan London. Remember that about two-thirds of adults on the block were foreigners and, even including their London-born children, the overall proportion of London-born residents in our census sample area was still under half of all residents. Compared with the rest of London this is exceptionally low. The proportion of London-born residents in inner London overall was about 65 per cent in 1901, rising to just over 70 per cent in 1920.

Very few parts of London matched Fitzrovia for diversity – Westminster was one that did, with a virtually identical proportion of London-born inhabitants in 1911, just below half.

Fitzrovia was uncharacteristic, also, in having fewer incomers from Ireland, Scotland and Wales than other parts of London, if indications from our sample census area are any guide. According to Jerry White in *London in the Twentieth Century*, 'The main reservoir of new Londoners in the first half of the twentieth century remained Ireland, as it had in the nineteenth century too'.[4]

Fitzrovia's small Welsh contingent did make an impact, though: Welsh dairy farmers often came to London to open dairies, and they did the same thing on the north side of Oxford Street. John Evans' beautifully blue-tiled dairy was opened in around 1916 at 35 Warren Street, according to Megan Hayes' history of Welsh dairies in London, *The London Milk Trail* (2015). Another dairy in Tottenham Street was kept by Dan and Getta Thomas. Charlotte Street had three dairymen at around this time: David John Richards at 21 Charlotte Street, David Henry Richards at 43–45 and George Williams at No. 65. A Welsh dairyman, David Davies, later to be Sir David Davies, became a Conservative MP and Mayor of St Pancras, 1912–22.

The 1911 census snapshot of more than 1,000 lives, young and old, all gazed upon by the infirmary, demonstrates how well Fitzrovia maintained its reputation as a haven for the outsiders who were drawn to this pocket of the capital city caught between the West End and its rougher northern reaches. We now need to put these lives in more context if we are to further understand the interaction of people and place at this time.

Fitzrovia's History of Immigration

As we can see, Fitzrovia by 1911 had a solid history of large-scale immigration and communal diversity. Hugh David sums up its singular character in *The Fitzrovians*:

> Well before 1883 … the district had been offering a haven to some at least of the tired, the poor and the huddled masses of Europe. By the first decade of this century Fitzroy Street and Fitzroy Square were at the heart of an area of London uniquely well used to the cosmopolitan lifestyle more commonly associated with the Latin quarters of other European capitals.[5]

E. Beresford Chancellor, in 1930, in fact called his book on the area *London's Old Latin Quarter*.

Jerry White, however, labels Soho – the area directly *south* of Oxford Street – as 'London's "cosmopolis"', invoking the magic and glamour of a quarter rich in clubs, theatres and restaurants – a hub of the night-time economy – as a magnet for foreigners.[6] But in Soho's northern counterpart – the Other Side of Oxford Street – the *daytime* streets were thronged with thousands of workers from the clothing, furniture and artisan trades, as well as the hotel, restaurant and many other businesses. Fitzrovia's daytime streets were perhaps not quite so exotically glamorous as Soho's night ones, but they were every bit as full of vitality and industry.

By 1900, growing numbers of Fitzrovians were Jewish. As V.D. Lipman records, the capital's Jewish population swelled from around 27,000 in 1858 to 35,000 in 1871 and 46,000 in 1882, due both to population increase and to migration.[7] This was even before the years of peak migration throughout the 1880s and 1890s. Adding to mid-century Jewish arrivals from the Netherlands was 'a steady stream' of Russian and Polish Jews. The Jewish Board of Guardians reported in 1872 that 'the poor Jews in England are now almost exclusively recruited from Poland', heralding the influxes to follow.[8] Some of these earlier nineteenth-century immigrants had already found their way to Fitzrovia, as the 1855 opening of the West End branch of the Great Synagogue in Portland Street testifies.

Henry Mayhew's *London Labour and the London Poor*, revised in 1861, outlines the ways in which the poorer mid-century Jewish arrivals made a living. If they possessed some financial means they might be wholesalers, or if not then street hawkers, in a variety of goods, '[W]atches and jewels, sponges – fruits, especially green fruits, such as oranges, lemons, grapes, walnuts, cocoa-nuts, &c., and dates among dried fruits – shells, tortoises, parrots and foreign birds, curiosities, ostrich feathers, snuffs, cigars, and pipes'.[9] Mayhew specifically mentions wholesale dealers in fruit, and notes that 'superior retail Jew fruiterers – some of whose shops are remarkable for the beauty of their fruit – are in … Oxford Street', as well as in Piccadilly, Cheapside and Covent Garden market.[10]

In those years, before the rise of ready-made clothing, the long-established and traditionally Jewish-dominated trade in old clothes occupied some immigrants; though this was a trade based mostly in the East End and it was spoken of as declining, even at this time. During the twenty years or so after the 1861 edition of *London Labour and the London Poor*, the ready-made clothing trade would become dominant, absorbing the bulk of the growing numbers of Jewish immigrants. The special importance of the women's outerwear trade to Fitzrovia will be examined in Chapter 5.

The Jewish presence was having more and more impact at the end of the nineteenth century and the first years of the twentieth. It has been estimated that there were around 15,000 Jews living in the West End and on both sides of Oxford Street in 1900, rising by 1925 to about 25,000. Numbers of the local Jewish community remained high throughout the 1930s. During these decades there was a significant increase in the proportion living north of Oxford Street and a reduction south of it.[11]

The German connection with Fitzrovia was also strong, including both Jews and non-Jews. According to Gerry Black, 'A strong German [Jewish] settlement centred around Goodge Street and Mortimer Street from 1877.'[12] The number of German restaurants and shops in Charlotte Street was such that it became known as '*Charlottenstrasse*'.[13] Fitzrovia's many German artisans were augmented, from the mid-nineteenth century, by communists escaping government crackdowns. The most famous, Karl Marx, lived in Soho, but some of his followers lodged in Fitzrovia. This included Marx's tailor, Friedrich Lessner, who lodged in Tottenham Court Road. Lessner worked in the English Labour movement and trade union politics his whole life, also co-founding the Independent Labour Party in 1893.[14] Unfortunately Marx often neglected to pay him.

Jerry White homes in on the importance of foreigners to London's tradition of political radicalism in the nineteenth century. He notes that French radicals, among others, went north of Oxford Street in preference to Soho:

> [After the Franco-Prussian War of 1870 and the Commune] these new arrivals marked a shift in the geography of French London. Many ex-communards settled in the streets between Oxford Street and Fitzroy Square, otherwise best known for its German community. They found Soho too much occupied by French prostitutes, who had moved there in the 1850s and 1860s. So 'to this day', remarked Adolphe Smith at the end of the century, 'we have the political foreign quarter in the Fitzroy square district, north of Oxford Street, and the non-political foreign quarter south of Oxford Street in the Soho Square district'.[15]

A vital part of German social life in the area was the *Verein*, the club for German workers. Its address kept changing, but by 1911, the year of our census survey sample, it was based at 107 Charlotte Street, where it's listed as 'The Communists' Working Men's Club and Institute', secretary Max Dittrich. We'll find out more about the political side of immigrant life in Chapter 6 on radicals in Fitzrovia.

Italians were later in arriving on the scene in Fitzrovia as their traditional centre in London was Holborn, where they had been established in numbers from the middle of the nineteenth century. Lucio Sponza attributes the Italians' spread out of Holborn to the slum demolition in this district that began in the 1850s.[16] Italians then began to be dispersed into St Pancras and Finsbury. Soon afterwards, with a growth in the catering trades favoured by Italians, there was a substantial increase in Italian immigration. Italians later became as famed throughout London for their domination of ice cream street selling as they had been in Victorian times for being street musicians.

Settling in Westminster, where many hotels and restaurants catered for Londoners and visitors to the city, Italians also fanned out to parts of Marylebone, including Fitzrovia, to carry on the same lines of work. Our 1911 census survey clearly shows this in the population of waiters and other catering workers centred on Charlotte Street. It's not surprising that eighteen Italians were found to be living in the block around the infirmary, given Charlotte Street's many eating establishments. Sponza also comments on the frequency of mixed marriages of Italian men to English women: there is one example in our census survey, of a couple living in Howland Street, John Pasotti from Milan, a restaurateur, and native-born Emma Pasotti who was listed as a 'waiter', most probably assisting in the same restaurant. Others like the Pasotti family also set up their own cafe or restaurant. The *St James's Gazette* observed that these Italian entrepreneurs 'remain behind the counter looking minutely after every detail until the last thing at night; and they will do this for years without a single day off'.[17]

One group of Italian heritage notable in Fitzrovia, the Ticinese, also made a big impact on the cafe and restaurant sector of the West End as a whole. They were Italian speakers from the southernmost Swiss canton of Ticino, bordering Italy. Driven by desperate economic times at home and facilitated by the opening of the Gotthard Tunnel in 1882, they flocked to London during the following two decades or so. Living often in conditions of great hardship, dozens of Ticinese waiters and cooks crowded together in accommodation above or near their workplaces. They worked long hours at their trade, in some cases creating highly successful businesses which transformed Londoners' experience of eating out. Chapter 8 will describe the contribution of these foreign arrivals to Fitzrovia's food and drink businesses.

All the above-mentioned groups of foreign immigrants were from Europe, which supplied the vast majority of newcomers to London. But, as we've seen, arrivals from other nations were scattered across the neighbourhood, from Scandinavia, America, Turkey, South Africa and elsewhere. What's missing in our sample block around the infirmary is an Indian presence (this period is, of course, decades before India was divided to create Pakistan and later

Bangladesh from the huge Indian subcontinent). But the sons of wealthy Indian families had already started to arrive from the mid-nineteenth century onwards and settle nearby as students, attending University College (UC) across the road in Bloomsbury. According to Rosina Visram, four Bengalis came to study medicine at UC in 1845, the first Indians to do so, two of them financed by Dwarkanath Tagore, Rabindranath Tagore's grandfather.[18] Others followed, with some having radical inclinations. By 1920 they were evidently numerous enough that a YMCA Indian Students Hostel was opened for them in Keppel Street, Bloomsbury, moving to Gower Street in 1923.

With both the UC and the YMCA hostel being situated just behind the east side of Tottenham Court Road, the streets of Fitzrovia must have seen some evidence of an Indian presence. And the rackety streets around Tottenham Court Road probably helped to foster official concerns over uncontrolled behaviour by some Indian students. Accusations of 'fast living' involving drink and English women had, indeed, brought about the setting up of the YMCA to regulate their reportedly wild behaviour. Fitzrovia must surely have played a part in furnishing the temptations that were feared by the authorities, perhaps for potentially threatening the racial status quo.

Immigration was an ongoing cause for concern in official quarters. The flow of immigrants into London during the 1880s and 1890s started to alarm the authorities and some members of the public, set as it was against a background of economic and social turbulence. The mid-1880s saw a severe trade depression with high unemployment. There was an ongoing housing crisis affecting working people to add to the distress. In such bleak conditions, the arrival of large numbers of Jews from Poland and Russia was viewed as greatly exacerbating the 'problem' posed by the working class for their social superiors. In the East End, civilisation teetered on the brink, if the evidence of social investigators like G.R. Sims (*The Bitter Cry of Outcast London*) and Beatrice Potter (later Webb) was to be believed: 'Respectability and culture have fled; the natural leaders of the working class have deserted their post; the lowest element sets the tone ... Alas! For the pitifulness of this ever recurring drama of low life ... bearing down to that bottomless pit of decaying life.'[19]

Ideas of the 'residuum' – a leftover, left-out class of irredeemables, almost subhuman and declining in health with each generation, frightened the middle classes. The condition of the poor became linked with theories of urban degeneration; and immigrants, many of whom were among the poorest inhabitants, became thought of as a toxic ingredient of the 'residuum'.

The political authorities and police also feared the influence of radical elements among the city's immigrant population in case it inflamed the artisan class – a substantial class in areas like Fitzrovia – and encouraged revolutionary insurrection at a time of increased unemployment and hardship. They thought these fears were coming true between 8 and 10 February 1886, when rioting, including shop-window breaking and robbery, followed a protest meeting at Trafalgar Square on the 8th. The protestors were unemployed dock and building workers, joined by members of the Social Democratic Federation who verbally attacked high unemployment under the Conservative government. The riot brushed Fitzrovia, as members of the crowd looted shops in Oxford Street and other West End businesses. *The Times* the next day declared, 'The West End was for a couple of hours in the hands of the mob.'

Tensions remained high on 9 February, though little took place except some gatherings in Trafalgar Square. But on the 10th, rumours were hysterically high over 'mobs' said to be on the march from Deptford and ready to attack. Tensions were such that the City and the West End were guarded, shops and government offices were closed, and troops were readied for deployment. The rumours themselves went some way towards causing a disturbance, drawing crowds at the Elephant and Castle to join the phantom 'mob'; they were eventually dispersed by the police. By the next morning public panic had finally subsided.

However, fears of revolutionary, rampaging mobs didn't disappear. The alien appearance of such events, and of the working-class poor as a whole, to the eyes of affluent citizens and politicians, meant that, in Michelle Allen's words, 'The riot … appear[ed] in the light of a foreign invasion, one that, moreover, seems to have permanently breached that imaginary dividing line between west and east [the wealthier London West End and its poorer East End]'.[20] In such an atmosphere, the presence of foreigners within the working class, often feared as radicals, revolutionaries and criminals, became a source of acute concern and a threat that had to be addressed. So, a Select Committee was appointed in 1888 to examine the question of immigration. It recommended in August 1889 that data on immigrants should be kept, and held out the possibility of future legislation limiting immigration.

During the 1890s unemployment rates were generally low and numbers of Jewish arrivals fell back. However, a Conservative Parliamentary Immigration Committee and an anti-alien lobby in Parliament generated a failed Aliens Bill of 1894, aiming to keep out destitute aliens and anarchists. There was opposition to such legislation from the Jewish community and from trade unions, although some trade unionists also favoured such an Act. The issue was sidelined for the rest of the 1890s but re-emerged in the 1900s with further Jewish influxes after Russian pogroms in 1903 and 1905, aided by shipping price wars making it cheaper for immigrants heading from Germany to America to go via England.

The diverse foreign communities of Fitzrovia never evoked the same level of anti-alien fear and disgust as the mass Jewish poverty of Whitechapel. Nevertheless, in many people's minds there was a sordid stain on the neighbourhood of Tottenham Court Road, and part of that stain was no doubt due to the presence of aliens. In areas where the 'lower classes' and foreigners lived and worked together there was always thought to be a powerful threat both to authority and morality. Robert Machray's *The Night Side of London* (1902), humorously but effectively recharging old stereotypes, plays on the moral danger posed by outsiders, especially Jewish outsiders, in Chapter XVI, 'A "Night Club"', that portrays them as exploiter and exploited. This club, 'somewhere off Tottenham Court Road', is run by a proprietor 'of a pronounced Jewish type': an ugly character, who is caricatured dancing with an attractive young woman in an accompanying illustration. And among the 'unfortunate women' who keep the men company are girls from Germany and Finland: in fact, the investigator finds that 'nearly all the women … are foreigners'.[21] This is the low life that, according to Machray, was being suppressed so vigorously that hardly any clubs of the type remained in London at that time.

Much was also being said about 'white slavery' during the last decades of the nineteenth century and the first decades of the twentieth. Again, immigrants were the focus for this sinister trade in girls and women, with Jews attracting much of the blame; another plank in the argument against immigration that produced the Aliens Act. The Jewish Association for the Protection of Girls and Women was founded in 1885, the same year the issue began to be widely publicised in media such as the *Pall Mall Gazette*, to 'rescue' young Jewish women arriving at Tilbury Dock bound for London and prevent them from being enticed into prostitution by other agents. Other groups of immigrants were blamed for trafficking as well: Member of Parliament Arthur Lee claimed that among the thousands involved in running the trade, the majority being foreign according to him, were 'dozens of negroes in the West End of London running white English girls on the streets'.[22] However, the black presence referred to here was probably in Soho rather than Fitzrovia at this date.

With national unemployment rising again at the turn of the century, anti-alien agitation took off once more. A smallpox outbreak in 1901 was blamed on the migrants, 'the scum of humanity', according to the British Brothers' League (*Jewish Chronicle*, 17 January 1902). A Royal Commission was set up against a background of steady anti-alienist agitation. It came out for restrictive legislation in 1903 and, after some delays, the Aliens Act was passed in July 1905 and began to be enforced from 1906. The Act provided for exemption for political and religious refugees from the Act's restrictions, but this was interpreted harshly, and numbers admitted under this provision fell from 505 in 1906 to just five in 1910, whereas thousands a year had been admitted before.

The Aliens Act began the process of choking off immigration, so that the diversity we see in the Fitzrovia of 1911 was at a peak, not to be repeated at least until after the Second World War.

Foreigners who embraced politically radical ideas were seen to be of an especially pernicious criminal type. According to some commentators, after the passing of the Aliens Act, these radicals were still not being kept out or summarily deported. Foreign criminals were thought to be heedless of all laws and desperately violent in their actions – and therefore somehow in a different league to British criminals. The *Daily Mail* of 10 January 1911, even though immigration had fallen to almost nothing by 1910, declared, 'We cannot consent longer to admit these thousands of undesirables to the cruel injury of our own people or permit indefinitely the scum of Europe to be poured into our country … That way lies the moral and spiritual death of our race.'

David Feldman, in *Metropolis London*, argues that there was a tendency by the authorities and the media at this time to speak more favourably than before of the working-class population – who had represented a social evil about twenty years earlier – at the expense of immigrants, particularly Jewish immigrants.[23] The shooting of three policemen during a raid on a jewellery warehouse at Houndsditch, that led to what was called the Siege of Sidney Street in December 1910, inflamed opinion against all aliens and strengthened the link in many people's minds between foreign immigrants, radicalism and crime. More will be said about this in Chapter 6.

Winston Churchill, as Home Secretary, even prepared new legislation that would have required aliens always to be deported if they committed any imprisonable offence, whatever its nature, and went as far as talking of deporting aliens even before any offence had been committed. However, this Bill was never made law.

By the summer of 1911, anti-alien agitation was fading. On the north side of Oxford Street, people like my mother's family were busy settling, finding jobs and raising children, not much touched by the eddies and swirls of hostility evoked by the immigrant presence in some quarters. My maternal grandfather had found it necessary, or convenient, to change his surname from Simkovitch to the very English-sounding Harris on his arrival in the 1890s; but my mother's father was Isaac Coshever to the rest of the world (though his name was still Anglicised somewhat from Koscheva). Perhaps a reassuring sign of calmer times?

There is evidence of a strong and continuing movement of the Jewish community into Fitzrovia until the start of the Second World War, linked in many cases with the growth of the clothing industry. The increase in Jewish arrivals was balanced by a decline in numbers among other groups of immigrants who had previously flourished in the neighbourhood. A major cause was the First World War, when those belonging to Britain's ally nations, like France, returned to be with their families, perhaps also to fight for their countries, and those from enemy nations such as Germany became *personae non gratae*. There had been over 31,000 Germans in inner London in 1911, but from August 1914 all Germans were registered as 'alien enemies' and from October that year many were interned in camps in and around London. There were outbreaks of anti-German hostility: riots and looting of German shops.

By 1921 there were only a few thousand unnaturalised Germans still resident in the city and numbers remained low, until the late 1930s brought in German Jews and others escaping Nazi Germany.

No such severe decline was seen in numbers of Italians, who were allies of the British in the First World War, but Italians were more numerous to the south of Oxford Street in Soho, and the Italian population in Fitzrovia was never as high as was the French or German one.

The historian Jerry White describes how the Jewish settlers became integrated in the decades following their arrival in London. White notes the evolving social and economic contribution made by the Jewish incomers as they were moving westwards:

> Jewish Londoners became prominent less in the pre-1914 domain of tailoring and bootmaking than in the professions (notably medicine and the law), in academic life, in the arts and in the entertainments industry, especially popular and classical music and the cinema. Wardour Street, Soho, the centre of Britain's interwar film industry, was called a 'glossy Ghetto' by 1933. As the influence of talented individuals expanded and held its own in the wider society, the 'small planet' of 'Jewish' trade unions or politics was abandoned for the bigger stage, giving another turn to the screw of assimilation.[24]

However, to White's observations it should be added that the clothing industry, and the Jewish contribution to it, remained very strong in Fitzrovia before the Second World War, while Jews were also branching out into other trades and occupations, and continued to be significant even up till the 1960s, as explained in Chapter 5 on the clothing industry. The westward movement noted by White was meanwhile continuing, as Jewish families moved on to suburban areas such as Golders Green and Hendon on a north-westerly trajectory.

The local German and Italian communities were affected in different ways by the Second World War, both fluctuating in size. Soho and Fitzrovia's Italian community declined as some members were taken away from London for internment as enemy aliens. Many Italian waiters were interned, and some restaurants were attacked in anti-Italian outbreaks. But German Nazism triggered an influx of German Jews into London between 1933 and 1939, some of whom found their way to Fitzrovia, although a majority of Jewish refugees went to north-west London. Some prominent organisations for aiding these refugees were close at hand. The Jewish Refugees Committee and other Anglo-Jewish organisations were based, from 1938, at Bloomsbury House in a former hotel in Bloomsbury Street, while the German Jewish Aid Committee was at Woburn House, Tavistock Square, in Bloomsbury.

The Anglo-Jewish community took much of the responsibility for fundraising and organising provision for refugees, and these relief organisations were vital in coping with the influx of Jews leaving Germany after the *Kristallnacht* pogroms of November 1938. They had to manage the arrival of nearly 10,000 unaccompanied children on the *Kindertransports* from December 1938, and to aid the many thousands of young women who escaped to Britain on domestic service visas.

Growing up on the Other Side of Oxford Street

What was it like to be a child of foreign immigrants growing up in Fitzrovia? For Trudie Flinder (born Gitra Spiegelman) who lived in Saville Street (later Hanson Street) it was 'mostly a Jewish ambience', although there were 'Irish in the area, there were a few Greeks and things'.[25] Her mention of Irish people shows that our infirmary-based census sample with its dearth of Irish people may not be completely representative of Fitzrovia. Trudie remembers that her family flat was:

> ... very close to Great Portland Street ... there were 12 flats to a block and each one had a separate family, so it was quite a little community in its own right, and these blocks went virtually up sort of right along the road, so it was a very Jewish community.

Her parents were from Czedlovska, near Lodz, and on first arrival in London went to the East End. From there they made the move westwards, although they still kept in touch with East End Jews who were 'landsmen' from the same

Polish town. Trudie was vaguely aware of tensions between themselves and other local communities. She says:

> Where we lived, parallel with that street … there was a Catholic church, there were groups of Irish boys … there were little gangs … we never went through Ogle street, which was where the Roman Catholic church was. I … never even called it anti-semitic, I knew that was the Irish lot and they would call us names, and we weren't very polite to them either. Or if they saw the boys going to Hebrew classes, but I don't think it twisted us … you know, I don't think it had a tremendous traumatic effect on us.[26]

Trudie did later suffer discrimination in employment, however. In 1937, as a 17-year-old, she asked her employer, the boss of an addressograph company near Tottenham Court Road in Bedford Row, Bloomsbury, for time off for a Jewish holiday, only to be told that they didn't employ Jews. Her father thought of Bloomsbury as being like 'a foreign country', highlighting the very different cultural atmosphere of Fitzrovia.

Sonia Birnbaum, of 57 Grafton Way, was the child of an East End family who moved west when Sonia was young. Her grandfather owned a business in Cleveland Street, where he sold boots and shoes and bric-a-brac. Her father opened a kosher butcher's shop in Charlotte Place, which had moved to 37 Charlotte Street by the time Sonia was born in 1927. She says that her father was known as 'the gentleman butcher in the West End'.[27]

Benny Green, the writer and musician, was yet another son of Fitzrovia (though actually born in his mother's home town of Leeds) whose ancestors had begun their lives in England in the East End then moved west. His father's father, a master tailor, had arrived before the height of Jewish immigration, in 1876. He moved to Fitzrovia's Greenwell Street (formerly Buckingham Street) from the East End, possibly because of Fitzrovia's proximity to Bond Street and the premier tailoring shops of Savile Row. Benny Green confirms the sense of a settled local Jewish community when he was a child in the 1920s: 'It was a very sizeable Jewish community round there, a very big one'.[28] His perception, too, was that the Jewish community and the tailoring trade were very closely intertwined, 'It … was full of trouser makers and waistcoat makers and pressers and tailors'.[29]

Benny Green speaks of the Jews north of Oxford Street being closely connected with the much bigger East End community, saying, 'We were an outpost because there was this Jewish community stuck in behind Marylebone Road – between Euston Road and Soho'.[30] At the same time, when asked by the interviewer about the difference between Fitzrovia and the East End, he captures the contrast by highlighting Fitzrovia's characteristic openness to alternative ways of living:

> I think that my standard of living in Cleveland Street was pretty low – it was poverty – no joking it was very harsh living, but I think the difference was: you went 100 yards and you were at the Nash Terraces of Regents Park and you saw how the other half lived. You went round the corner into Fitzroy Square, literally round the corner and you saw another life. Whereas in the East End, I think it was all pretty dodgy or there were no monied people living there. Whereas I only had to go 150 yards and there would be the really rich could be living there and I think that made a difference. It didn't make me envious but it made me fascinated that you might be able to end up with them or in those houses.[31]

Reuben Falber, also of Polish-Jewish parentage, was born in 1914 in Tottenham Street, his parents having arrived in London in the 1890s. Although Reuben doesn't say which number he was born at, the 1911 census reveals that his father, David, his mother, Eve, and his two older sisters, aged 3 and 2, were living at 35 Tottenham Street. His father is listed as a fruiterer. Reuben recalls his parents' struggles to establish themselves:

> They had a very precarious livelihood, my mother had a little stall for drapery and things like that in a small market at Goodge Street … And my father, whose mother died when he was 14, he was more or less put into a position of having to earn his own living. He'd been apprenticed as a [brick polisher] and he gave that up and he just earned his living as best he could, which effectively was what you called a barrow boy. And then after he and my mother had met and were married, he then got a few pound together and opened a greengrocer's shop in Tottenham Street.[32]

There is no sign in the census that Reuben's mother, Eve, was employed outside the home in 1911. Perhaps she had given up the stall when she got married and had children, or possibly the stall was not a regular daily occupation. The family greengrocer's shop was at the Falbers' living address. Living accommodation for Reuben's family was as squashed as it seemed to be for most local families:

> We had two rooms, one at the back of the shop and one above the shop and the one above the shop was my parents' bedroom, the one at the back of the

shop was the family's living room and the bedroom for my two sisters and myself. The rest of the house was … I suppose my parents … we were probably tenants, as were the people who lived in the other room.[33]

In fact, barring any great change in home conditions between 1911 when the census was carried out and the time of which Reuben is speaking several years later, their address at 35 Tottenham Street would have been shared with many other people when he was a boy. In 1911, several households were jammed into No. 35, despite some of the space being given over to the shop. Nineteen other people occupied the building besides the Falber family. Reuben, as a young man, became a Communist Party member and his early experiences no doubt influenced his political choices.

These reminiscences of Fitzrovia's second-generation Jews, who were growing up in the 1920s and 1930s, reinforce an impression that the area by this later period was even more distinctively Jewish than is indicated by our 1911 census-based survey. The 1920s and 1930s saw the continued growth of the Jewish community north of Oxford Street. The existence of a vibrant community is reinforced by the oral testimony of Benny Green and others, and also non-Jewish residents.

Joyce Hooper was born in Birmingham in 1927 but settled in Fitzrovia when she was young. She remarks, 'When I moved to Seymour House [in Hanson Street] it was mainly Jewish people who lived here … There were a lot of Jewish shops in Hanson Street … There was a large Jewish community.'[34] Local-born Nellie Muller comments on the 'lovely Jewish fish shops along Cleveland Street' when she was young, and says, 'There were a lot of Jewish people round here'.[35]

'Asphodel's' (not her real name) parents were Polish-Jewish immigrants who had met and married in Portsmouth and both died while Asphodel was still very young, leaving her in poverty with her stepmother's family. In 1937, after leaving school, she left on her own for London; she had passed the preliminary exam for Oxford but couldn't go as she had no way of maintaining herself until she was the required age of 18. Asphodel took refuge in Fitzrovia:

I had half a crown and I got on the bus and went to Victoria Station … Eventually somebody who appeared to be a railway policewoman came up and asked me whether I was waiting for someone. I said I'd run away from home … She asked me what my plans were, and I said I didn't know. She asked if I would object to going to a girls' hostel, and I said I'd be delighted. Arrangements were made and some other woman accompanied me in a car

– I don't think I'd ever been in a car – to a hostel at 49 Cleveland Street, at the back of Middlesex Hospital: the Emerson Bainbridge Hostel for Young Women and Girls in London. It was next door to the Emerson Bainbridge Hostel for Fallen Women, so they got me to the right one first. In those days they were very worried about what was called the White Slave Traffic and I'm quite sure that that was the reason that the policewoman came up to me.[36]

Asphodel was very happy at the hostel, staying in a dormitory which housed about ten women. She got a job the next day earning 30*s* a week, paying 15*s* to stay at the hostel. She later worked at London County Council (LCC) and became a member of the Communist Party. Emerson Bainbridge House still stands but has succumbed to gentrification and has been sold for development as a block of upmarket apartments.

New Arrivals: Post-War Immigration

By the 1940s, new communities were springing up and growing in Fitzrovia. A small but distinctive, almost exclusively male, Japanese group of settlers began to appear there just before and after the Second World War. As described in Chapter 4, they specialised in Japanese paper lantern making and intermarried with British women, becoming long-term residents.

Another much larger group of immigrants were from Cyprus, escaping economic hardship and civil war and coming to England after the Second World War as British subjects. Athanasios Papathanasiou, after being refused a visa for the USA due to his 'revolutionary and anarchistic principles' was sponsored by relations living in Camden Town and arrived in 1949 to join them in their crowded flat.[37] He found work in Fitzrovia as a shoe machinist, a trade familiar to generations of immigrants:

In a few days I had found a job as a shoe machinist in a small workshop, a basement in Hanson Street, W1. The owner was a Greek Cypriot and another young man from my village was working there, making three of us in all. As I could not understand the language my only contacts were Greek Cypriots. In the beginning it was very lonely, work, home, then from home to work again.[38]

Athanasios continued his political activities in London as another contributor to Fitzrovia's radical tradition, becoming involved in disseminating and selling the left-wing paper, the *Vema*. He recalls 'selling the paper outside Warren Street Station and all along Tottenham Court Road'.[39] After a few years he moved on to Hammersmith and Fulham where many Cypriots settled and where he became closely involved with the Greek Cypriot Association.

Some other arrivals from Cyprus were decorators Christofi Kyriacos at 41 Howland Street and L. Christodoulou at 67 Cleveland Street. A boot repairer, Euripides Papsou, lived at the same address as Christodoulou. Some of the earlier Cypriot settlers, arriving in the 1930s, were involved in trouble with Italian street sellers in Soho, as established immigrant groups perforce made space for newer migrants. Like Italians, Cypriots often tended to enter food-related trades, so perhaps competition was to blame for the conflict between the two groups.

By this time, there was a perceptible African presence in Fitzrovia. Many locals remember the Howland Street resident, Prince Monolulu, a boisterous character who was a horse-racing tipster and whose popular catchphrase was 'I gotta horse!' At 146 Great Titchfield Street lived Winifred Ekpenyon, who married an African law student based at London University. They met in her father's antiques shop during the Second World War and had two children before he died in 1951.[40]

There was evidence also of a settled Asian community to add to the numbers of transient students passing through University College and the University of London. One sign was the presence of several small local Indian restaurants: Nick Bailey's *Fitzrovia* contains a photograph of one of the earliest, the Khan Restaurant at 137 Whitfield Street, shown in 1945.[41]

Meanwhile, older immigrant communities remained. The Welsh continued to run their dairy businesses. Joyce Hooper recalls that when she moved to Seymour House in Hanson Street before the Second World War, 'There were a lot of dairies … which usually were owned by Welsh people'.[42] The Evans' Dairy at 35 Warren Street survives today: it still possesses splendid original fittings such as tile pictures of cattle, framed in the same glorious blue as the shop's exterior tiling, lined along the elegant frontage of its counter. The last Evans to own the dairy retired in 2000 and it is now (2017) run by Turkish people.

Conclusion

In this chapter we've seen how immigrants came to Fitzrovia to settle from across Europe and beyond. They landed in a corner of the city that was exceptionally responsive to their presence, where job and business opportunities abounded in new or expanding industries such as clothing, hospitality or entertainment and where almost every new arrival could find support from pre-existing communities and networks. The immigrant households took their place in a part of the city with a tradition of immigration stretching back to the French and German artisans who helped to build Fitzrovia in the eighteenth century; and they had arrived at a time of unprecedented immigration which was only slowed down by the restrictive legislation of 1905.

Fitzrovia was a safe part of London for immigrants: the sense of threat that must have been felt by an East End immigrant during the anti-alien agitations of the 1890s and 1900s or the heyday of Oswald Mosley and his fascists in the 1930s was almost unknown here. Yet Fitzrovia's 'unsavoury' reputation with some other Londoners, Parliament and the police surely owed much to a xenophobic distrust of its foreignness, and immigrants on the Other Side of Oxford Street must have had some idea of the suspicion with which they were viewed in many quarters.

Foreigners had been instrumental in creating Fitzrovia from semi-rural fields and scrubland. And an outsider taint lingered. At the same time, Fitzrovia, with its 'invasive' foreigners, was within London's urban barricade of Euston Road, right inside the city, making it even more dangerous in the eyes of some Londoners. Even to Fitzrovia's looked-down-upon Soho neighbours, the Other Side of Oxford Street was 'the wrong side of the tracks'.[43] As Judith Summers puts it, 'If a Soho family moved north of Oxford Street, it was as if they were going into voluntary exile.'[44] Perhaps to end up north of Oxford Street, as increasing numbers did in the first half of the twentieth century – coming from far abroad or simply making the short journey from the city centre – was to enter a land full of exiles. For all that, it proved a welcoming first home for many whose later generations were to spread and prosper.

2

Moving Around Fitzrovia: Transport and Public Space

Testing Fitzrovia's Boundaries

Fitzrovia, by 1900, was an evolving part of an ever-moving, rapidly growing city. People and traffic washed southwards through it across Oxford Street and into the West End towards their workplaces, shops and leisure activities. In the opposite direction, they flowed up Tottenham Court Road towards Euston Road and London's spreading northern districts, perhaps going home to the suburbs at the end of the day.

Given the constant overcrowding and blockages caused by its awkward street topography and inadequate traffic management, crossing these southern and northern boundaries of Fitzrovia became true rites of passage. The barriers to access, into and out of Fitzrovia, gave extra force to the idea of Fitzrovia's being a discrete space in the city, existing on the Other Side of both Oxford Street and Euston Road. Within its boundaries, Fitzrovia's communities were in a struggle for spaces to shelter, work, shop and play.

This chapter explores the opposing forces governing the streets and public spaces of Fitzrovia: the need for constant free movement through it against the need of local people to congregate, to trade or, in desperate times, to find a temporary roof over their heads. It charts the sporadic efforts to impose order on the street space and people's movements into, out of and around Fitzrovia through road developments and transport innovations. It also shows how that attempted order was sometimes resisted.

Certain spaces in Fitzrovia have historically proved the point that 'spaces are not merely locations in which politics takes place, but frequently constitute objects of struggle in their own right ... politicized in contests over access, control and representation'.[1] The chapter will describe two such fought-over spaces: the second-hand car market in Warren Street and the Tube stations used as bomb shelters during the Second World War. Fitzrovia's borderline qualities, its ambiguous status within the city, were at the fore in these spaces that were, literally or metaphorically, underground. But, long before either of these contentious spaces existed, Fitzrovia was defined by its major roads.

Euston Road: The Key to the City

Euston Road, a key east–west artery of London, was of major importance in controlling movement into and out of Fitzrovia. It was an essential part of the cordon by which early Victorians 'delineated their version of London' that consisted of the central area enclosed by the city's main railway termini.[2] Three of these major termini, King's Cross, St Pancras and Euston, lay along the Euston Road itself. As we've seen, the Euston Road was both a physical and a psychological barrier between the centre of London and the shoddy streets of north London. Nevertheless, it daily had to allow and facilitate large traffic flows into and out of the centre of the city. Improved transport communications across it to other parts of the city and suburbia had become a more and more urgent need by 1900.

The Metropolitan Railway had opened in 1863, built just below Euston Road by the 'cut-and-cover' method. Now Euston Road, below surface level, was acting as a much-needed gateway to some of the outer reaches of London. Suburbs to the city's north and west were given great impetus by this intra-urban railway. A station had also been built next to Fitzrovia: Great Portland Street Station, in Marylebone Road, along which Euston Road continued westwards. Yet, above ground, Euston Road continued to be a barrier to London's movement. The Metropolitan Railway couldn't do anything to aid transport flow from there into the West End because the railway didn't run through the centre of town. In fact, none of the overground railway routes into and out of London were allowed to penetrate the very centre of the city.

London's developing tramways were also prohibited from running into central London, since the metropolitan boroughs that controlled them consistently refused the building of lines into the centre. The one exception to this ban on city-centre tramways in London was a tramway running down the new Kingsway–Aldwych road development, introduced in 1905. So, trams from north London heading south towards Tottenham Court Road had to stop at the end of Hampstead Road, just short of Euston Road. Proposals by LCC to extend the Hampstead Road tramway down Tottenham Court Road were rejected in 1904 by a Commons Committee. This was due to the fear that the tramway crossing Euston Road – occupying space at the junction while bearing the slow-moving trams – would cause 'great delay … and render the traffic there almost unworkable'.[3]

Tottenham Court Road was already notorious for its heavy, slow-moving traffic, even with all the restrictions on trains and trams crossing into it. And the junction of Euston Road, Tottenham Court Road and Hampstead Road was a major bottleneck that seemed almost incapable of being freed up, due to the narrowness of Tottenham Court Road, the amount of traffic decanting into it, and the awkward turning from Hampstead Road westwards towards Marylebone Road. It was 'a monstrous condition of affairs, day after day and week after week', as Horace Crawfurd put it in the House of Commons in 1927.[4]

In fact, a bottleneck had always existed at the north end of Tottenham Court Road. In the eighteenth century, before the making of the New Road (later named Euston Road), a turnpike had controlled access to London at the junction of the 'road to Highgate' (later Hampstead Road) and Tottenham Court Road. Roque's 1746 map shows the junction to be encumbered by the turnpike kiosk. It was also narrowed by what were probably farm buildings at the top of Tottenham Court Road, projecting into the lane to Marylebone. The cumbersome junction was never effectively opened up to traffic in the subsequent centuries, despite periodical attempts at smoothing and opening the way to the city at that point.

At the other end of Tottenham Court Road, the junction of the road with Charing Cross Road and Oxford Street was almost equally notorious for jams as Westminster-bound traffic flowing into the constricted Charing Cross Road fought for right of way with the Oxford Street traffic bearing thousands of shoppers. Transport problems here were as intractable as at the Euston Road end, with no satisfactory solution found to move the traffic along.

By 1900 the seething traffic of Tottenham Court Road, lacking trams or local train stations, was almost all horse-drawn. Passengers used hansom cabs and omnibuses. The London General Omnibus Company was operating 1,372 horse-drawn buses just along Oxford Street by 1900. However, horse-drawn traffic posed its own problems. Trudie Flinder remembers when a horse drawing a brewery cart fell over on the ice in winter: 'I remember the sparks as his hoofs … and his eyes were rolling in fear, it was a terrible thing to see'.[5]

Only a few wealthy West Enders had motor cars, which were still not widely regarded as a viable means of transport. Many pedestrians mingled with the traffic and it was possible to cross central London north of the river in less than half an hour on foot, as did many workers.

But London was growing tremendously. The need for circulation in the great urban body was vital if it was not to succumb to total paralysis, not least in its ever-busier central shopping district of Oxford Street and the increasingly important Tottenham Court Road with its growing number of large stores.

Down the Tube

An answer to the traffic problem lay deep underground with the beginning of London's Tube. The Central London Railway from Shepherds Bush to Bank opened on 30 July 1900, with a station at the junction of Tottenham Court Road and Oxford Street. In 1908, the station became an interchange for the Central and Northern Lines.

The 'Tube' railway was immediately popular. In its first year, it carried almost 15 million passengers, charging a flat fare of 2*d* and becoming known as the 'Twopenny Tube'.[6] Unlike the Metropolitan Line and other surface railways, the underground Central London Railway's carriages were all of one class. In this way, the enterprise had a modern feel to it, while the Metropolitan preserved its system of separate classes.

At first, the Central Line's daily operations were extremely cumbersome. Eight railway staff worked on each seven-car train, including four gatemen posted throughout the train and a front and rear guard. Starting the train at stations was complicated, with each gateman holding up his hand when the gates to the carriages were shut:

> When the front guard saw the correct number of hands he showed a green light to the rear, to which the rear guard responded by showing a green light forward and blowing a whistle. On receiving these signals the front guard showed a green light forward to the driver or his assistant, and then the train could start.[7]

This system must have existed partly to assuage public fears of travelling deep below the ground, but it's no surprise that it was soon simplified and the number of staff on the trains was reduced.

The Tube running along Fitzrovia's southern border along Oxford Street very soon became a vital part of the city's transport network. However, it didn't help to solve the pressing problem of access, via Tottenham Court Road, to and from the northern parts of the city across the Euston Road. Another underground line did that in June 1907: the Charing Cross, Euston and Hampstead Railway, known as the 'Hampstead Line' or the 'Hampstead Tube'.

This became the Northern Line in the 1920s, when the Hampstead Tube was joined up with two other lines and was extended northwards and south-wards. It was one of three Tube lines financed by an American, Charles Yerkes – the others were the Bakerloo Line and the Piccadilly Line which had already opened in 1906.

The Hampstead Line ran right through Fitzrovia along Tottenham Court Road. Starting near the River Thames at Charing Cross, it ran northwards through stations at Tottenham Court Road/Oxford Street, Goodge Street and Warren Street, before crossing Euston Road to Mornington Crescent and Camden Town. It then split in two directions, ending at Highgate and Golders Green.[8] *The Times*, on 24 June 1907, reported that Mr Lloyd George had 'switched on the current to the motors' of the train carrying him and other guests on the inaugural run, using a golden key. The line carried 25 million passengers in its first year, growing to about 30 million a couple of years later. By then, the Tube network and the mainly surface District Line had been jointly named the Underground.

The Tube was a new space for Londoners, working all day and deep into the night. As of October 1908, the last train of the day left Piccadilly or Leicester Square as late as 1 a.m. on weekdays, later than it does now. Subterranean travel influenced ideas about the shape and workings of London and surfaced in the imagination of many writers, such as Aldous Huxley, Agatha Christie and Margery Allingham, during the first half of the twentieth century. Literary visions of the city as a body expanded to contain images of the Tube network as a series of blood vessels, drawing people in from the suburbs and sending them outwards again at the end of the day.

Sometimes the whole city was thought to have moved underground, espe-cially when the public started to use Tube stations as deep-level shelters in the First World War and, to an even greater extent, in the Second World War. Later in this chapter we'll see how ordinary Londoners from Fitzrovia and the sur-rounding areas made these protective underground spaces their own during the Second World War, in the face of official disapproval. But the Tube was also thought of as a framework linking people at street level as they met each other at stations or traversed London by walking from one station to another. This was an even truer image of the city after 1908 when Frank Pick produced his first definitive map of the underground with colour-coded lines and inter-change points clearly marked out.

However, the Tube also gained more negative associations. Old fears of London being overwhelmed by a tide of excess population were transferred to the overcrowded Tube. It was sometimes visualised as 'a kind of overflow for London', much as the suburbs themselves had been envisaged, except that underground the overflow never had a stopping point but was continually in motion.[9] And, of course, the persistent anxieties about criminal 'outsiders' being able to reach the heart of the city were exacerbated by knowing that criminals could just as easily travel around by Tube as more orderly types of passenger. Patrick Hamilton's trilogy, *Twenty Thousand Streets Under the Sky* (1929–34), features the Tube as 'a vast urban network' that brings marginal figures to the centre of London and where criminals and the police encounter each other at West End underground stations.[10] And the overflows of people on the Tube, washing through Fitzrovia, no doubt heightened ever-present concerns about unsavoury overflows of poverty and criminality pouring across the Euston Road from the north and overflowing Oxford Street from seedy Soho in the south into more respectable districts of the West End.

Meanwhile, the Tube works also caused disturbances on the surface. In Fitzrovia, perhaps the most significant disruption took place in a small but densely built-up area around Warren Street, where houses were knocked down in 1906 to accommodate the building of Warren Street Station. Comparing the Ordnance Survey map for the Euston area (Sheet 49) dated 1894–96 with one dated 1916, there are clear alterations in the block enclosed by Euston Road, Tottenham Court Road, Warren Street and Upper Fitzroy Street. The maps show the entrance to the station on the Tottenham Court Road side replacing about eighteen older buildings. Additionally, a hotel has been built on Tottenham Court Road next to the station entrance, replacing a couple of buildings giving onto Tottenham Court Road, as well as several structures at the back of those buildings, perhaps workshops or storerooms. Presumably the hotel was built to take advantage of the increased passenger traffic arising from the new Tube line. The maps also show that the creation of the Goodge Street Station entrance on Tottenham Court Road necessitated the removal of several more buildings.

Some idea of what these demolitions must have meant for people who had lived or worked in these buildings is given in the 1906 Medical Officer of Health (MOH) Report for St Pancras. These reports include issues relating to overcrowding and insanitary or unsafe housing. The MOH writes:

Recently a site on the west side of Tottenham Court Road … had been cleared, consisting of some 15 houses and shops, and two blocks of artizan's dwellings, containing some 264 rooms and displacing about 500 persons. No proposition appears yet to have been made to provide housing accommodation to re-house these displaced persons.[11]

So, around 500 of Fitzrovia's working people must have had to find alternative accommodation because of the Tube workings. If they wanted or needed to stay nearby, close to their workplaces or extended families, they would find housing to be in short supply. Working-class neighbourhoods in St Pancras, as in many London boroughs, were chronically overcrowded. They may have had to move to rougher areas like Somers Town, north of Euston Road. Little Clarendon Street in Somers Town, for example, had whole families living in each room of a four-roomed house on its western side. The MOH believed that, due to this extreme overcrowding, 'Little Clarendon Street has attracted to itself the most undesirable element of the population within a large radius assisted by the centrifugalized force imparted to the crowded residents of central London by demolitions and changes in the use of dwelling houses'.[12] A family forced out of Fitzrovia may have had little choice but to put up with accommodation like this, suffering worse housing conditions than they had before. Meanwhile, the travellers, tourists and businessmen taking advantage of the new hotel in Tottenham Court Road might have welcomed the 'sanitisation' of the area brought about by the developments around Warren Street Station and the consequent removal of 'undesirable' poor families.

On the Buses

The omnibus was one form of public transport allowed to cross Euston Road from the north. Motorised buses were beginning to replace horse-drawn buses by 1900, but motor buses were late to take off in London. London's road surfaces were often bad, probably due partly to the roadworks for the new rail developments, and their condition was a factor in delaying the growth of motor buses, so that in 1907 the old horse buses still ran in Oxford Street. Laura Philips, who was born in 1905 and at different times lived north and south of Oxford Street, remembers how she used to run, somewhat riskily, after the horse buses and jump aboard.

The development of robust, good-quality motor buses took years and there were several failed experiments in electric and steam propulsion before reliable petrol-engine buses reached the roads. The first proper petrol-powered motor-bus service, starting in 1905, was the London Motor Omnibus Company's service between the suburb of Brondesbury and the law courts in the Strand, skirting Fitzrovia along Marylebone Road.

In 1907, even with all the delays in putting motor buses on the roads, 1,205 were already operating in London. It's possible that, had motor buses come in just a few years earlier than they did, Tube lines such as the Hampstead Line might not have been built, as customers would have preferred the cheaper buses that charged half a penny to a penny fare, compared with 2*d* or 3*d* on the Tube.

The No. 24 and 29 motor-bus routes came into existence in 1910 and 1911 respectively. They still run northwards up Tottenham Court Road and Hampstead Road through Camden Town towards Hampstead (No. 24) and Wood Green (No. 29). Both routes were operated by the London General Omnibus Company (LGOC). For several more years the horse buses carried on running, not phased out completely until August 1914. By then, LGOC had introduced the new B-type bus, a lighter, more reliable model which now dominated the market for bus transport in the capital.

However, horse-drawn goods traffic was still plentiful long after this: in 1946, MPs in the House of Commons were still agitating to the Minister of Transport about congestion from horse-drawn vehicles, and Wilson Harris MP complained about 'the large number of horse-drawn railway vans in the neighbourhood of the great termini on the Euston Road'.[13]

Londoners living in or visiting Fitzrovia or the West End often depended on the buses. As a young woman, Laura Philips used to see the Jewish boys up from the East End at dances on Saturday nights, 'You'd see them all marching on Oxford Street towards Bloomsbury at midnight, to go home to get the last bus, trams'.[14] Sonia Birnbaum, born in 1927, recalls visiting her aunts in Stamford Hill by bus at a young age, in the care of the bus conductor: 'Sometimes [my parents] used to put me on a bus, which in those days you could do, the bus conductor would look after me and my uncle or my aunt would meet me at … the end'.[15]

Fitzrovia's Public Transport Workers

The railways, Tube and buses offered employment to local people as well as faster, easier, more comfortable transport. The 1911 census shows that in Howland Street, where my mother's family was to live in the 1920s and 1930s, at least two residents were railway workers: Gidney Wells of 52 Howland Street, who is listed as a railway messenger, and Arthur George Edwards at No. 58, who was a railway clerk. Tube workers were most probably listed simply as railway workers, so we can't tell if they worked on the new Tube or the older overground railways.

The first decades of the Tube and motor buses saw long initial working hours being reduced and decent wages being established. On the Tube around

1913–14, motormen earned 38s 10d for a six-day week of fifty-four hours, while signalmen got 31s 11d and gatemen 24s 7d. These wages were around the national average for similar skilled manual jobs and had the advantage of being very secure.

An eight-hour day was achieved for railway staff in 1919. The majority of railway staff received paid annual holiday of between three and seven days. On the buses, drivers in 1914 were earning between 7½d and 8½d per hour and worked for eight or nine hours a day, earning similar wages to the Tube motormen. A drawback was that bus drivers' working hours were spread over twelve or fifteen hours a day.

Like railway staff, workers on the buses quickly saw their pay and conditions improve, with bus drivers by 1922 working a forty-eight-hour week and enjoying a greatly improved hourly pay rate of just under 1s 10d, which took their weekly wages to £4 10s. Equally strong pay rises were seen on the railways. Unionisation undoubtedly helped, with most transport staff being unionised by 1933. Discipline on the Tube was severe, with smoking or gambling punishable by the loss of one's job.

Initially, few women benefited from job opportunities in these transport sectors. As Mike Horne puts it, 'Female staff were grudgingly tolerated as station cleaners and ladies' waiting room attendants', but were denied the chance to learn new skills and received lower pay than men doing similar types of work.[16] Neither management nor unions conceded the principle of equal pay for women, although women struck for equal pay in 1918 when more women were working in transport, due to the First World War creating a labour shortage.

The Motor Car and Fitzrovia

The first few motor cars – experimental models – were being seen in the West End during the 1890s. Important as the Tube lines and buses were to residents, the growth of car ownership was in some ways just as significant for Fitzrovia's economic development. From its earliest days, the car trade flourished in Fitzrovia, becoming centred on Great Portland Street, while the area sprouted businesses and occupations arising from this new means of private transport.

When car owning was starting to spread beyond wealthy West Enders to the middle and working classes in the 1920s and 1930s, Fitzrovia's established business in new motors was being mirrored by a thriving, if somewhat shadowy, trade in used cars centred on Warren Street. Much of this popular used car trade was carried out on the streets, a factor enhancing distrust of the market in official quarters and attracting attention from the police, especially when it attracted criminal low life. As we'll see, the public spaces of Fitzrovia that housed the car market were sometimes areas of contention between buyers and dealers, on one hand, and disapproving officialdom, on the other.

In the early 1900s, the motor car was leaving behind the experimental days that made driving a form of extreme sport engaged in by enthusiasts, and was becoming a viable means of transport, at least for the wealthy. The Locomotives on Highways Act of 1896 had already removed the severe restrictions on motorists that had imposed a speed limit of only 4 miles per hour and had insisted on vehicles being preceded by a man bearing a red flag to alert other road users.

Even before the 1896 Act, a wealthy local businessman, Henry Hewetson, had owned a large shop stocking motors in Tottenham Court Road, and had begun to import Benz cars from Germany:

> Hewetson claimed to be 'Britain's first motorist' and to have made Britain's first car import in 1894 after meeting Benz officials at a German trade show where he had gone to discuss the purchase of coffee. However, modern research has shown he was being 'economical with the truth' by a year or so!
>
> But he was certainly driving his little Benz 'Velo' when the law compelled motorists to drive at 4mph with a man walking in front – he got round this by having a boy ride ahead on a bicycle to detect police presence, whereupon a second boy jumped off and walked ahead with a strip of red ribbon on a pencil to serve as a warning 'red flag'![17]

After 1900, motoring was being participated in by more sober spirits than Henry Hewetson and was established and popular enough to generate regular news and opinion in the press. The weekly *Illustrated London News* published the first of a long series of columns on motoring called 'The Chronicle of the Car' on 30 March 1907, while C.G. Matson in the *Daily Mail* was writing on 'Motor Matters' in July of the same year. On 24 July 1907, Matson wrote, 'Cars are being supplied to the public at moderate prices and without any undue delay.' However, the affluent nature of this 'public' was given away by the theme of the article which was, how the prosperous car owner could find a competent chauffeur! Matson opined that ex-Royal Marines, after following a six-month 'chauffeur's course', would make excellent drivers.

Car transport was good for local employment. The 1911 census of Howland Street shows residents listed as chauffeurs, motor drivers and motor mechanics. Other local occupations derived from motor vehicles were recorded in the census, too: living at 37 Howland Street were a motor cleaner and an automobile engineer. And, proving that other new transport technologies were having an impact on working lives, a motor cycle engineer is also listed in the 1911 census, at 52 Howland Street. Motorcycles had begun to be mass produced by British companies like Royal Enfield in 1901 and Triumph in 1902, and quickly achieved popularity – above all, with young men.

Great Portland Street was becoming a hub of the car trade that was beginning to be concentrated on the middle-class market. By November 1911, when the Third Annual Exhibition of Motor Cars was in progress, an *Illustrated London News* feature on a lower-priced car, 'The Little Six', mentioned that it was being shown at 85 Great Portland Street. The car sales industry starting to grow up there is repeatedly publicised in the *Illustrated London News* at around this time, with a feature in 1912 on the Austrian Daimler Motor Company of 112 Great Portland Street, and a 1913 report on the reasonably priced Torpedo de Luxe sold by Byrom & Co. of No. 85. The emergence of British-made cars is also reflected on Great Portland Street, with Vauxhall Motors owning a big showroom at 174–182.

By the 1920s, when car ownership was increasingly attracting the middle classes, we can see further proof that Great Portland Street had become firmly associated with car sales and was predominant in 'the light-car business' at the cheaper end of the car market. 'The Chronicle of the Car', *Illustrated London News* of 4 February 1922, gives a brief history of the London new car trade, marking 'the gravitation of the trade westwards'. It traces the very beginnings of the car trade in London to Long Acre near Covent Garden, before Great Portland Street had become 'easily the favourite locality' soon afterwards. Despite declaring, 'Bond Street is becoming the fashionable headquarters of the motor trade', the piece acknowledged that Great Portland Street 'is still [the centre], in so far as the number of motor firms doing business there is concerned'.

Great Portland Street's reputation for car sales must have remained solid for, even in the late 1930s, retail space there was dominated by the car trade, with long stretches of the street consisting of showrooms and at least forty-nine sales firms represented.[18] Reuben Falber of Tottenham Street worked in a car showroom after he left school; he must have been one of many young men to do so by around 1930.

The importance of the trade to Fitzrovia was echoed in the growth of associated businesses supplying car parts and accessories. Businesses associated with driving and car manufacture opened in Great Portland Street to add to the many car sales firms. And by 1920, Tottenham Court Road had several businesses selling car tyres, including a well-known company, Firestone, as well as firms manufacturing brakes, lighting and ignition. The brake manufacturer, the Herbert Frood Company, as it appears in the *Post Office Directory* of 1920, evolved during the 1920s into Ferodo Ltd, another long-lasting brand name. Situated at 222 Tottenham Court Road, it remained there until the 1940s.

UK private car ownership rocketed to more than 2 million by 1939, due to rising incomes and lower car prices (the 1931 Morris Minor SV cost only £100), but especially the growing availability and popularity of hire purchase (HP) for buying cars. In fact, *The Times* for 28 May 1936 notes, 'Of the 300,000 new cars sold last year at least 70 per cent were acquired on hire-purchase … the Popular Ford saloon, a new model ready for the road, is obtainable for a first payment of only £25'. At the same time, though, the HP system or 'the never-never' (you seemingly never stopped paying!) was looked down on by many middle-class customers, even by car dealers, as not respectable and unreliable and buyers would often not admit to using it.

The rapid expansion in car ownership in the 1920s and 1930s eventually took in all levels of the middle classes and was beginning to involve working-class consumers. It naturally caused a relentless increase in daily traffic through Fitzrovia to and from the West End. By September 1929, the *New Survey of London Life and Labour* tells us there were 97,843 private motor car licences in London as well as 47,443 current motor cycle licences.[19]

Added to this motor traffic were numerous motorised taxi cabs. Since being introduced in 1903 they had quickly replaced horse-drawn hansom cabs, with very few hansoms remaining after 1918.[20] However, there was still a lot of horse-drawn goods traffic to add to this unruly street-clogging mixture.

Freeing the Streets?

Fitzrovia's high street, Tottenham Court Road, was still choked with traffic as the twentieth century advanced. The crossing from Euston Road into Tottenham Court Road was an everlasting bottleneck. Meanwhile, the junction of Tottenham Court Road, Charing Cross Road and Oxford Street continued to be notorious despite the building of the West End's Tube lines. The *New Survey of London* records a great increase in traffic accidents, from 571 accidents in 1921 to 1,362 by 1929.[21] The danger of death from a traffic accident doubled during this time.

Traffic occasionally came to a complete standstill due to unforeseen events, as in 1930 when a water main burst near Oxford Street and the area was flooded. The flood breached Tottenham Court Road Tube Station where passengers were 'suddenly caught in a swirling flood which swept down the escalators, over the platform, and on to the lines' according to the *Manchester Guardian* of 16 December 1930. Many road surfaces were damaged in the affected area, with shopkeepers worrying about their Christmas trade being hit. The newspaper reported:

> The junction of Oxford Street, Charing Cross Road and Tottenham Court Road, normally one of the busiest points in London, was impassable, and long detours had to be made. Every street, even the narrowest, within a half-mile radius ... was full of vehicles all seeking a way out of the congestion ... Every bus was packed with bewildered passengers uncertain where they were being taken.

Floods apart, the Tube system that served Fitzrovia was under great pressure, despite the upgrading in 1933 of Warren Street Station to cope with the increasing traffic on the Northern Line, as the Hampstead Line was now known. The station underwent extensive works to move the station entrance to the corner of Tottenham Court Road, where it is today, to make room for the installation of escalators.

Horse-drawn and even hand-drawn vehicles continued to clog the streets in the 1930s. Simon John, whose policeman father, David Thomas John, was based in Tottenham Court Road from 1929 to 1939, remembers the police 'barrow':

> Until *c.* 1932 when [police] motor vehicles arrived dead bodies and drunks were conveyed on a barrow. This was a long wooden affair with two wheels, two long handles and was similar to those used by 'Barrow Boys'. The barrow had straps and a tarpaulin. The straps were used to secure drunks. The barrow was most in use on a Friday for drunks and two policemen were assigned to it. The tarpaulin was used to cover a dead body. Whichever its use as the police wheeled the loaded barrow to the station they would be accompanied by catcalls and often followed by a crowd.

By 1936 the pressure on Parliament to act on traffic congestion in London had resulted in the Ministry of Transport prohibiting horse-drawn vehicles using Regent Street and adjacent streets during peak hours. It also extended a 'no waiting rule', already in force in Oxford Street and some side streets since 1930, to more streets including Wigmore Street.

The efforts to control the traffic arteries of central London brought about another proposed restriction with unwelcome consequences for small traders and the public who used Fitzrovia's streets as their selling and shopping space. Street traders were not going to be permitted to sell goods from a vehicle in selected streets unless they were selling from an authorised stationary pitch. Working people, as traders and as customers, would have been hit by an official move such as this towards tighter demarcation of public space and the curtailment of the street activities that had always been associated with the life of London. Some were doubtful of the benefits of eliminating roving street traders from the streets. A *Manchester Guardian* journalist, writing on 9 September 1936, observed:

> The barrow salesmen, at whom this is presumably aimed, do not appear as a very noticeable menace in the London streets. They go along at a fairly brisk rate, without taking up an excessive amount of room. However, they are to go, and we shall see whether our London 'bus rides are any less stagnant as a result.

In the event, this effort to repress itinerant street trade didn't happen and the subject was still being debated in Parliament in the 1950s. However, that wasn't the end of official attempts to impose control on the public spaces of Fitzrovia.

There were incessant calls from all quarters to improve the traffic flow in the centre of the city. Alfred Hacking, of 191 Tottenham Court Road, a director of the Society of Motor Manufacturers and Traders and the author of *A Transport Policy for the British Empire*, wrote a letter to the *Times*, appearing on 10 May 1937, stressing that a 'highway running within the circle of King's Cross, Euston, Paddington, Victoria, Waterloo, and Liverpool Street is no longer a luxury to be contemplated as a vision, but a sheer necessity'.

As we know, this road version of what sounds a bit like London's present Crossrail project never materialised. Road improvements were promised but not delivered. The 1955 London Roads Development Plan proposed roundabouts at the intersection of Tottenham Court Road and Euston Road, and at the junction with Oxford Street. But it was felt that these expensive roundabouts might simply push traffic towards the already crowded Cambridge Circus and Leicester Square and therefore worsen the problem.

It wasn't until the end of the 1950s that major solutions began to be proposed to the blockage of traffic at the Euston Road/Tottenham Court Road/Hampstead Road junction. One solution aimed to ease the flow of traffic along Euston Road across this junction. Euston Road itself had been a notorious site of traffic jams for decades and in 1959 a four-lane underpass was proposed by the LCC, spanning the junction.[22] But this raised the question of how pedestrians bound for Tottenham Court Road would cross this formidable new barrier in Euston Road.

Both subways and pedestrian crossings were felt to be needed. However, due to the Circle Line running beneath the road, it was thought that the subway would have to be deep and that this would put off pedestrians.[23] The underpass was built in the 1960s and Euston Road was widened at the same time, easing traffic, but with no new pedestrian subway, creating an even bigger barrier between north and central London.

In a potentially momentous move, during the same year of 1959, LCC also considered widening Tottenham Court Road to 90ft on its western (Fitzrovian) side, to carry six lanes of traffic. Its actual width was between 50 and 68ft. A 'comprehensive redevelopment' of the whole area was being thought of, including opening Tottenham Court Road's side streets up to traffic more widely, according to council minutes dated 11 November 1959. The site clearances caused by wartime bombings, heaviest at the northern end of Tottenham Court Road nearer to the main railway stations at Euston and Kings Cross, probably made this redevelopment seem more feasible.

This development would have had very significant impacts on Fitzrovia, which might have changed its character completely, but the widening of Tottenham Court Road never happened, even though there seems to have been no objections made by St Pancras Council to the scheme. It was placed on LCC's 'road improvement priority programme' to start in 1968 but was delayed to 1969–70, then seemed to simply fade away, with schemes in other parts of London taking precedence.

What did happen was a one-way scheme, beginning in 1961 and still in operation today, entailing southbound traffic towards Tottenham Court Road being diverted to run via Gower Street to its east. Only northbound traffic now flowed up Tottenham Court Road. I am old enough to remember this change in how we north Londoners reached the West End, and I recall the feeling of surprise and dislocation I felt as a 9-year-old when the southbound No. 29 bus suddenly swung left at the bottom of Hampstead Road to turn into Gower Street instead of carrying straight over the junction into Tottenham Court Road as it had done before. The one-way scheme didn't eliminate the traffic problem, but alleviated it enough to forestall more drastic answers to it.

So, instead of being comprehensively redeveloped, Tottenham Court Road and most of its side streets continued to be pretty much their old cramped, crowded and slightly rackety selves – and the Euston Road continued to act as a giant barrier between Fitzrovia and points north of it. Traffic circulation lost out for reasons that don't appear to have been fully explained but probably owe a lot to insufficient government money for large-scale traffic projects and their associated redevelopment, especially given the need to compensate local businesses and satisfy the claims of numerous landowners. It seems to have been a fortunate overlooking in many respects, given that road developments might have almost destroyed the area and few voices would probably have been raised against the destruction at that time, as conservation movements only started to gather force in the 1970s. As it happened, Fitzrovia carried on being tucked away behind the busy highway, a distinctive part of central London that was entered only with some sense of struggle.

Warren Street Car Market: A Shadowy Trade?

There were sometimes struggles over the use of public spaces within Fitzrovia, as I've already suggested, where public rights and customary usage met official attempts to clamp down on 'undesirable' activity. This was true of perhaps one of the duskiest patches of Fitzrovia: Warren Street second-hand car market. This was one of the busiest used car markets in London, huddled directly behind Euston Road. It traded almost next door to the glass showrooms of the new car market in Great Portland Street. Warren Street car market had a reputation for dodgy dealing and crooked agents. Yet its importance to local people and to other Londoners comes across in the words of May Thomas, a long-term resident, who says, 'It was the centre of all the cars, there wasn't anywhere else you would go if you wanted a car apart from Warren Street. You would walk in one end and by the time you come out the other end you would have your car.'[24]

The market endured for many years. Responses to an excellent blog post on the website nickelinthemachine.com, dealing with the Warren Street car market in the days when it was connected with the notorious murder of the car dealer Stanley Setty in 1949, date its disappearance to the 1980s. May Thomas, interviewed in 2010, says it came to an end 'about fifteen years ago'.[25] A Volvo car showroom on the corner of Warren Street was the market's last echo until recently, but that too has now disappeared.

The market's trade naturally depended on the presence of a large pool of potential customers for second-hand vehicles, and this customer base materialised surprisingly early in the history of the car trade. A *Picture Post* feature, 'Car Dealers of Warren Street', dated 19 November 1949, states that the used car trade began as far back as 1912, an extension of the car trade on the Euston Road: 'There were a few original models that had become three years out of date and were enough to start Friswell's second-hand auction rooms on the corner of Euston Road'.[26]

Traffic, however, grew on the main road and, ironically, squeezed back the car trade. The dealers in the original showrooms discovered their premises had a back entrance opening onto Warren Street, which was a more reasonable parking ground for their stock.

It seems as if these motor businesses must for some time have kept their main presence in Euston Road since, according to the 1920 *Post Office Directory*, the only motor trader listed in Warren Street is Cass's Motor Mart Limited, but by 1930 Cass's had been joined by five other car dealers. The 1940 *Directory* lists eight car dealerships in Warren Street itself and several others in neighbouring small streets like Fitzroy Street. By 1950, the number of establishments on Warren Street had risen to fifteen, including the specialist American Autos Limited.

Fitzrovia's working people, like other Londoners, must have taken advantage of the new avenues of car ownership. The growth of second-hand car markets was a potent factor in the spread of car ownership, greatly helping those who were not in the 'respectable' middle-class salaried occupations deemed necessary to obtain a car on HP. O'Connell says of the new working-class car buyers that they 'were willing to share the purchase or running costs of a car within the extended family, or amongst friends – they thereby brought traditional working-class cultural and spending patterns to the sphere of motoring'.[27] Sometimes these lower-income car buyers worked in motor or transport sectors, or had close connections who did so and could help with buying and maintaining a car.

Not everyone liked the prospect of universal car ownership. A more mobile working class supposedly held dangers for those concerned about criminality spreading via transport systems, as we've seen in the case of Tube travel. Much of the dislike of HP arose from the perception that car transport was being made available to disrespectable and undeserving consumers. For instance, a 'Weekly Purchase Plan' put forward by Ford in 1924, where you could make a minimum payment of just £1 per week for two and a quarter years and get a new car at the end of it, had a poor reception from at least some motor dealers because it was assumed that a buyer who couldn't put down the normal deposit of £25 on a Ford car 'must be in a very bad way and an undesirable customer [*Motor Trader*, 26 March 1924]'. In the 1930s and even later, Hire Purchase schemes for cars were regarded with such doubt, and even shame, by many car buyers that those using HP would sometimes travel outside their local areas to buy. This was one reason why the large London salerooms were so busy. And the so-called 'undesirables' who couldn't even qualify for HP terms had all the more reason to head for markets like Warren Street, where they just might get a bargain.

However, these less than financially solid customers sometimes received a distinctly less than solid bargain at Warren Street. Its registered car dealerships were, as time went on, augmented by casual street dealers who kept no paperwork, sealing a deal with a handshake instead. These pavement car traders became more numerous after the Second World War, when the market reportedly attracted discharged servicemen who couldn't find a job, and other drifters. Darkly shaded *Picture Post* illustrations of the Warren Street market present almost a gangster image of the traders, showing photographs of men in mackintoshes and fedora hats gathered in deep conversation next to a car or lingering on the corner of Warren Street and Fitzroy Street.

With these street dealers, the buyer really had to beware in case they ended up with a bad bargain. Back in 1928, the columnist of 'The Chronicle of the Car' in the *Illustrated London News* had warned prospective buyers:

> There are establishments where you can buy what are known as 'crashes', for example, – attractive looking cars of aristocratic descent which have unfortunately met with disaster and been patched up. To what extent and with what lack of success this painful operation has been carried out you will discover for yourself – afterwards. Be very careful about these. Deal only with firms which have a reputation to lose and never with those which have one to make – of the proper sort, I mean [2 June 1928].

Cars like these 'crashes', one suspects, were often sold to unwary or uninformed customers on the pavement in Warren Street. The 1949 *Picture Post* article, permeated by strong scepticism about the entire market's respectability, pointed out that numerous parking offences were committed by its car dealerships, and also hinted that the police largely ignored the offences except when new constables were sent there as a sort of training school for dealing with motoring offences.

The Warren Street market was also quietly selling *new* cars – a most unwelcome activity to the established car dealers a stone's throw away in the Great Portland Street showrooms. This established trade had already been badly hit by the Second World War with the number of dealers on Great Portland Street plummeting by 1945. It was in no condition to take any form of competition (or rule bending!) from Warren Street traders. It hit back with court cases. The *Times* of 21 December 1948 reports a case brought against some pavement traders, 'Salvadori and others', in the High Court of Justice by the British Motor Trade Association (BMTA). The case concerned breaches of the BMTA's motor car covenants that prevented car owners selling their new cars within twelve months. Cars were in very short supply just after the war and the 'starved public' for new motors, together with the restrictions imposed by the BMTA, encouraged an illicit trade in new cars. The dealers would pay above list price to anyone prepared to sell a new car to them, then sell them on to customers willing to pay up to twice the list price. The *Times* explains that the defendants in the Salvadori case couldn't buy new cars through reputable suppliers as they weren't members of the Trade Association or were on the association's 'stop' list, probably for being detected in shady practices. So, they relied on paying 'reputable' purchasers over the odds to obtain new cars in breach of covenant.

The Warren Street dealers (these particular defendants were actually based in Fitzroy Street just around the corner from Warren Street) argued in court that they were providing legitimate competition with the established car market. However, the judge rejected their claim, adding that he 'had suffered from a spate of false evidence' and some of the documents in the case 'were melancholy touchstones of mendacity'. The judge granted an injunction restraining the Warren Street dealers from dealing in new cars in breach of covenant and awarded the BMTA costs against them. He added, 'The Warren Street kerb market was the forum of an organized counter-attack on the covenant system' and the defendants were 'a ring within that market' conspiring to breach that covenant, according to the *Times* of 22 December 1948. His words, when set beside May Thomas' assertion that Warren Street was 'the centre of all the cars' give an idea of the threat posed by the market to the 'official' car trade, which would undoubtedly have liked to have seen the market disappear completely.

The market's reputation received another blow about a year after the court case, when it suffered by association from the murder of one of the car dealers, Stanley Setty. The accused murderer was Brian Donald Hume, known in the market as 'the flying smuggler', according to the *Times* report of 24 January 1950. Hume was a pilot and was accused of dropping Setty's body parts from a plane onto Tillingham Marshes in Essex in October 1949. However, after being given a retrial because the first jury couldn't agree a verdict, Hume was cleared of the murder and was sentenced instead to twelve years in prison for being an accessory after the fact.[28]

After Setty's murder, the market became a continuing focus of police interest and media attention, with the *Picture Post* article of November 1949 homing in on the market's daily business. Fairly or not, the article cast doubt on the entire trade of the market, making few allowances for anyone's probity:

Plaintively the car-dealers say they cannot do anything about it. They were only too anxious to show us the details of their trade. Mr. Clayton produced his books, Mr. Knott, who has been in the street for many years, took us specially into his office to show us a framed letter. It was thanks from Scotland Yard for helping to trace stolen cars. And we were given the freedom of one showroom to test if a car had been stolen. The dealer phoned through to a central bureau that checks the numbers of cars for hire-purchase and the records of ones which have been stolen. The car was cleared in a few seconds or, in simpler terms, '*It's not hot*'.

The slang phrase, 'It's not hot' must have been more striking in 1949 than nowadays. It seems designed to persuade readers that those who used such language were dubious characters that knew a lot more than they wished to reveal and it reinforced an impression which the words 'only too anxious' had created. The reporter's tone of moral superiority spiced with sarcasm undermines any evidence that honest business was ever carried on. The disdainful tone of the whole piece is shown in the final paragraph:

It is this constantly presented two-sided aspect of Warren Street, its trade and its people, which is rather confusing. We found a host of people who were frank, open and honest. But we ran into strange silences when we asked the standard of current prices. Or how a dealer could buy a car he had never seen over the phone, and confidently see it at a profit by the next telephone call. Or how a man who was not a mechanic, but had made his capital out of a small dress establishment, could enter the market as a dealer and know a second-hand car was fit and safe to sell again. These are trade secrets.

The *Picture Post*'s presentation to its middle-class readers of an exotic corner of urban life evokes the 'split personality' of Warren Street associated with it being 'the northernmost boundary of Soho'. We can see Fitzrovia and Soho being conflated here, perhaps to further exoticise Fitzrovia and to muddy its reputation even more, since Soho was even more well known than Fitzrovia for sleaze at this time. The market's geographical position, the journalist says, has led to the place attracting 'a fair amount of gutter garbage from the hinterland'. This vague but threatening 'hinterland' might not just have been Soho; it might also have been the seamy parts of north London. Euston Road, as we know, was seen to be a barrier – often alarmingly permeable – against London's northern hinterland of working-class districts. And Brian Donald Hume, the accused murderer of Stanley Setty, came from Finchley Road in north London. So, far from being situated inside a protected zone in central London, the Warren Street market and its neighbourhood could have been receiving a double dose of contamination, from within and outside the city centre, which the regulatory authorities felt they had to repel with double the vigour.

However right the *Picture Post* was to highlight illicit dealings in Warren Street, the blanket suspicion and contempt emanating from the above article also seems to display a prejudice against working-class, non-Establishment traders who were pitched against a wider car trade that undoubtedly had its own cartel to fix prices. The fact that many street dealers were from immigrant backgrounds also seems to attract disdain: for example, an anonymous trader is sneeringly described as having run 'a small dress establishment'. This is almost certainly a coded reference to a Jewish dealer since Jews were predominant in the textile trades of the area at that time.

Whatever dubious dealings took place in Warren Street, its importance as a used car market for as long as seventy or eighty years tells us that many Londoners, and non-Londoners too, turned to it at a time when other sources were beyond their reach. The thriving kerbside trade within the market is an example of street enterprise at its liveliest and perhaps its most challenging to the authorities, with shady deals and criminal connections. The market took over street spaces for use by traders and the public in ways that potentially threatened law and order. It thrived for many years in the face of official distrust and disapproval, filling a public need, and apparently no attempt was made to close Warren Street to the market and its customers.

Taking Over the Tube

The spaces inside the Tube network were tightly controlled by the railway authorities and government legislation, and ordinary customers had little power to change how they were used. However, there were rare times when the public, including the people of Fitzrovia, imposed their will upon the Underground. During the Second World War, London's population insisted on using the Tube stations as bomb shelters, resisting official deterrence and quickly forcing the authorities to accept what was, in effect, an occupation by members of the public.

During the intermittent London bombings of 1917 people had sheltered in the Underground, therefore it was to be expected that Londoners would head to the Tube when war broke out again in 1939. But the question of whether Londoners should shelter in the Tube this time round was left hanging by the authorities.

To follow debates in the House of Commons shortly before war broke out is to realise that the government just could not make up its mind what to do about deep-level shelters in London. It was still dithering when the war began and prevaricated for many months after. Some politicians were against people using the Tube in bombing raids, fearing that people would be reluctant to come out of the shelters after raids had ended. Sir Gifford Fox, speaking in the House of Commons on 1 March 1939, about six months before the war began, urged the government to make up its mind, rejecting this argument:

> … it is important that we should really try to solve the problem of the deep bombproof shelter and build these shelters when there is peace, and not suddenly start digging as we did in the last crisis. I cannot believe that there is anything in the argument that if you have a deep bombproof shelter which is perfectly safe for people to enter that they will not come out again and continue their work. I do not believe that that is the spirit of our people. If they can have shelter for the time being when there is a great air raid on, it will be of great benefit.

Some other MPs pressed very strongly for action to protect the population. Megan Lloyd George, speaking on civil defence on 5 April 1939, said:

> What do the Government contemplate that these people will do? … there are numerous areas in London where there are no trenches, no open spaces and no parks within 10 minutes' walk, or even more. We are told that there may be only five minutes' warning. I am thinking of places like New Oxford Street and the Mile End Road … in all probability the basements in the area will have been adapted for the number of workpeople employed in the particular factories or shops to which they are attached. I can visualise a real panic if an air raid happens in the day-time and in the rush hour in a place of that kind, where there is no special protection available [Hansard].

But other MPs participating in the same debate opposed the provision of deep shelters in Tube stations. Sir Ralph Glyn viewed Tube shelters as potential hindrances to the flow of traffic:

> In regard to tubes, I would point out that in an air raid it would be a matter of great concern to keep the traffic running and to prevent an ugly rush of

people whose nerves were not altogether normal, and that there would be great danger, both on the lifts and on spiral steps, far greater than any of the dangers from the raiders.

Sir Ralph was concerned at the balance of the debate being too much in favour of the population at large. He also believed in looking ahead at future uses for such shelters:

> There is a great danger that people will get an impression, though I am sure hon. Members do not intend to convey that impression, that we are paying too much attention to the protection of individuals here, and not giving sufficient attention to what really matters most – our offensive and defensive power … If you are going to make deep shelters for use in time of war you must devise shelters which will bring in some sort of commercial return in time of peace, such as car parks …

Whatever the thinking in government circles, nothing was done before the war or during the first twelve months of the 'phoney war' either to advance the building of deep-level shelters for Londoners or to legislate against using the Tube for shelter. The transport authorities, meanwhile, wanted to block the public from taking refuge there.

During the phoney war, a London population made smaller by evacuating many schoolchildren in 1939 began to swell again, as a number of these children re-joined their families in the city and weren't re-evacuated when the raids started. And when the bombings began in August 1940 many people simply decided for themselves that they and their families felt safest in the Underground and occupied the Tube stations, ignoring official warning notices against sheltering in stations. Fitzrovia's Tube stations, Tottenham Court Road, Goodge Street and Warren Street, were all heavily used.

During this movement to safety underground, the Communist Party was heavily involved in campaigning for better shelters for all and in taking direct action to open Tube stations to the sheltering public. Ted Bramley of the Communist Party of Great Britain (CPGB), in the pamphlet *Bombers Over London* dated 12 October 1940, declares:

> Londoners have had to take things into their own hands. Three times the authorities said that the Tubes must not be used as shelters. But the people went to the Tubes. At many stations police and officials barred their way, gates were closed; but at Warren Street, Goodge Street, Highgate, etc., gates,

police and officials were swept aside and every inch of stairs, corridors
and platforms taken by the people ... Thousands of East London workers
streamed to the West End to seek safer shelters.

The people's will was acknowledged by Parliament during the continuing
debates on air-raid precautions. Arthur Woodburn, speaking in the Commons
on 19 September 1940, suggested enlarging the Tube tunnels, 'In view of the
fact that some people in London have decided on *tube* stations as deep shelters', which suggests a fait accompli. At some places on the network, deep-level
shelters were constructed as the war went on.

Sir Percy Harris, the MP for Bethnal Green South-West, speaking on
9 October 1940, said:

The case for a certain number of deep shelters has been absolutely made
out by the action of the people themselves, by the way they rush down into
the tubes ... [Miss Lloyd George] pleaded two years ago for the reorganisa-
tion of the tubes as deep shelters, but she was told that it was not a practical
proposition. It might not have been practical, but the matter has solved itself
because the people of London have taken possession of the tubes.

By October 1940 there were signs that the nightly Tube sheltering was being
organised. A Commons statement by Mr Mabane on 10 October states:

In the tube stations definite instructions have been given for people to go
to stations which have not, perhaps, been fully used. Those instructions are
being carried out, as I know full well, because last night I was in a shelter
of excellent character that was not fully used ... every effort is being made
by publicity and by the actual direction of people to shelters that are unoc-
cupied to distribute the people better among the available shelters.

In effect, Londoners had forced the hand of government. Rather than accepting the official line that the Tube should remain solely a transport network,
there purely to ensure freedom of movement around the city, they had insisted
that it should provide living space in time of urgent need. By their actions in
occupying Tube stations, they had created 'counter-spaces' in the city. Fran
Tonkiss explains, 'Counter-spaces are the work both of political imagination
and of practice. They are implied in the criticism of normal spatial arrangements, and realized when existing spaces are remade in contrary ways.'[29] And,
for the duration of the war, the transitory spaces of the Tube, due in the end

more to the common-sense practice of ordinary people than to political imagination, were remade as long-term shelters.

Once stations were being used by thousands of people night after night
during the Blitz, which lasted for several months, it became desperately urgent
that proper sanitation and other facilities should be provided. Photographs
taken in the Tube shelters early in the war show hundreds of recumbent people
squashed against each other without any bedding to provide even a minimum
of comfort. Some pictures show them lying even on the rails in what must
have been disused stations.

These extreme conditions were worsened at first by the absence of sanitary
facilities. The smell must have been almost unbearable. The Minister of Health,
Malcolm MacDonald, took steps to improve conditions, with local Medical
Officers of Health made responsible for enforcing them. Sanitary equipment
was being provided, ventilation and heating were being looked at, overcrowding was to be reduced by trying to disperse people to less-used shelters, and
first-aid posts were to operate in shelters holding more than 500 people, with
a medical officer posted in the large shelters.

By January 1941, the work to equip the Tube stations for efficient sheltering
was well under way, although not complete. On 16 January, Muriel Harris of
the *Manchester Guardian* reported on progress, trying for a note of reassurance,
even cosiness:

> In many shelters the bunks are already up, three-tiered, with a sacking or,
> more cleanly, steel base … Own bedclothes may be left there, also preventing
> much dragging about of heavy suitcases. Upper bunks have the advantage of
> light for those who are readers. Lower bunks can be sat upon, three at a time,
> and are thus productive of friendly converse.

Muriel Harris emphasises the mixed nature of the population in the shelters:

> [A] blue-eyed Norwegian with all but perfect English; a French Jewess with
> blue-black hair; a young Polish mother in green trousers with a scarlet band
> around her hair, bending over a two-month-old baby; German refugee Jews,
> one of whom, a picture dealer, gave his address as X Tube Station and had
> letters delivered to him there.

Max Minkoff, a teenager during the war, has vivid memories of what it was
like to shelter on the platform in Warren Street Tube Station. He recalls that his
family were allocated bunks in the station by organisers: 'We … had to go to

the underground in the evening to get our bunks, we had to go seven o'clock, six o'clock, whatever it was, straight after work'. He doesn't remember people being turned away, 'I don't think it ever happened, I think there was always more bunks than people ... my mother ... went every night with my sister'. Max's father, on the other hand, stayed at home with one of Max's brothers, sleeping in the basement under a table.[30]

Max recounts how the tube trains carried on operating while they were occupying the platform. And Nellie Muller, living at the time in Great Titchfield Street, remembers, 'When it got really bad everyone was living down the shelters. Everyone was so friendly and nice, we had parties down there and singing', though she added, 'It was sad times because you knew the men'.[31] One of Nellie's best friends was caught in an air raid and killed after leaving Great Portland Street overhead shelter to go home to her father.

Muriel Harris points out that the shelterers were 'a vast potential of labour only waiting to be utilised' in support of the war effort, and many of those who sheltered at night were actually doing war-related work during the day, like Nellie Muller who was 'making guns and stem [*sic*] guns, down Cleveland Street'.[32] Harris evokes the embrace of the British Empire and Britons' good-humoured 'friendly pity of the foreigner' in the atmosphere of the shelters. She sees the often-stated British values of order and tolerance permeating this underground world, with supervision carried out by shelter marshals drawn from the civilian population who may be 'porters, retired business men, socially minded women'. But there were cracks in the surface of this cheerful image: there was conflict over space on platforms despite the best efforts of the marshals. My mother, a girl of 14 at the time of the Blitz, remembered arguments breaking out with their regular neighbour, a German woman, caused by the woman's many belongings overflowing into their own little platform plot.

The Tube sheltered 'up to 177,000 people' a night while continuing to circulate people around the city almost as before.[33] During the war, eight new deep shelters, each sheltering up to 8,000 people, were eventually constructed under Tube stations including Goodge Street, but work wasn't completed until 1942 and they weren't opened to the public until 1944.[34]

As David Welsh points out, the Tube shelters became a part of wartime mythology, recorded in the drawings of Henry Moore and locked into generations' memories. The city temporarily moved underground as domestic life for large numbers of Londoners took root below the street surface. And for communities on the Other Side of Oxford Street, the underground shelters were a vital refuge.[35] Fitzrovia, abutting major railway lines, was heavily bombed, with much damage done both in 1940–41 and in the doodlebug era of V-2 bombings in 1944. The destruction included the bombing of Maple's, the big furniture store in Tottenham Court Road, and large parts of Howland Street where my mother's family had lived and where few houses survived the bombing on the north side. For many in Fitzrovia, the Tube became a world in itself; a world that ordinary people had claimed and helped to shape.

Fitzrovia: A Space of Resistance

Fitzrovia's ambiguous insider/outsider relationship with central London and its great northern barrier of Euston Road became even more complex after Fitzrovia became part of an underground Tube network that transported people through both ground-level physical obstacles and symbolic social obstacles. Its 'protected' status at the centre of London became, in some people's minds, even more vulnerable to disrespectability and crime, even more threatened by the rough urban territories to its north as well as sleazy Soho to the south. Meanwhile, Tottenham Court Road escaped major changes towards free traffic movement that might have altered Fitzrovia beyond recognition and continued to be the stubborn traffic bottleneck it had always been. This meant that Fitzrovia could resist the social impact of post-war planning and continue to be an urban space that was somewhat undefined and accommodating to marginal activities like Warren Street car market and the Tube occupations. Overground or underground, it was never fully amenable to outside control.

Fitzrovia's Push for Healthcare Provision

The 'Other Side' of Healthcare

Between 1900 and 1950, the development of healthcare in Fitzrovia gave several new meanings to the phrase 'the Other Side'. Firstly, it meant a divide in healthcare because of the two separate boroughs in which Fitzrovia lay: St Pancras and St Marylebone. These borough councils, set up in 1900 with healthcare responsibilities, could in some respects be understood as 'the Other Side' of each other, with increasingly distinct variations in healthcare. St Marylebone was more affluent than St Pancras and hosted an exclusive area of expensive private healthcare centred on Harley Street. But it also possessed pockets of deprivation and poverty, especially in Fitzrovia around Tottenham Court Road. St Pancras was unquestionably a poorer borough overall. But, in the pre-National Health Service (NHS) decades of the twentieth century, public health and healthcare on the St Pancras and St Marylebone sides of Fitzrovia diverged from each other in ways that complicate a picture of poorer people receiving poorer care. Nevertheless, this fractured care was itself one of many obstacles to improving the health of Fitzrovia's people.

There were also two sides to the nature of public health itself. One was concerned with the care and cure of the sick. But there was a more coercive side where public and official attitudes to health and sickness were connected to class, nationality and ethnicity. The oppressive side of healthcare found expression sometimes in health institutions and also in the laws that upheld and regulated them. It could even affect people's freedom of movement when restricting movement was perceived to mean controlling infection and maintaining the health of the city.

In the late nineteenth century, ideas of the poor as a degenerate mass who embraced filthy ways of life were not uncommon. The poor were seen as being 'sanitary perpetrators' who threatened the classes above them.[1] In some people's minds, poverty itself became a disease. Michelle Allen, writing about Victorian London, mentions a belief among some urban reformers that 'the acquired defects of the poor could be passed down through the generations – a process referred to as "hereditary urban degeneration"'.[2] Slum clearances and the moving of poorer families out of the city centre became a way of cleaning the city. But the uncontrolled movement of workers, and even more so of foreign immigrants, within the city spelt danger to urban authorities. Racism, anti-Semitism and xenophobia played their part in fears about contamination from sections of London's population. These attitudes hadn't disappeared by 1900, although by then a wave of social reform had begun to soften and change them.

One clear example of these linkages is in attitudes towards the prevention and treatment of tuberculosis (TB), where the urge to isolate sick people gave way to surveillance of communities to try to control disease. Fitzrovia, even more than many parts of London, thrived on constant influxes and circulation of people. This made it a potential threat in the eyes of the affluent public since the mass circulation of poor people generated fears of disease mixed with a sense of a wider nameless 'contamination' by their unwanted presence.

A truly dangerous contagious and incurable disease like tuberculosis caused high anxiety among local health authorities and the public. Of all the notifiable diseases, it was the one that elicited the most precautions against its spread. Many London families would have known someone who had the disease: my mother's cousin Rose died of it in the 1930s. Poor housing and health conditions meant that TB could flourish in a street like Howland Street where my mother lived, just yards away from upper-middle-class residents in Fitzroy Square. We can imagine affluent West Enders' anxiety about 'grubby' neighbourhoods like Fitzrovia right on their doorstep.

In 1900, working people who fell sick in Fitzrovia received poor care, as was true across the nation. Healthcare and welfare at that time was a patchy mixture of care provided by charitable hospitals, like the Middlesex Hospital located at the centre of Fitzrovia, and basic local services funded by the boroughs with some government funding.

The Middlesex Hospital already had a long history by 1900. It was founded in 1745 in Windmill Street and was the first hospital in West London. In 1757 it moved to the site it was to occupy permanently until 2005, the block now enclosed by Cleveland Street, Mortimer Street, Nassau Street and Riding

House Street. Next door, in Bloomsbury, University College Hospital (UCLH), was built in 1835, next door to its parent University College in Gower Street, and also served Fitzrovia's population.[3] In 2005, it was to absorb the Middlesex and plant its outposts in Fitzrovia, which today hosts much of UCLH's neurology department. These two institutions were the area's major hospitals.

The Middlesex, unlike the later-built UCLH, was originally sited in semi-rural surroundings, on the Marylebone side of the old parish boundary line. Roque's 1746 *Map of London* shows where it was soon to stand: at the corner of a small field, with another marshy field between it and the just developing Tottenham Court Road. Market gardens lay north and south of it. Its location reflected the tradition of hospitals being situated on the edge of their communities to separate the sick from the rest of society and minimise the risk of contagion to healthy people. However, to its west, city streets were already laid out and coming closer.

By 1769 the land around it was rapidly being developed and, before the end of the eighteenth century, streets and houses had densely surrounded the hospital. Between 1757 and 1900 the location of the Middlesex Hospital relative to the rest of Fitzrovia and to London itself was transformed. The hospital that had been on the very edge of the city was now in the city centre and had also assumed a central place in the neighbourhood, almost equidistant between Tottenham Court Road and Portland Place.

The hospital's altering position in the city seemed to repeat the oscillation between margin and centre so typical of Fitzrovia, as London shaped itself around the Middlesex. The embedding of the Middlesex Hospital within the city was a sign that the sick poor were no longer outside the city boundaries but inside them. The risk of contamination from the sick was now internal to the urban body, with ramifications such as developments in treatment of tuberculosis which emphasised control and surveillance rather than isolation.

By the early years of the twentieth century, both St Pancras and St Marylebone had dedicated tuberculosis dispensaries staffed by tuberculosis officers and nurses. In these clinics, people were screened for TB, diagnoses were made, outpatients treated and their progress followed up using a rigorous set of procedures. These separate clinics were a sign of the social, as well as the medical, importance to the authorities of controlling this, as yet incurable, disease. As David Armstrong comments, 'The dispensary radiated out into the community. Illness was sought, identified and monitored by various techniques and agents in the community co-ordinated by the dispensary.'[4] In other words, the dispensary, though needed and useful, became another means of surveillance of communities, especially poor working-class communities, in which TB most tended to flourish. It was not until the discovery of effective drug treatment in the 1950s that fears of TB could start to diminish.

The Middlesex Hospital was generally highly thought of by the community around it. It was 'a lovely hospital' where 'the care was amazing', according to one local resident, Juanita Braithwaite.[5] But from 1778, after the area's urbanisation, it had a grimmer partner in care: the local workhouse for the destitute. The Covent Garden Workhouse, as it was known at first, stood almost opposite the hospital in Cleveland Street, across the parish boundary line in St Pancras. In 1900 it was known as the Cleveland Street Infirmary. It was absorbed by the Middlesex Hospital in 1926, as the workhouse system came to an end. Today, the eighteenth-century buildings are preserved as a site of historical interest and are still standing, although about to undergo redevelopment.

Many of the chronically sick and elderly had no choice but to enter the workhouse. The Covent Garden Workhouse was later renamed the Strand Union Workhouse and was a notorious Victorian institution satirised by Dickens in 'A Walk in a Workhouse' (1850). By the 1860s it was overcrowded and in unsuitable buildings. It had 460 or more sick, infirm or insane inmates, no professional nurses whatsoever and a miniscule allowance for medicines. Astonishingly, the workhouse guardians had allowed a highly profitable carpet-beating business to be set up in the yard. Dust from it constantly entered the wards and aggravated patients' illnesses. The only light in the picture was the presence of a good master and matron, and an outstandingly hard-working, capable medical officer, Dr Rogers, who, over time, brought about many improvements in care.

Workhouses like these often seemed to have more to do with confining the poor and sick than with caring for or curing them. It was a mechanism of social control at a time when poor and overcrowded London neighbourhoods like Fitzrovia raised fearful images among officials and wealthier residents of poor communities themselves being reservoirs of infection. This workhouse, the Cleveland Street Infirmary as it later became known, had a frightful reputation that must have terrified anyone in danger of entering its doors.

The struggle to contain and eliminate disease within Fitzrovia's communities was closely bound up with keeping its streets, public spaces and buildings clean. Annual MOH reports describe actions taken to clear away rubbish; to closely control, and eventually to eliminate, noxious industries such as tanning and animal slaughtering; to ensure a pure water supply (cases of typhoid were reported in 1900 in St Marylebone) and food that was free from contamination; and to prevent filthy conditions in and around residential and commercial buildings.

The borough's duties extended to keeping the population 'clean' by providing 'cleansing stations' for the destruction of vermin – fleas, lice and bugs – in clothing, bedding and furniture and on people's bodies. The numbers treated in each category were duly recorded in the annual reports. In 1900, St Marylebone Council had erected an extra steam disinfector next to the public baths for cleansing dirty clothes of vermin. Its boast that year was that 'no district in the Metropolis has a more complete [cleansing] installation than St Marylebone'.[6] For larger vermin, St Marylebone appointed a rat officer, after the Rats and Mice (Destruction) Act came into force in 1920. It was reported that he 'is taking the greatest interest in the work'. That same year, two 'Rat Weeks' were held 'with good results'.[7]

Ideas about public cleanliness and disease had, as we've seen, a tendency to become linked together. For instance, notifiable diseases such as smallpox, typhoid, scarlet fever and measles generated concerns about contamination from clothing and bedding, meaning that certain local cleansing stations dealt with the burning or disinfection of these items. And ideas about cleanliness and disease reflected social attitudes to social class, poverty, immigration and public order and disorder. Perceptions of Fitzrovia as the domain of tainted outcasts – poor, working class and often foreign – are undercurrents to media perceptions of its public health and hygiene, and sometimes to the local authorities' approach to it.

Since overcrowded housing was often linked with disease, the sanitary approach to housing prevalent at the end of the nineteenth century saw slum areas knocked down as a way of dispersing the poorest families and 'purifying' the city for more affluent Londoners. But 'the migratory class' of paupers were an insoluble problem, and perhaps a danger, for reformers like Lord Shaftesbury, who had 'not a notion what to do with them'.[8]

Migration, both inward and foreign, was perceived to be importing disease into the urban community. Churning populations were seen to be a menace to public health, necessitating official oversight and control. In this view, the constant movement of people so characteristic of Fitzrovia was making both its foreign immigrants and its indigent native-born into 'shock troops' of 'a diseased and dangerous new "race" of the London poor'.[9]

Fitzrovia's twin institutions, the hospital and the workhouse, were on 'the Other Side' of each other: they were in two separate boroughs while reflecting different aspects of care and control. They had a huge impact on the lives of working families, both for good and ill. They were also part of a pre-NHS network of care that thickened and strengthened over the years, much of it created by the local boroughs. This chapter will trace the growth of this whole mesh of services and its distinctive character in Fitzrovia, sketching its contribution to a big improvement in the city's healthcare and to local working people's lives.

'Midwives Did the Dinners': Pre-War Healthcare in Fitzrovia

Healthcare in early twentieth-century Fitzrovia was often haphazard but could also be an appealingly personal service for those who could afford to pay for medical attention. Some doctors were regarded as community physicians. Some Jewish former residents born in the 1920s mention a Dr Yale as their regular family doctor. 'His surgery was in Hampstead Road,' Sonia Birnbaum remembers. 'He'd come and visit … in those days it was entirely different with doctors. They made a prescription up in his surgery … he did his own dispensing … I think he was most people's doctor.'[10] Max Minkoff also mentions his family using the services of Dr Yale and paying 'about two shillings or two and six a visit'. Max Minkoff also recalls going to the charity-run 'University Hospital' (UCLH) to have his tonsils out as an outpatient. 'I came home in a taxi still bleeding in my throat, didn't stay in,' he says.[11] These reminiscences remind us, not only that a large part of the local community at this time were Jewish but that the majority was not prosperous. Dr Yale had to keep his charges comparatively low, and few people were private hospital patients.

For many working people, paying a shilling or two for a doctor was their last resort, and not many workers could rely on getting medical treatment when they needed it. Exceptions were the minority of men, and the even smaller band of women, who had taken out private health insurance through their trade union or friendly society or had contributed to a church sick loan society. In any case, financial arrangements like these were unlikely to cover women for the high cost of pregnancy and childbirth. A doctor attending a home birth charged £1 in the 1900s, a week's wages for some workers, while a midwife, often with only rudimentary training, cost 10s a week, or 12s if she did the family washing.

Laura Philips, born into comfortable circumstances and living in Soho at the time of her pregnancy, paid £4 a week for a midwife from the East End recommended by her husband's sisters. The nurse 'wore a nurse's uniform and all that … but she cooked … when there was no one there. You know those midwives did the dinners … for the husband when he came home.' Laura's mother stayed with her at home when she had her children. 'I wouldn't go to a hospital. I've never been in a hospital. I wouldn't go away from home …,' she says.[12]

London's standards of hospital care improved from 1900 with better professional training, rigidly enforced antiseptic cleanliness and better treatments for
the big killer diseases. The Middlesex Hospital had a growing reputation for
the treatment of cancer, a disease starting to afflict more and more people as
lifespans grew longer. The University College Hospital was equally influential, specialising in cardiology and neurology. But other health improvements
took place in homes and communities as health and welfare concerns came
more and more to the attention of government, health officials and the public.
Health gains were set against sharply falling populations in Fitzrovia and
nearby areas as people moved away to the suburbs over these decades.

A lot of pioneering community health work was done in Fitzrovia after
1900. On the St Pancras side, there was a very active and influential MOH,
Dr John Sykes, who played a key role in improving community healthcare.
Dr Geffen, his successor, credits Dr Sykes with being largely responsible for
'the establishment of the child welfare movement in this country'.[13] St Pancras
was the first borough to open a School for Mothers, introducing health checks
for infants and advice and classes for mothers on raising healthy children. The
school was started in 1907 by Alys Russell and Dora Bunting in co-operation
with Dr Sykes. The borough and the local government board also worked
with UCLH to open a hospital Infant Welfare Department in 1916. On the
St Marylebone side, the voluntary St Marylebone Health Society, founded
in 1906, carried out a lot of work with mothers and children at around the
same time. Margaret Llewellyn Davies, later General Secretary of the Women's
Co-operative Guild, which strongly championed women's rights including
the provision of healthcare, gained experience of working women's lives from
being a sanitary inspector in St Marylebone.[14]

After 1900 there were successive waves of intense medical and public concern
about different aspects of ordinary people's health. This concern produced the
seeds of a public health service initially aimed at the working poor. The twentieth century brought a shocked recognition of the enormous death rate of infants
under 1 year old: a rate that was much higher in working-class children.

The lack of attention previously given to these infant deaths is shown by the
fact that there was no obligation for MOHs to record them separately from
overall deaths. However, a special force was given to these losses when first
the Boer War of 1899–1902 and then the First World War focused the minds
of politicians and the public on 'the competition and conflict of civilisations'.
This competition required, on the British side, 'a sufficient mass of numbers' to
succeed, as Herbert Samuel put it when he was president of the local government board.[15] Efforts to reduce the huge infant death figures (St Pancras' 161

deaths per 1,000 live births was about average for London) were often directed towards the health and education of the mother. This was a controversial position as it risked blaming the mother for the social causes of infant deaths.

Meanwhile, groups such as the Women's Co-operative Guild (WCG) and the Women's Labour League were fighting for more economic support for women, such as maternity benefit. This came in with the National Insurance Act in 1911 and was made the property of the mother in 1913. The campaigns were also supported by groups, such as the Fabian Society, that had a connection with nearby Bloomsbury. It was Virginia Woolf, for example, who helped and encouraged Margaret Llewellyn Davies to publish her ground-breaking book, *Maternity*, a collection of married working women's letters about their health and healthcare in pregnancy and childbirth. The book became a key part of the WCG's campaign to establish better support for mothers and infants. Campaigners argued vehemently that health advice and even good medical care couldn't improve women's and children's health without changes in their economic and social conditions.

The National Insurance Act came into force in 1912, covering workers earning less than £160 a year. Men, and a minority of women, who worked full time and paid 4*d* per week became entitled to sickness, disablement and maternity benefits, the service of GPs, and free treatment for tuberculosis. But there was an enormous drawback to the scheme: only the workers themselves were covered. Women who stayed at home and children were not entitled to benefits. Neither were the many part-time and low-paid women workers, or unemployed men and women. As Jane Lewis puts it in *The Politics of Motherhood*:

> Responsibility for the care of women and children was assumed to rest in the hands of a male provider. There was, therefore, great reluctance to intervene directly in the private world of the family and its economy … while it was recognised that any failure on the part of the male breadwinner to provide for his dependants left them helpless victims, it was also believed that family responsibilities provided the greatest incentive for men to work.[16]

Lewis also points out that, for the government and local authorities, 'The main aim behind national health insurance … was to keep the insured man out of the workhouse and to prevent pauperism caused by ill-health', thus reducing the cost to local rate payers.[17]

National Insurance excluded yet another group that was numerous in Fitzrovia: foreign workers who had lived in the country for less than five years. Even the five-year residency concession was only given after vigorous lobbying by Jewish friendly societies and reformers, and it only applied to members of an approved benefit society. It was therefore likely that a substantial number of immigrants in Fitzrovia didn't qualify for National Insurance.

So, the ever-growing Middlesex and University College Hospitals and their overburdened outpatient departments provided the lifeline for Fitzrovia's working-class families. Only the very sickest patients were admitted to the wards, not only due to lack of beds but because few workers could support themselves or their families while they were in hospital. They had to carry on working for as long as they possibly could. Going into hospital was often the last resort of the dying.

Joyce Hooper, a long-term resident, describes how the system at the Middlesex worked for families like hers:

> If your kids had anything wrong you didn't go to the doctor, you went round to casualty where Sister was. She used to take the children in, and decide if they needed to see a doctor or not. If you had to see a doctor they would ring up to the Children's Ward and bring them down.[18]

A *Morning Post* newspaper feature of 11 April 1912 describes a bustling but homelike atmosphere in the hospital's outpatients department. It was clearly written to give a boost to the Middlesex Hospital's fundraising efforts, adding plenty of local colour. Like most hospitals then, the Middlesex was an independent charity depending on donations for its daily running costs:

> By two o' clock the outpatient's department was full of patients who were waiting to see the doctor in whom they have learnt to have confidence … there is a freemasonry among them. To many, who are chronic attendants, the waiting-rooms act as a club … Most of them discuss the progress of symptoms as the white-capped nurses and the white-coated students move to and fro among them.

The writer continues, 'A rather overdressed Jewess sits beside men and women who are far less well clad than she, but the authorities have learnt not to judge of patients' means by their clothes.' The journalist's inference that the 'overdressed Jewess' may be choosing to receive free outpatient treatment when she can afford to pay, besides reflecting anti-Semitic bias, reminds us again that, for many working people in Fitzrovia as in other communities, receiving medical services as a charity was their only option. The feature concludes with a charitable plug, 'The hospital has dreams of a new department, adequate for its requirements, and looks to the time when it will be able to complete its buildings'.

Albums of old hospital press cuttings reveal almost non-stop activities held in support of the Middlesex's work. These ranged from a 1911 performance of Verdi's *Requiem* at the Queen's Hall, in memory of a deceased royal patron, Prince Francis of Teck, to a popular stall called 'Fragrance and Fair Women' at an All-British Shopping Week at Harrods the same year, where young actresses sold perfume to customers, raising 1,000 guineas.

An appeal regularly placed in the local Marylebone press at this time was directed specifically at residents of Marylebone, which included a wealthier section of Fitzrovia, reminding them of *their* stake in the hospital. 'No less than 45% of the patients treated at the Out-patient department of the MIDDLESEX HOSPITAL, together with a large proportion of the In-Patients, ARE DWELLERS IN THE BOROUGH OF MARYLEBONE', it declares in bold capitals.

The Middlesex's testament to the success of these campaigns is a set of post-cards made from photographs of the hospital, showing comfortable-looking wards with gleaming floors, white bedcovers, immaculately uniformed nurses, potted plants, and, in the children's ward, a large rocking horse and other toys. Some of these postcards were sent to family or friends by 'Nurse Nell', a student nurse at the hospital at the beginning of the century. 'I would like you to see the hospital,' she writes, 'it has every comfort.' Perhaps it wasn't always so comfortable for the nurses: in the Founder Ward, Nell says, a little ambiguously, 'the men want a good deal of sitting on'.[19]

The hospital buildings extended underground as well as above. Their rambling, unexpected turns were evocatively described by a former nursing student and sounded typical of Fitzrovia itself in their changeableness: 'I … loved the underground corridors where you could pop out in another part of London altogether'.[20] As befitted such an old hospital, there were ghost stories about the Middlesex. 'A patient on the oncology wards told me that he had seen a kind lady in grey who asked if he was alright, then she vanished. He died shortly afterwards,' recalls a former senior nursing officer who trained in the 1940s.[21] A former chair of the League of Friends remembers, 'You could hear trolleys in the basement that you never met.'[22] Perhaps there was a supernatural 'Other Side' to Fitzrovia!

There were earthier tales about the Middlesex, as well, according to Simon John, who says that it was reported that people were stealing rings from the fingers of corpses in the morgue in Middlesex Hospital, so a bell was rigged up to ring when the morgue's door opened. Simon John's father, PC David John, was hiding close by when the bell rang. He rushed into the morgue, only to discover a doctor and a nurse together on the mortuary slab, investigating each other's nether regions.

The Middlesex made efforts to spread health messages among its community. In 1927–28 it brought out an extensive series of leaflets on various conditions and diseases.[23] Topics included cancer prevention and treatment, care of the teeth, the prevention of deafness, house flies and disease, and eye strain.

A leaflet on infantile diarrhoea shows how widespread and deadly this disease still was at the end of the 1920s. It states, 'Eight thousand children, under the age of five years, die in England every year of Diarrhoea; nearly two thousand die each year in London alone; in many of these cases death could have been prevented by prompt medical treatment.' The leaflet goes on to caution against allowing flies in the house and permitting children to put dirty things in their mouths. It advises covering food with muslin, boiling all milk and making sure all food is fresh.

Another leaflet, perhaps an unusual one at this time when such subjects were not generally discussed, is on the menopause or the 'Change of Life', as the leaflet is called. The tone is mostly practical, the leaflet warning, for example, about the dangers of missing signs of womb cancer through ignoring irregular bleeding that might not simply be linked to menopause. It tries to address women's worries about their sometimes disturbing symptoms and to reassure them that these are normal. Yet the prevailing cultural attitude to menopause is hinted at in its capitalised last lines, 'THE "CHANGE OF LIFE" DOES NOT CAUSE MADNESS … [symptoms] can be greatly relieved if the women will consult a fully qualified doctor'. The emphasis on 'fully qualified' doctors seems to indicate that some women were resorting to unorthodox remedies for relief.

There is evidence that the local community strongly supported the Middlesex, as it supported them. *Ebb and Flow in Fitzrovia*, the series of interviews with local pensioners collected by the Fitzrovia Neighbourhood Association, is thickly scattered with reminiscences and praise of a hospital loved by many. Nellie Muller was born in the Middlesex in 1919 and remembers:

> When I was a kid I used to take my grandmother to the Middlesex about once a month and they used to give her great big bottles of medicine. I think it was for her chest or something, nothing too serious. My mum used to say 'Go on Nell you can have a day off school, go and take grandma to hospital and you can carry the medicine for her.' We had a doctor on the corner where we had to pay 3 shillings 6 pence, or we could go to the Middlesex

and pay 6 pence into the almoner's box. If they thought you were really poor then you didn't have to pay.[24]

Juanita Braithwaite says of the hospital post-NHS:

> I had my daughter in the Middlesex Hospital, and it was lovely. It was really very nice, a nice classy hospital. The care was amazing, I think maternity was on the sixth floor, whether you were private or NHS everyone was on that floor. I was very disappointed when it was knocked down. I hate to pass there to see what a lovely hospital being knocked down that served the community, for I don't know how many years ... people talk about The Old Middlesex and sometimes it brings a tear to the eye ...[25]

Beatrice Malta, a local resident born in 1925 in Portugal, worked at the Middlesex as a domestic supervisor. She was the only one who could speak both English and Portuguese and lived in hospital accommodation at York House for twenty years. During the Second World War Beatrice was a Red Cross nurse, trained by and working at the hospital.

When the hospital was rebuilt in 1935 the cost of rebuilding was borne by donations alone. The local community responded generously:

> [A]lthough there were some very large contributions, there was a wonderful response from less wealthy individuals including patients, staff, local traders and students. The appeal 'The Middlesex Hospital is falling down' was seen on hoardings, on buses, in papers and magazines ... with remarkable results. Within three years the foundation stone of the new building was laid ...[26]

Two of the new ward names, Bond Street and Dressmakers, reflected the fundraising done for the hospital by members of the clothing trade belonging to the Bond Street Association and the Dressmakers Association. Dressmakers was a male ward, reflecting the historically heavy male bias of the fashion trade.

Cancer research and treatment, for which the hospital was well known, had begun as far back as 1792. The Middlesex's cancer researchers did a lot of important work in the first few decades of the twentieth century, particularly on breast cancer. This was the most common cancer, with numbers of cases rapidly growing, to the consternation of doctors and the public. The hospital researched how cancer spread within and outside the breast; the grading of cancers; how best to operate to prevent the cancer recurring; and, above all, pioneering radium treatment.

Early experimental treatments tried by doctors at the Middlesex now sound bizarre and often gruelling to patients. Remedies tried in the first half of the nineteenth century included compression of the tumour after putting powdered chalk into the cavities on its surface; ulcerating the tumour with a caustic made of zinc paste and the herb sanguinaria, a treatment whose details 'make gruesome reading'; and making the patient take turpentine or Condurango bark, a South American herbal remedy, by mouth.[27]

Having large numbers of poor patients receiving free care at the hospital perhaps predisposed some doctors who were busy searching for new treatments to be more adventurous about which experiments they tried. All doctors were probably not as conscientious as W. Sampson Handley, father of R.S. Handley, who wrote a history of the hospital in 1924. Handley Senior said, in his book about cancer research at the Middlesex, the doctor 'is debarred from the method of experiment ... [t]he duty of the surgeon or physician is to heal the sick person ... [o]nly if the case is otherwise hopeless, and then only with the full consent of the patient, may an untried method be used'.[28]

R.S. Handley compares the survival results of patients he himself has treated to historic cases where few survived, saying:

Of the first 100 patients in my own practice who were operated on 15 or more years ago, 33 were still alive on the 15th anniversary and only 4 of these had shown recurrent disease. *I cannot help feeling that a 33% survival ... shows that modern treatment does at least achieve something.*[29]

The hospital had its own medical school on site, opened in 1835, to which women were not admitted as students until as late as 1947. In 1938–39, females only represented 11 per cent of students accepted by the University of London as a whole, compared with 20 per cent for the rest of the country. The Middlesex, like many other London medical colleges, dragged its feet on admitting women. It only changed after a 1944 government interdepartmental committee had recommended non-payment of grants if colleges continued to refuse women students.[30]

The hospital also had its own nurses' training school with a nurse's home. Young women who had reached the age of 20 could apply and were expected to complete a twelve-week preliminary training course for which they paid 10 guineas. They studied elementary anatomy, physiology, hygiene, nursing, sick-room cookery and bandaging.

Nursing standards in hospitals had risen considerably since the late nineteenth century as the professionalisation of nursing continued. In 1919, State

Registration of nurses came in and a General Nursing Council was created. It was required that State Registered nurses should have three years' training at a recognised hospital. By this time, there was a network of training schools for nurses attached to hospitals such as the Middlesex.

Apart from the Middlesex and UCLH, care for the local community was provided by the area's leading maternity hospital, Queen Charlotte's, in Marylebone Road. The Elizabeth Garrett Anderson Hospital for women, opened in 1890, stood in Euston Road, almost opposite UCLH, and to the west, in Great Portland Street, the Royal National Orthopaedic Hospital, a charitable children's hospital, opened in 1907. Its light, airy, pavilion-type wards displayed the emphasis on fresh air that was then thought to be particularly good for children.

The London Skin Hospital opened at 40 Fitzroy Square in 1891, receiving inpatients and treating outpatients with skin disorders like tuberculosis of the skin and psoriasis by X-ray treatment, high-frequency electric current and ultraviolet light. In addition, outpatient treatment was provided at the London Foot Hospital, founded in 1913 as a clinic in Charlotte Street before moving to 33 Fitzroy Square. It was the first centre in the country to formally teach chiropody.

Care in the Home: Saving Fitzrovia's Mothers and Children

Nursing care at home was even more greatly needed than hospital care. Most women gave birth at home and required reliable nursing and midwifery care which they often failed to obtain. Besides, many of Fitzrovia's working people couldn't afford the services of a doctor when they were ill, which made good home-nursing provision even more urgent. In response to this need, the Metropolitan Nursing Association was set up by Florence Lees in 1874 as a training body for home nurses or district nurses and was the first association to provide systematic nursing training. The association ran a nursing home situated close to Fitzrovia in Bloomsbury Square. It was followed in 1887 by the Queen Victoria Jubilee Institute for Nurses, later named the Queen's Nursing Institute, headquartered in Henrietta Place just west of Fitzrovia, off Cavendish Square. The institute's nurses became known as Queen's Nurses.[31]

Reasons for these two leading nursing institutions choosing this vicinity must have included the presence of several great teaching hospitals there, including, of course, the Middlesex and UCLH, and proximity to wealthy West End potential patrons, as well as large numbers of the needy poor who required home nursing. The Queen's Institute set the standard for nursing for many years. In 1936 the Midwives Act was passed, requiring all local authorities to employ salaried midwives; but it was not until 1948 that the National Health Service Act required home nurses to be provided by all local authorities.

It was a taxing life. A former Queen's Nurse, recalling her working day before the advent of the NHS, tells us:

> [W]e used to report to the Queen's Institute in the morning … half past seven, at quarter to eight we were on the road … we had to collect equipment and we had to collect our lists … you had to get your bike out … and off we'd go, with our bags in the basket at the front … we had five diabetics which we had to do first … And then you started on either some TBs or your leg dressings or your general nursing cares … the evening ones went out at half past four, and we were lucky if we were back by eight or quarter to nine. So it was a long day.[32]

The advice and care given by nurses in the home, often to new mothers, was usually greatly appreciated. And it was often desperately needed because, at the beginning of the twentieth century, there was no special provision for mothers or infants before, at or after childbirth. Midwives were often untrained and not dependable. One correspondent in *Maternity* says, 'When I was pregnant the second time, I heard that the midwife I had the first time had started drinking, so I was afraid to have her.'[33]

Fitzrovia's infant mortality in 1900 was shockingly high. That year's MOH Report for St Pancras recorded a death rate of 160.9 per 1,000 live births for infants in their first year. This disastrous rate was nevertheless average for London boroughs; and the poor Tottenham Court Road subdistrict of St Pancras showed an even higher figure of 182 deaths per 1,000.[34] Another 118 died later, from reasons related to prematurity. The rate for St Marylebone wasn't recorded – there was no obligation to do so at this time – but the borough's later recorded rates suggest that they were somewhat lower at this time. Stillbirths were not recorded but were numerous.

If babies survived past their first year, the diseases of childhood were still big killers. In 1900, 123 infants died of measles and 104 of whooping cough in St Pancras. Some 228 infants succumbed to diarrhoea, another constant danger to the young. These diseases killed far fewer in St Marylebone at that time: thirty-nine died of measles, forty-eight of whooping cough, 137 of diarrhoea and seventy of prematurity. St Marylebone's figure for diarrhoea included adult deaths, although it was mostly the very young who died. St Marylebone's toll was still substantial and, as we have seen, the death rate varied by subdistrict. In the predominantly working-class streets of Fitzrovia, the rate would have been closer to that of St Pancras.

However, by 1910 the MOH Report for St Pancras clearly shows how attitudes to infant welfare were changing. Dr John Sykes devoted several pages to his new arrangements for improving infant vitality and welfare. The first paragraphs set out his vision for the programme, '[W]e must commence with the child at the very earliest age possible. But we cannot reach the young infant directly, we must reach the infant through the mother ... not infant consultations, but medical consultations for mothers and infants – mothers first.'[35] (We have to remember that consultations did not stretch to treatment at this time.)

Dr Sykes was convinced that mothers should be advised to breastfeed only. He credits this policy, introduced in 1902–03, with producing an extraordinary fall in the summer mortality of infants in St Pancras compared with other boroughs and towns. The mention of summer mortality indicates that the reduced deaths were primarily due to preventing diarrhoea in infants. Numbers of deaths from diarrhoea in St Pancras fell dramatically to thirty-eight by 1910. The prevention of childhood disease had also been boosted that year by a vaccination programme against diphtheria. Dr Sykes reported that local legislation, the Diphtheria Anti-Toxin (London) Order, had enabled free provision of the vaccine to poorer residents.

Sykes, in the same report, proudly notes the opening of the St Pancras School for Mothers at 37 Chatton Street, Somers Town, north of Euston Road. It provided 'medical advice, dinners for mothers suckling their infants, and educational demonstrations in mothercraft at the School and in the home'. He also reports that the school had begun to work with older children up to school age. It included in its scheme the St Pancras Day Nursery in Cartwright Gardens and the St Pancras Nursery School in Crowndale Road, with a programme of medical inspections, the weighing of babies, and home visiting from health visitors.

Sykes triumphantly concludes his report, 'We have got beyond the mere prevention of infant mortality, beyond the diminution of infant sickness, we are now steaming ahead to the greater improvement of infant health and physique ...'.[36]

Although Sykes' exhilaration is understandable, it isn't, at this early date, conclusively borne out by the results. The figures certainly show a great drop in the borough's infant deaths, down to 107.8 per 1,000 live births. However, this rate is in fact a little higher than the 1910 London average of 101.6, although we must allow for St Pancras being a poor borough whose figures would normally be much higher than average. It's possible that broader factors such as improved economic and housing conditions, and London-wide measures such as vaccination for childhood diseases, had more to do with the reduced deaths than the St Pancras School for Mothers and other local programmes. But, at the same time, other London boroughs were starting to put in place many similar local provisions for infant welfare which might have acted to bring the death figures down across the city.

St Marylebone, where the infant mortality rate had fallen to 98.9 per 1,000 in 1910, was carrying out some of the same work aimed at mothers, such as tea and talks on domestic subjects and hygiene, through the voluntary work of the St Marylebone Health Society and its clinics and health visitors. Clinic consultations with mothers covered feeding methods, sleeping arrangements, bathing and outings for fresh air. Babies were weighed at each consultation. According to Jane Lewis, '[D]ummies were discouraged because of the dirt they accumulated when they were dropped and also because they were believed to distort the shape of infants' mouths. A writer in *National Health* … commented, "Remember that a baby that had had a dummy is like a tiger that tasted blood".'[37]

Both the Marylebone Health Society and the St Pancras School for Mothers recommended putting the baby in a separate cot instead of the family bed. The poverty of many local families made this ideal very hard to reach. Makeshift cots were common. Lewis says, 'The St Pancras School sold banana crates as cots for 1s each.'[38] My mother and her twin brother slept in furniture drawers after they were born in 1926 – not an unusual arrangement where they lived.

The MOH for St Marylebone, as was the official tendency then, puts responsibility for infant vitality and welfare firmly on the mothers in his 1910 report. He says of infant deaths, 'Many of those who died … did so because their mothers were in bad health or careless of themselves.' The MOH seems convinced that the Health Society is combating a tide of maternal carelessness and ignorance.

However, in 1907, Mrs Barbara Drake, a member of the City of Westminster Health Society, began an innovative twelve-month investigation of the connections between living conditions and infant death rates. She used Health Society records to analyse the effect of various socio-economic conditions on infant health. Results consistently showed 'a close link between low income, poor housing and high morbidity and mortality among both infants and mothers'.[39] Drake defined a 'comfortable' family income at 25s a week: a modest sum which, nevertheless, many families failed to receive. She demonstrated that those receiving a 'comfortable' income were also the best housed and healthiest.

Barbara Drake commented that areas like Fitzrovia with many home-run businesses tended to produce families with comfortable incomes and good standards of mothering. While this was perhaps true, 'comfortable' incomes were far from universal in Fitzrovia, and the proliferation of tailoring and other home workshops in the first decades of the century must have meant severe pressures on space and difficult home conditions. While London's local authorities made efforts to provide new housing for working families, they couldn't accommodate all the families displaced by slum clearances. The new housing also wasn't affordable for many poorer workers, since rents in the new estates were usually higher than before. According to Anthony S. Wohl, even though St Marylebone and St Pancras lost over 10,000 in population between 1901 and 1911 they were more overcrowded than before. This was partly due to a need for commercial space that squeezed out space for housing.[40] If over-crowding in Fitzrovia eventually became less of a problem, it was probably due much more to an intensifying movement out to the suburbs than to families being rehoused in the locality.

Many local people must have had to tolerate the sort of conditions roundly criticised by Benny Green, who talks of his grandfather living in a 'warren' in Greenwell Street off Cleveland Street. There was a workshop on the first floor and Green's relatives, including his grandfather's adult children and their families, occupied the rest of the house. Green describes his own parents' 'disgraceful' flat, Howard House, in Cleveland Street. He says, 'They had an indoor toilet – yes – but there was no hot water … My mother put in a bath when she moved in … it was subhuman to take money for those flats.'[41]

My own mother's family of six was crammed into a bug-infested two-bedroom flat in Howland Street. It wasn't until 1938, when their house was knocked down to build the Museum telephone exchange, that their accommodation improved after they were moved by the council to Tufnell Park, a couple of miles north of Euston Road.

The housing problem was long lasting and, adding the later damage and destruction of the Second World War, insoluble for many decades. A Communist Party pamphlet of 1945 issued after Labour's post-war election victory declares:

St Pancras has one of the worst 'Tenement Problems' in London … out of the Borough's 24,250 houses and flats … 14,250 cast-off houses of the well-to-do are inhabited by an average of three working-class families each. These families have no separate front door, and usually no separate sanitary arrangements. The conditions in some of them are quite deplorable.[42]

Given the poverty of much of Fitzrovia, as well as heavy war damage, conditions must often have been very similar to those described above. Howland Street itself was badly bombed, with its north side almost destroyed, and must have become uninhabitable for many of its residents.

Home conditions began to concern the medical authorities to the extent that, after 1910, health visitors began visiting mothers' homes, tasked with reporting back to the local authority where home conditions were inadequate for the proper care of babies and young children. After 1915, all births had to be notified to the authorities, so that a health visitor could arrange to see the parents at home and mothers could be encouraged to attend their local infant welfare centre. In 1918 a Maternal and Child Welfare Act was passed, requiring each authority to set up a maternal and child welfare committee. Some authorities included salaried midwives, day nurseries and free milk and food for mothers.

But health visitors were quite often seen as patronising intruders into working-class homes. In any case, health visitors, like the staff at infant welfare centres, gave only advice, not medical treatment. Their remit and resources were limited by government reluctance to take economic responsibility for family health, and by the pervasive attitude that infant and maternal mortality was related to maternal ignorance.

What women in working families wanted themselves was free medical treatment, financial help to afford care at childbirth, post-natal care, including help with housework, and better household wages. These concerns come through time and again in the married women's letters in *Maternity*. Even after maternity benefit of 30s started to be paid to the mother directly in 1913, it didn't cover all a woman's expenses. A letter called 'Heavy Expense of Childbirth' explains that the benefit 'is only a trifle to the large expense that is incurred, when you have paid £1 1s for your doctor, your nurse 10s per week, a washerwoman 2s per day (you cannot get a nurse here under, and if she does the washing she will charge 12s per week)'.[43] Other letter writers stressed the financial burden of motherhood, even though many made a point of praising the maternity benefit.

In *Maternity*, the Women's Co-operative Guild put forward their own proposed scheme for maternal and infant care. This included higher maternity benefits which would also be paid during pregnancy, free treatment at mother and infant centres, better training for midwives, more maternity beds in hospitals for complicated cases, free milk and the provision of home helps.

By 1920, the borough authorities in St Pancras were working to address these needs. The 1920 MOH report shows that by this time there were thirteen

Maternity and Child Welfare Centres (renamed from Schools for Mothers) in the borough. One was within walking distance of Fitzrovia in Bloomsbury's Tavistock Square. Besides free or cheap milk for poorer mothers, they provided a free dental clinic for mothers and young children, as well as other services. Home helps were provided for sick mothers by a voluntary body, the St Pancras Home Helps Committee. By this time, there were also four district nursing associations providing home nursing in St Pancras. The council was also subsidising the provision of midwives for residents, but this subsidised charge had been raised to £1 in 1920 and was still a very large chunk out of a modest family budget.

The 1920 MOH report for St Pancras includes a breakdown of exactly who was treating expectant mothers at childbirth. There were nearly 2,000 private and institutional midwives and 1,453 doctors attending births; however, medical students also attended women, in similar numbers to doctors. This doesn't just indicate that more women than before were giving birth in hospital; it suggests, as well, that labouring women in hospital weren't always given the specialised attention from fully qualified doctors that they might have needed.

At UCLH an Infant Welfare Department had begun in 1916 under Dr E.A. Barton. It ran two clinics a week by 1919, with 770 infants, known as 'Barton's Babies', on the register at that date, and four cots for sick babies.[44] There seems to have been close co-operation between UCLH and borough infant welfare facilities, with sick infants being transferred from the hospital to the care of the borough when they were well, while the borough centres moved their sick children to the hospital.

The harsh local conditions after the First World War are reported on by a health visitor at the time, Miss Brooke. She says, 'Economic conditions have caused much distress – mostly owing to lack of employment and the price of food and coal.' She grimly comments, 'It was not unusual to have infants brought up [to the hospital] in a moribund condition and sometimes they died in the department before they could be conducted to the Ward; two in one family died in one afternoon.'[45]

Despite these fearsome conditions, the infant death rate for St Pancras in 1920 was down to seventy-three per 1,000 live births, the lowest figure to date, against seventy-five for London as a whole. This improvement, now giving St Pancras a lower than average infant death rate, does perhaps start to give force to Dr Sykes' earlier enthusiasm about the borough's approach to maternal and infant care. However, childhood diseases were still a danger in St Pancras: twenty-one died of measles and eighteen of whooping cough. None died of diphtheria, due no doubt to the vaccination programme. Fifteen deaths were from inherited syphilis, another intractable disease.

In St Marylebone, the infant death rate had dropped to sixty-five, also the lowest ever recorded. As before, the relative affluence of the borough might have affected the statistics. Deaths from childhood diseases had plummeted in the borough since 1900: one child died of diphtheria and one of scarlet fever, while measles claimed two lives. 'Prematurity' was still responsible for fifty deaths of infants below 1 year old.

By 1920, St Marylebone was also attempting, like St Pancras, to provide a better service to mothers and young children, although it was less comprehensive than in St Pancras. There were ante-natal clinics close to Fitzrovia, in Salisbury Street and Marylebone Lane, as well as at Queen Charlotte's Hospital, where many local women went to have their babies. There was also a free home help service organised through health visitors. This must have been only for the neediest mothers, since health visitors obtained help for only twenty-nine women at a cost of 25s per week.

It appears that, in 1920, Fitzrovia's mothers and children were significantly better off in terms of healthcare facilities if they lived on the St Pancras side of the borough boundary. Furthermore, the death rate for all residents, as opposed to infants, was slightly higher in St Marylebone (12.7 per 1,000) than in St Pancras (12.4 per 1,000). This might indicate that the general population also felt the benefit of better care in St Pancras, even though St Pancras was the more deprived borough.

But maternal mortality was still a huge problem in both boroughs and had been long neglected nationally. Every local MOH report of this period records several mothers dying each year through childbirth, a rate well above one per 1,000 births even in the late 1930s.

In 1926, Dr F.J. Browne of UCLH wrote:

Mortality and morbidity rates in child-bed and the puerperium are almost as high as they were in pre-antiseptic days. I believe ... in this country alone about 3000 women lose their lives every year ... When we add to this the thousands of women who survive but are more or less permanently injured ... we are face to face with a condition that calls aloud for remedy.[46]

Dr Browne blamed doctors unskilled in midwifery for much of the toll. The opening of a new Obstetric Hospital in 1926, run by UCLH and incorporating Dr Barton's Child Welfare Department, would, it was hoped, mark a turning point for women's health provision. However, the local networks of infant and maternal welfare clinics were still crucial in giving help and support to mothers. They started to provide free health checks and advice (though not medical treatment) for women as well as babies and, in some cases, free meals as well as government-subsidised milk.

Fitzrovia's Borough Divide: Two Sides of Public Health?

In 1931 the Metropolitan Boroughs gained extra responsibilities for healthcare provision under the Local Government Act of 1929, including taking over health services from hospitals formerly run under the Poor Law. Public Health Surveys were carried out in St Pancras and St Marylebone, as in all the London boroughs, after this legislation. The final reports were written in 1933 and give an official assessment of their services' range and standard.

Comparison of the two different borough healthcare reports is revealing and fascinating. By the 1930s, an 'Other Side' existing within Fitzrovia itself was clearly visible, depending on which side of the borough boundary line you lived. The individual surveys for St Pancras and St Marylebone not only show the extent of public care in Fitzrovia in 1933 but also reveal sometimes striking differences in provision, particularly in the care of mothers and children. Although joined-up healthcare across the boroughs was beginning to be seen some years before the coming of the NHS in 1948, there was also an unevenness between them, meaning that local people living only streets apart could experience very different levels of care. Fitzrovia's population experienced a more problematic version of our present complained-of 'postcode lottery' in health services.

The Public Health Survey reports for both boroughs highlighted the Tottenham Court Road area as an area of need. The survey for St Pancras began, 'Some of the meanest houses and poorest people are to be found … round about Tottenham Court Road, while the extreme north of the Borough [the Hampstead area] is the abode of wealthy residents …'. The survey for St Marylebone described much of the borough as being 'inhabited by comparatively well-to-do persons living in well-built houses provided with all the amenities', but adds:

> … other parts … are inhabited by the poorest classes housed for the most part in badly built and dilapidated working-class dwellings or, as in the corner between Oxford Street and Tottenham Court Road, in houses each of which formerly accommodated a family of the prosperous middle class but are now let out in tenements for the working classes.

It is obvious that Fitzrovia at this time was still regarded as one of the poor parts of London with, no doubt, many urgent healthcare needs.

St Pancras appeared to be rapidly assuming control of many local health services and employed substantial numbers of staff in health roles. The St Pancras Survey is largely devoted to maternal and infant welfare provision, as might be expected not only from the strong national focus on this issue but also from the borough's pioneering work in the field. The report says, 'Much good work for the welfare of mothers and children is being carried out in the Borough.'

St Marylebone directly employed far fewer staff and provided fewer health facilities than its neighbour. In fact, the St Marylebone Survey noted that an 'outstanding feature' of the borough's maternal and child welfare work was 'the large part played by voluntary societies, especially the St Marylebone Health Society'. The reporter commented that this arrangement was much less expensive for the borough!

St Marylebone's infant death rate actually increased temporarily after 1920, despite the survey report saying that there are 'admirable facilities for hospital treatment of mothers and children within or closely adjoining the Borough'. St Marylebone's average infant mortality rate for the five years before 1931 was 72.6 per 1,000 live births as against the London average of sixty-five. The borough was twentieth in the list of London boroughs. The St Pancras rate for 1930, by contrast, was sixty, 'the lowest ever recorded', according to that year's MOH report, with no five-year figure given.[47] Even ten years later, the gap between the boroughs was equally wide, although rates were lower: fifty-four in St Pancras (1939) and sixty-seven in St Marylebone (1940). St Pancras' more centralised, consistent approach to reducing infant deaths over the years might have been measurably paying off, but the borough's record could still bear criticism. St Pancras was slated in a 1936 Communist Party pamphlet for inadequate care in its mother and baby clinics.

There was a similar contrast between St Pancras and St Marylebone when it came to maternal mortality. St Pancras' 1931 MOH report recorded the deaths of four mothers from childbirth – equivalent to 1.6 per 1,000 births – compared with the far higher St Marylebone figure of four per 1,000 births. But again, St Pancras had much room for improvement, according to the Communist Party: its maternal mortality in 1935 was unfavourably contrasted with Labour-run Bermondsey, where no mothers had died of childbirth at all.

The St Pancras Survey clarified that local services for mothers and infants, apart from those in hospitals, were now being largely council run and funded. St Pancras had ten Maternity and Child Welfare Centres. One was in Grafton Road in Fitzrovia, and another was close by in UCLH. The Grafton Road

Centre was small, but through it, women and children could access a widening network of health services. During 1930, this centre sent nine mothers and eleven children away to council convalescent homes and referred eighteen children to its Artificial Light Clinic for the newly popular 'sunshine treatment' for rickets, catarrh, malnutrition and other conditions. Additionally, most of St Pancras' health visitors – twenty-five full-time staff – were now employed by the council, against only six health visitors in St Marylebone. In fact, Dr Cameron, who wrote this section of the St Pancras Survey, thought that there was overstaffing when it came to health visitors.

In 1931 St Pancras had forty-six midwives, mainly employed by the council: only seventeen of them were private. On the other hand, St Marylebone only had twenty-two midwives in total which, the survey noted, was an inadequate number. St Marylebone relied on hospital midwives to make up the numbers. And St Marylebone's ante-natal clinics were mainly run by St Marylebone Health Society, whereas in St Pancras the council ran all the ante-natal clinics not provided directly by hospitals. There was still some voluntary activity in St Pancras – 'a good deal' of maternity nursing in St Pancras was being done by the voluntary Maternity Nursing Association headquartered in Camden Road. More than 40 per cent of births in St Pancras were now taking place in hospital, with the borough paying £1 towards care for each patient who couldn't afford hospital treatment.

Children's educational welfare was also better catered for in St Pancras. The borough owned five nursery schools and also contributed to the cost of the four day-nurseries. One of these was in Fitzrovia: the Whitfield Day Nursery at 53 Whitfield St. According to the survey it was underused, 'said to be due to the rapidly changing character of the district and its increasing industrial development'. (In fact, the Whitfield Day Nursery was to be closed before very long, possibly given the final blow by bomb damage during the Second World War.) In contrast, St Marylebone had only two council day nurseries, neither of them near Fitzrovia.

The surveys of local services clearly showed two different pictures existing in St Pancras and St Marylebone in the 1930s. There did seem to be distinct advantages for mothers and children living in the St Pancras-controlled area of Fitzrovia. We might even say that Fitzrovia was split down the middle as far as healthcare for mothers and children went. With health services starting to be grouped together and centrally run by local authorities, people's health was benefiting overall, yet the powers given to the authorities in 1929 had not yet resulted in evening up healthcare across the city. Indeed, perhaps provision had temporarily become yet more uneven as boroughs like St Pancras moved at speed to implement their new responsibilities whereas others, including St Marylebone, were slower to respond. Fragmented arrangements like this allowed far too much opportunity for women to fall through gaps in care. We can appreciate the drawbacks involved in this patchwork evolution of services, while perhaps also being impressed by the amount of public healthcare already existing in London before the NHS, especially in places like St Pancras.

Some of the impact of these pre-war changes in healthcare governance can be seen in the words of George E.S. Ward of the Middlesex Hospital Medical School. Ward says, in his introductory address to students in July 1936, 'It is apparent to all that the Government, through the Ministry of Health and by its system of State grants, is getting more and more control over the many and varied problems of vital importance to the bodily welfare of the Nation'. Ward calls this project 'a stupendous task'.[48] However, during the 1930s much health-care and nursing continued, as before, to be paid for privately from workers' often tiny budgets or provided by family and neighbours. Although substantial numbers benefited from the free clinics, many others never used them. Only the introduction of the NHS could begin to properly address these imbalances.

Flying Bombs at the Middlesex and the Coming of the NHS

When war broke out in September 1939, the Middlesex and UCLH carried on through the raids. The authorities thought that London would immediately be the target for air attacks, so plans were made to put the hospitals on a war footing and to evacuate many patients and staff, keeping the London premises mostly for emergency use. But when no air raids materialised immediately, hospital departments, in many cases, moved back to their London buildings; and when raids started in the autumn of 1940 it wasn't practicable to re-evacuate on the same scale as before, so the hospitals carried on much as usual through the war. Many bombs fell around them, since the important rail connections close to Fitzrovia were bombing targets.

An anti-aircraft shell broke through one of the windows of the Middlesex some months after bombing first began in 1940. Luckily, it failed to explode, and patients had already been moved to the lower floors, so were unharmed by the shell's violent entry. In April 1941, a 500lb bomb dropped onto the roof of the hospital's east wing, while explosions and a fire affected the top floor of the outpatient annexe. Both incidents caused severe damage to the upper floors but, again, no one was hurt, due largely to the efforts of the roof patrol made up of Middlesex staff and the solid construction of the 1935 hospital building.

Meanwhile, UCLH had some narrow escapes: a landmine destroyed the library and great hall of University College, next door, and a bomb caused a huge fire in Maple's department store in Grafton Way, behind the main hospital building.

Both hospitals received constant casualties at times of bombing raids, with surgical operations continuing throughout the night. Later in the war, the Middlesex Hospital weekly return of outpatient cases marks, in red ink, clinics cancelled on 24 June and 1 July 1944, due first to an air raid on Whitfield Street and then a flying bomb in Howland Street. The Whitfield Street bomb led to about 200 casualties arriving at the hospital.

In 1948, after the turmoil of the war, came the legislation that brought about the NHS. The changes brought by the introduction of the NHS are far too vast to go into here. Its impact on ordinary people's lives was immense. It's easy to imagine what a relief it was not to have to scrape money together to see a doctor and to buy medicines. Fitzrovia's working families could feel a new sense of dignity when charitable hospital services became theirs by right. Nevertheless, the flourishing private medical clinics of Harley Street still signal that there are two sides to healthcare in Fitzrovia, as in the rest of London and the UK.

In 1948, institutions like the Middlesex Hospital could be slow to fully understand the transformation caused by the coming of the NHS. J.J. Astor, the chairman of the Middlesex Hospital Board, declared in his 1949 Annual Report:

> In spite of the changes wrought by the National Health Service, the work of the Hospital has suffered no interruption, and indeed, has gone forward with increasing intensity … With the Medical School, although it has now become an independent body, the Hospital has continued to work as closely and happily as before … in all things we have tried to preserve continuity … Our constituent Institutions, St Luke's Woodside, The Hospital for Women, Soho, and the Arthur Stanley Institute, were deprived by the Health Service act of much of their independence, but it has been the Board's aim that they should retain their identity, and, as far as possible, their freedom of action.

It's evident here that J.J. Astor greatly prized the independence given to the hospital by its charitable status. He appeared to fear an interruption to its work from the NHS but was keen to reassure those involved with the hospital's running that nothing had changed. There is a suggestion that, in the mind of the chairman at least, the aims of the Middlesex and the new NHS did not fully coincide – the hospital's work continued 'in spite of' the NHS. It was likely that some other hospital boards had similar reservations about loss of identity, until the NHS itself had had time to become a central part of British hospitals' identity and, indeed, of British identity.

Fifty Years On: The Struggle for Healthcare

The 1950 Annual Report of the MOH for St Pancras noted that it was 'a year of celebration for the Metropolitan Boroughs, for it represented the fiftieth anniversary of their establishment'. To mark it, the St Pancras report opened with comparative statistical snapshots of 1900 and 1950. Some of the key figures are reproduced below, set beside the equivalent figures for St Marylebone:

	St Pancras		St Marylebone	
	1900	1950	1900	1950
Population	243,076	141,300	141,188	78,260
Birth rate (per 1,000 pop.)	26.5	15.5	21.9	10.99
Death rate (per 1,000 pop.)	19.1	11.5	18.9	11.64
Infant death rate (per 1,000 live births)	161	30.6	N/A	22.09
Diphtheria deaths	71	Nil	36	Nil
Typhoid deaths	63	Nil	13	Nil

Dennis Geffen, the MOH for St Pancras, proudly noted, 'These figures speak for themselves.' They broadly reflect the progress achieved in London in reducing the burden of disease and early death; progress that had begun in the closing decades of the nineteenth century when health legislation and improving living conditions had seen the overall death rate begin to fall.

It is not until the dawn of the NHS, though, that we begin to see in local MOH reports, such as the 1950 St Pancras report, a move away from previous anxieties about child and maternal health that suggests battles being won, and a concentration instead on the welfare of local elderly residents that coincides with the ending of the last remnants of Poor Law provision for the elderly.

There emerges a recognition that shutting old people away in workhouse-type hospital wards or housing accommodation could no longer suffice. Over fifty years, it appears that things have moved from tackling a large-scale loss of life at birth to what seems a very current preoccupation with the other end of the human lifespan.

For several decades after 1950, the Middlesex continued to stand in Fitzrovia and serve its residents. The building finally closed its doors in 2005, after the hospital merged with UCLH. Now, the walker along Howland Street passes several of University College's medical outposts, and on the corner of Charlotte Street and Howland Street is a newly built research centre, the Sainsbury-Wellcome Centre for Neural Circuits and Behaviour. Around the corner in Cleveland Street, awaiting redevelopment, are the deserted Victorian buildings of the hospital annexe that was the old workhouse infirmary: some of the last remnants of the old Middlesex.

The Furniture Trade: Fake Fitzrovia?

The furniture trade grew up with Fitzrovia. Wood yards and carpentry workshops were woven into its fabric as it became fully urbanised in the decades before 1800. The burgeoning of the furniture and carpentry trade was, in fact, linked to Fitzrovia's marginality at the border of London. As the frontiers of the city changed and London expanded northwards, the frantic pace of house building around Euston Road, with all the necessary fitting out and furnishing involved, meant that carpentry and furniture making were natural industries to find there. The evolving Fitzrovia of the eighteenth century also possessed larger and cheaper workshop and storage space for woodworking than did the more central and built-up Covent Garden where the trade had been based before.

Historians old and new have commented on the area's tradition of furniture making as it developed from the eighteenth century. Nick Bailey, in *Fitzrovia* (1981), devotes some valuable pages to tracing the history of Fitzrovia's 'unrivalled place as a major centre for cabinet and furniture making'.[1] Bailey dates the link with the furniture trade as far back as 1752, at a time when few streets there had even been laid out, when two former employees of Thomas Chippendale (who worked south of Oxford Street in St Martin's Lane, Covent Garden) set up a workshop near the Swan in Tottenham Court Road. Others also took advantage of the low rents in the area to start their businesses. Christopher Fuhrlohg, the Swedish cabinetmaker patronised by the Prince of Wales, had a workshop at 24 Tottenham Court Road. François Hervé, the chair maker, worked at 32 Johns Street – now Whitfield Street – from 1785.

The new housing developments in Bloomsbury, and in Fitzrovia itself, drew carpenters, cabinetmakers and many other artisans in related trades – gilders, silversmiths, French polishers and upholsterers – both British and

foreign. A cluster effect also operated to ensure that wood suppliers, craftsmen and then large retailers, benefiting from their proximity to each other,
all thrived within this same small area. The emergent large stores contracted
out orders to a network of existing small workshops, driving and expanding
the industry.

Other urban developments drove the trade, too. C. Edwards, in a study of
Tottenham Court Road's furniture trade, argues:

> Apart from local sources of supply, the retailers benefitted from develop-
> ments in infrastructure. In 1818, the Tottenham Court Road was equipped
> with street lighting, which must have had a beneficial effect on business. The
> Regents Canal passed nearby so this was useful for timber deliveries. By the
> mid century, a transport infrastructure included buses that used the street as
> a thoroughfare, and useful rail links. The Euston mainline terminus and the
> Metropolitan line underground stations were close by. It was at this stage that
> a critical mass was established.[2]

As we know, by 1900, Tottenham Court Road was overflowing with omnibuses, with the Central and Northern Tube lines hovering on the horizon. The
street was one of the busiest in London.

Fitzrovia's carpentry trades were supported by the City-based Worshipful
Company of Carpenters, which set up the Trades Training School in Great
Titchfield Street in 1893 – an example of the growing movement towards
technical education and away from the old apprenticeship system. The Trades
Training School, later a college, remained there until 2001 before moving
to Stratford in East London. It trained a whole range of carpentry, furniture
making and building workers who were already working in their industries.

Another mark of the trade's importance locally was the presence of the
Woodcarvers' Society, founded in 1833, in Tottenham Street. Furniture making,
then, was established well before the opening in Tottenham Court Road of big
home-furnishing department stores such as Heal's, Maple's and Shoolbred's,
which propelled the trade forward as the nineteenth century progressed.

By 1861, there existed what P.G. Hall calls 'a considerable West End branch
of the trade', much of it clustered off Tottenham Court Road.[3] Quality-wise,
Fitzrovia's furniture products were placed second in Hall's four ranked categories of the trade. They were labelled 'High-class ready-made', ranked in
quality below 'West End Bespoke' but above both 'East End ready-made' and
the lowest 'factory trade' that was also mostly East End based.[4] Hall described
this second tier of furniture making as being 'centred in the "trade" or "piece-

masters" shops, in and around Tottenham Court Road and Euston Road'. According to Hall, 'It is these shops which account for the well-marked West End furniture quarter of the nineteenth century.'[5]

Good craftsmanship didn't always mean wages to match, however. Furniture making was, in general, a lower-paid trade and, although the East End tended to bear the brunt of poor pay, the small makers of the West End were increasingly squeezed by the big retailers upon whom they were often dependent for all their orders, so that the small masters had to keep prices and pay down. The potential for 'sweating' therefore existed in this higher-class branch of the trade, also. Increasing mechanisation de-skilled workers, contributed to low wages and eventually led to the decline of the 'high-class ready-made' sector and the virtual demise of the old craft in Fitzrovia and other parts of the West End.

However, in 1901 there was a dense mixture of workshops belonging to cabinetmakers, chair makers, and general furniture makers on both sides of Tottenham Court Road, according to Hall's area map of the local furniture industry. Carvers, turners and French polishers were sprinkled into this mix of trades. The cluster extended eastward into Bloomsbury and westward as far as Great Portland Street, with a scattering even further west, between Wigmore Street and Oxford Street. Yet another huddle of workshops lay north of Euston Road, adjacent to the main road and rail lines. Two sawmills operated in the area, behind Tottenham Court Road and Newman Street.

All of these small carpentry and furniture businesses were run by men. This contrasted with other types of businesses in Howland Street and across Fitzrovia where women did feature: food retailing and catering, for example, or dressmaking and associated trades. The furniture industry was, in fact, heavily male dominated, with the few women working in it being found mainly in furniture polishing or in some sections of the upholstering process, although the situation began to change a little during the First World War when women were drafted in to fill men's jobs.

In 1901, Fitzrovia's furniture industry was even bigger than the 'considerable' 1861 industry. Yet, relative to the East End, it was already in decline, even though Hall's 1901 area map of the West End furniture trade shows a large concentration of workshops. The decline in the West End furniture industry continued, so that by 1951 few workshops remained in Fitzrovia. Hall's 1951 map shows how the industry had shrunk.

Lingering public perceptions about 'sordid' Fitzrovia persistently tinged its reputation as a producer of good furniture. The place was distrusted, even though consumers crowded into its big stores and experts on domestic furnishings admitted its dominance in the market. Stores like Heal's and Maple's prided themselves on making good-quality furnishings available to the growing middle-class market of the 1900s, and public recognition of their influence gradually diminished the snobbish suspicions attached to wares from Tottenham Court Road. However, to some middle-class taste formers, less expensive automatically meant worse, and attitudes like these took a long time to alter.

Ideas about the worth of Tottenham Court Road's reputation for furniture production were also closely linked to wider debates about taste and style, such as whether furniture design should seek out new forms or reinterpret old ones. The consumer demand for old styles of furniture at this period led to debates about what value to attach to the 'reproduction' furniture which became a substantial part of the industry.

The prestige market in original antiques, which began to grow in the nineteenth century, later in the century became blended with the wider market in newly made furniture that copied the old, in ways that confused many people. By 1900, Fitzrovia was a major centre for the better-quality side of this reproduction work – another reason why it was harshly judged in some quarters as a producer of 'fake' furniture and a vector of 'inauthentic' standards of taste. Even a retail dynamo like Ambrose Heal had to work very hard to soothe these public misgivings.

In this tangle of taste wars there erupted small but surprising phenomena, like the little Japanese and British-Japanese 'families' of lampshade makers that popped up unannounced in Fitzrovia, Bloomsbury and other patches of London. Why did they suddenly appear, what was their role in Fitzrovia's home-furnishings market, and how did their presence play into or out of stereotypes concerning domestic taste and style? This chapter will try to provide some answers to these questions.

The Furniture Stores of Tottenham Court Road

By 1900, Heal's, Maple's and Shoolbred's home-furnishing department stores had already been open for decades and were well-established, well-regarded features of Tottenham Court Road. Shoolbred's, at 155 Tottenham Court Road, opened in the 1820s, the first department store in the area, although it didn't sell furniture until the 1870s. It was followed by Hewetson's (1838), Heal's (1839), Maple's (1841) and Oetzmann & Co. of Hampstead Road (1848). By the end of the nineteenth century the stores' importance was displayed in extensive buildings whose massive and imposing appearance we still associate with the West End department stores.

The *Illustrated London News*, marking Maple's new premises in an advertorial
dated 17 June 1893, exclaimed at 'the handsome blocks of buildings whose
ruddy tones give colour and warmth to the northern end of Tottenham Court
Road'. Behind Maple's store, it noted, there were 'great yards, where huge
stacks of timber are ripening for use' and 'numerous great factories and workshops fitted up with every modern labour-saving appliance'.

On 15 May 1914, *The Times* surveyed 'the varied length of the Tottenham
Court-road', where 'at intervals, the towering plate-glass discloses … to a
prying public the comfortable hearth of a nameless home'. By 2 April 1921
the newspaper was marking the impact of local transport improvements on
these great stores:

> The shopping woman knows that [trade] follows the omnibus. One of the
> busiest streams of traffic in London is that which, fed from many centres,
> rushes with ceaseless clatter down Tottenham-court-road … one can almost
> see it grow as its businesses one after the other rebuild or extend. Furniture
> is the first idea that the name … evokes.

These major department stores aimed to be places to which the rapidly growing numbers of middle-class customers wishing to fit out their homes could
trust their entire home-furnishing budgets, in the confident expectation of
receiving both value for money and tasteful products.

Increasingly, during the nineteenth century and into the twentieth, Maple's,
Heal's and the other Tottenham Court Road stores were striving to anticipate
and satisfy consumers' growing home needs. The *Illustrated London News* article
of 1893 recognised a change in consumer aspiration, declaring that Maple's
existence was due to 'the growth of the natural and legitimate constituents of
house furnishing'. The article claimed:

> Maple's … may be regarded as perfect house furnishers – supplying, and
> in many instances manufacturing, every item, large or small, for the entire
> equipment of a home, or, for the matter of that, guiding one to the selection
> of a home, and then decorating and furnishing it.

Taste wise, the *Times* of 15 May 1914 described the modern 'British house-
holder' as possessing a newly 'critical spirit':

> With his modern eye he is now looking to 'effects,' and has, more and more,
> in furnishing his house some idea of what the completed whole is to be. His

purchases are more careful, and he is not content, as was his father, to but haphazard those characterless chairs and glassy sideboards which are now the stock-in-trade of the second-hand shop.

To satisfy the demanding modern middle-class buyer, the big stores had their own factories close at hand. But they were also sustained by a network of smaller suppliers in and around Tottenham Court Road. Heal's opened its own cabinet factory in 1897, behind the store in Alfred Mews, but continued to use other suppliers. In 1911, there were twenty-two furniture-making workshops in Tottenham Court Road and three more in Charlotte Street.[6]

Oliver S. Heal, writing about Ambrose Heal and the heyday of the store, reveals the closeness of the relationship that grew up between the big stores and their supplier workshops:

> Some of these workshops were evidently very small and little is known of them other than the fact that their relationship with Heal's was so close that the same piece of furniture might sometimes be manufactured by Heal's own factory or sometimes by the subcontractor.[7]

One of Heal's major suppliers in the late nineteenth and early twentieth centuries was Frederick Coote of 187a Tottenham Court Road, only a few doors away from Heal's at 195–198 (at that time the numbering was sequential, not split into odd and even on opposite sides of the road). Coote, previously trading in Warwick in the Midlands, moved his business to Tottenham Court Road in 1870 and lived at 17 Charlotte Street. He supplied bedroom furniture to Heal's until his business was taken over by Heal's itself in 1920. Oliver S. Heal says:

> From the bedroom furniture stockbooks that survive from 1897 onwards, it is evident that Coote was an important supplier of bedroom furniture to Heal & Son, which in the main was painted white, thereby suggesting that it would mostly have been made of deal. Heal's bedroom furniture range in 1900 included no less than twenty-six suites from Coote – by far the biggest single supplier. He had evidently decided not to continue with the same standard of top quality cabinet work with which he had been associated in Warwick.[8]

These remarks on Coote's using 'deal' (a cheap softwood like pine), and his move to doing lesser-quality work for Heal's, highlight the store's difficult balancing act in regard to its products. Heal's had to maintain a reputation as an arbiter of taste and a deliverer of high standards in homeware but also make goods available to a broad middle-class market, including some on a very limited budget. The 'deal' comment gives a certain force to accusations from some quarters that Tottenham Court Road stood for shoddy goods; however, Heal's reputation was shored up by it also providing furniture for the wealthy who needed no budget at all. As Oliver S. Heal points out, 'For Heal's, Coote even made a mahogany bedroom suite that was priced at £112: right at the top of the range.'[9] Ambrose Heal could even turn this variation in standards to his advantage. Tim Benton makes the point, in 'Up and down at Heal's: 1929–1935':

> [Heal] understood to perfection the mentality of his customers, who were prepared to pay for good workmanship and simple forms intelligently presented. There was enough similarity between the really expensive, inlaid pieces and the more modest, workaday models for the distinction of the one to rub off on the other.[10]

Unlike the famous big furniture stores, most of the small independent craft workshops in Fitzrovia left little trace of their activities. Many were perhaps humble enterprises working solely for the large retailers. However, there were a few independent furniture makers who sold their own goods and had their own 'name'. One of these was A. Davis & Sons Ltd of 209 Tottenham Court Road. It was founded in 1830 and was listed until the 1920s as a 'house furnishers', but it had changed its designation to 'antique furniture dealers' by 1930. Davis sold goods under his own name – an antiques website (sellingantiques.co.uk) features a 'Davis' Taper Leg Piano Stool' in mahogany with 'spade feet and leaf-patterned fabric' dated to around 1910. According to William I. Massil, A. Davis & Sons was taken over in 1921 by the firm of Shard which had previously supplied Davis. The firm's name remained the same but the change in the business description noted above might owe something to the change in ownership. Massil recounts a poignant wartime story about the company that re-emphasises the immigrant contribution to the industry so typical of Fitzrovia:

> Shortly after the outbreak of World War II, The War Office decided that a number of Shard's Italian cabinetmakers were aliens and they were deported. They chose to take their families to North America but all were killed tragically when the ship in which they were all travelling was torpedoed.[11]

Davis, under Shard's, grew and continued to operate in Tottenham Court Road until 1978, when it moved to Barnstaple in Devon.

The Furniture Makers

Furniture making in 1900 was a common form of employment among men in Fitzrovia. Up to 1900, the clothing trade was still largely based in Soho, and furniture making and its associated crafts were predominant on the north side of Oxford Street. In 1861, St Marylebone and St Pancras between them accounted for about 20 per cent of the 25,809 Greater London furniture workers, according to the 1861 census. The great majority must have worked in Fitzrovia, to judge by P.G. Hall's industry maps. However, by 1951, things had changed so that the two boroughs contributed only 4.9 per cent of the workforce to what was, however, a larger trade in general than in 1861. There were still 3,066 furniture makers left in Fitzrovia and surrounding areas in 1951, but it is probable that by this date furniture workers were employed in factories rather than the small-scale workshops that had been common fifty years before.

Howland Street, my mother's birthplace, had several furniture-related businesses at this period. In 1910, firms trading there included Henry Kerby, a carpenter's; Harding and Dupuis, wood carvers; Jonas Wolff & Son, carvers and gilders; Herbert George Scarlett, a white wood worker; Joseph Powell, trunk maker; Joseph Crisp & Son, leather gilders; John Delicata, wood carver; and Leslie Tucker, furniture dealer. There were also other associated trades, such as a furniture remover. The sprinkling of French, German and Italian names gives a flavour of the national diversity existing among these small businessmen.

Moreover, the 1911 census returns for Howland Street reflect the continuing presence of foreign artisans in Fitzrovia, showing that numerous European workers were engaged in the furniture trade there. There were polishers from France living at Nos 10, 16, and 60; a Venetian cabinetmaker at No. 13; a marquetry cutter from Bohemia at No. 24; an Italian carpenter at No. 26; a cluster of foreign wood carvers working for Harding and Dupuis' business at No. 41 and also at Nos 42 and 46; a Swiss upholsterer at No. 43; two Swiss cabinetmakers at No. 47; and Giovanni Delicata, who ran a woodcarving business at No. 56. The census indicates that Fitzrovia's old artisanal immigrant communities, established up to 150 years before, were still flourishing.

This mixed European community of artisans followed a trade with sharp distinctions among its different branches. The main occupations were cabinet making; the separate division of fancy cabinet making, at the higher end of the trade and well represented in Fitzrovia's workshops; chair making; turning; carving; French polishing and upholstery.

Those who entered the industry almost always learnt one main branch of it, where they would probably stay for their whole working lives. Wages were low, and by the late 1930s, experienced furniture makers in the numerous work-shops that paid below union rate were earning perhaps only 90*s* a week, even if they were in the senior post of foreman cabinetmaker. Pay was as little as 50*s* a week for a journeyman carpenter. Juveniles under 21, and the relatively few women in the trade, earned much less than even this low wage.

At the cheaper end of the trade, mainly located in the East End, further spe-cialisation existed linked to mass-production techniques. Relatively low-skilled 'beginner' workers, perhaps only making table legs for example, could be used instead of the fully trained craftsmen who tended to work in the West End.

However, a fully trained cabinetmaker producing high-quality work needed a multitude of skills. The 1938 Report to the British Furniture Trades Joint Committee evoked a long tradition of careful workmanship when it wrote:

> In cabinet-making, the following stages in the treatment of the timber are typical:- Preliminary smoothing; marking out the wood before cutting; cut-ting to length and breadth; planing to thickness; moulding; jointing; joining; veneering; smoothing; assembly; carving; fitting; filling; staining and colour-ing; polishing; finishing and touching-up.[12]

Many of the initial stages of cabinet making were carried out or aided by the machines that had been introduced into the industry from the nineteenth century. Wood cutting was, by the twentieth century, almost always done by machine, with small specialised workshops often taking their wood to 'trade mills', who would cut it to order. There were two such sawmills in Fitzrovia.

Planing was also done by machine. Soon after 1900, sheet materials became available to make drawer bottoms, for example, and birch plywood sheets were being imported from Finland and Russia for this purpose. Massil explains that sheets 'eliminated many of the processes associated with solid woods, such as drying, cutting and jointing, allowed furniture to be lighter in weight and lower in material and reduced costs'.[13] Mouldings were cut on a spindle-moulding machine, and joints could be made by hand or machine. Even veneer pat-terns could be created by machine as well as by hand. The workshops around Tottenham Court Road were among those that did the most hand work.

The 1938 report explains, 'In a shop where the old tradition of hand work is most nearly adhered to, the Cabinet Maker himself selects and cuts the wood to the size required, and does all the work necessary on the pieces'.[14] But, by the date of this report, relatively few workshops operated in such a way.

Chair making was almost a sub-industry, with a number of chair-making workshops operating in the area. In 1901 there were seven such workshops in

Fitzrovia itself and another six clustered just east of Tottenham Court Road in Bloomsbury, as well as another huddle of chair makers immediately north of Euston Road. Additionally, some of the local general 'furniture makers' must also have made chairs.

Carving was the most skilled of the traditional woodworking crafts carried out near Tottenham Court Road. In the 1930s, fine carving work was still being practised in the Trades Training School in Great Titchfield Street. The director, Banister Fletcher, reported in its 1934–35 Annual Report that the woodcarving students had executed elaborate carvings, 'A panel of shells and seaweed, a festoon of flowers, fruit and birds and also one of flowers and fruit after Grinling Gibbons – all in lime wood – and a panel of the Jacobean period in English oak'.

However, wood carving was one specialism that suffered as the twentieth century progressed and styles of furniture changed. The 1938 British Furniture Trades Report says, 'Modern styles have not required much of the carver's art, and wages, which used for special work to be the highest in the trade, are often depressed.'[15] Wartime Utility furniture, with its basic approach to design, did nothing to bolster carving. Of the sixteen carvers' workshops listed in Fitzrovia in 1901, only two workshops remained in 1951.

Furniture polishing was one of the trickiest arts of furniture making. The 1938 report summarises, 'Polishing by hand is a skilled operation, in which it takes about four years to become proficient in the better kinds of work.'[16] Hall's map identifies eight French polishers working locally in 1901. This was a branch of furniture making in which some women participated. An article in the *Women's Industrial News* of March 1902 explains the painstaking process of polishing in detail. The piece was seemingly written to alert girls and young women to opportunities for women in this trade:

> A good piece of furniture passes through several processes before it is ready to take the polish. It is sandpapered and then stained. Then the process known as 'bodying in' takes place, i.e. the wood is rubbed with a mixture of Plaster of Paris and linseed oil since neither planing nor sandpapering gives sufficiently smooth surface to receive the best polish. This is rubbed in vigorously and fills up every unevenness in the surface … the pad, made of cotton wool covered with a piece of rag, dipped in the polishing mixture, and the work at this stage is chiefly a matter of much rubbing and elbow grease. Often a piece of furniture is put away after its first polish, and a day or two after taken out again to go through the process a second time. Finally it is well rubbed with a pad dipped in methylated spirits to take off the excess of oil.[17]

At this time, most girls from 'better' working families rejected furniture making as a 'dirty' trade, carried on in an unsavoury environment with obstreperous male workmates, which was entered only by rough and poor women. The article optimistically highlighted the good conditions existing in a few of the largest firms, where women and men worked separately in large, clean workshops and women could earn, after a three-year apprenticeship, between 14s and 20s per week: higher wages at that time than the vast majority of female workers could earn.

The processes of hand polishing hadn't changed for hundreds of years. In the 1920s, as in the eighteenth and nineteenth centuries, French polishing a large item like a sideboard by hand took nine and a half hours.[18] But, by the 1930s, spraying with nitrocellulose had come in and soon virtually took over the polishing branch of the trade. It then took as little as twenty-five minutes to polish an item of furniture, but the process often caused skin reactions in the workers. These were reduced by the general use of barrier creams, as a former worker reveals:

> At the start of the morning and the afternoon shift, the foreman came round and squeezed some barrier cream on your hands. You rubbed it in while he was there; not everyone liked it, but it did stop the dermatitis and was much better than the old system of washing your hands in a bucket of washing soda at the end of each shift.[19]

The art of polishing, then, was fast fading out in the 1930s, along with the small high-class furniture workshops in Fitzrovia, years before the far greater trade disruptions of the Second World War.

The upholstery section contained more women workers than any other trade in furniture making. Pat Kirkham notes that upholstery was 'often referred to as the "soft" side of the furniture trade and was considered somewhat genteel and refined ... because it was carried out in dust free conditions and workers could wear clean and decent clothes to work'.[20] Most of the work was in seat covering. P.G. Hall surprisingly doesn't map the upholsterers like the other furniture workers, but they were specialists who had their own workshops near the chair and other furniture makers they served. In 1910, Charlotte Street, for example, had two upholsterers at Nos 34 and 41, just up the road from a cabinetmaker and a carvers and gilders workshop.

There were further subdivisions within the craft of upholstery, with the work on seats being divided into stuffing and covering. The different tasks were regarded as being either men's or women's work. The women's side of the trade was classed as unskilled, or less skilled, and remunerated accordingly. This sex discrimination was long lasting. The trade was employing women by the mid-nineteenth century, while giving them lower-skilled jobs and even paying them less for equally skilled jobs, and little seemed to have changed nearly 100 years later, to judge by the 1938 Report:

> The cover, cut generally by men but sometimes by women, is sewn by women and then is put on and stitched or nailed by men. Women finish off the sewing, sew on the plain back part of the cover, and do all necessary braiding and cording. Loose cushions are generally made by women. When loose cushions are fitted with patent springs, the work is heavier and may be done by youths.[21]

To the untrained observer, the tasks detailed here show little (if any) difference in skill level between those of men and women; but the difference in wages was huge, with a male upholsterer on weekly rates being paid on average 60*s* per week, while an upholsteress took home only 35*s* per week. These male rates were in any case below the London trades average for men, with 80 per cent of male upholsterers earning below the London Minimum Rate that had been negotiated between employers and the trades unions. Juveniles earned a pittance. Meanwhile, only 21 per cent of women outside the provisions of the London Minimum Rate earned less than this rate: a sign that the rate was set shockingly low for women in the first place.

Low pay across the furniture industry reflected the fact that many of its workers, most of all women, worked in unregulated small workshops and weren't unionised. By 1924 only 4 per cent of NAFTA members were women. And anyhow, in some cases, the trade unions were opposed to women workers in the trade. The United French Polishers Society had at this time resolved to fight the 'intrusion' of women into their trade and their union.[22]

Women workers comprised only 4 per cent or 5 per cent of workers in the furniture trade for much of the twentieth century. Percentages only rose during the First and Second World Wars when women were replacing men who were away fighting. In 1935, despite their low numbers and lack of union support, there was a big upholsteresses' strike of women who worked in the large West End workshops, including Maple's and Heal's. These women workers were all on timework and, very unusually, were completely unionised within the Amalgamated Union of Upholsterers. In 1935, trade was improving after the Depression years and the women asked for an increase from their rate of 10*d* per hour. The employers offered 1 farthing per hour (equal to one-quarter of an old penny and roughly one-eighth of a new penny!) and refused negotiation. The women went out on strike. They stayed out and picketed; the strike remained completely solid, and after twelve days the women won an increase of 1*d* (half a new penny) an hour. However, strikes like this were comparatively rare in the industry.

Unionised members experienced high rates of worklessness, with almost one-third out of work at times during the 1930s, presumably because employers were reluctant to pay official union rates, least of all in an economic downturn. Unionised workers in the furniture industry were undermined by the many non-unionised furniture workers who were employed, by and large, in producing the cheaper goods.[23]

Trade unionists bitterly resented unregulated firms squeezing furniture workers. The union campaigned in London for 'fair firms' that implemented union agreements. These firms were rewarded by being given access to the important Co-operative trade. But unregulated firms sneaked in. Hew Reid quotes the words of NAFTA official Alf Tomkins: 'Yet another "Rat Shop" has been discovered supplying bedroom suites to the London Co-operative Society. This shop is paying 1/1*d* per hour as top rate on a 54-hour week.'[24] The London rate at the time was 1*s* 7*d* per hour for a forty-seven-hour week. (NAFTA was active in the National Hunger March of 1934 which ended in Hyde Park with a large demonstration against a range of measures like the Unemployment Bill and the Means Test, while simultaneously protesting against the growing threat of Fascism and impending war.)

The dominance of large retail stores like Maple's and Heal's could facilitate 'sweating' on the part of some suppliers, with small manufacturers having to cut costs to retain the stores' custom. C. Edwards explains:

> One of the downsides of the powerful positions held by the large stores in Tottenham Court Road was the possible abuse of this power in relation to their suppliers. Maple's were particularly identified with the practice of 'sweating', whereby they set off subcontracted makers (often from the East End) with one another, and even with their own workshops, to push down prices … Allegations included the notion that Maple took advantage of the need for the individual maker to sell one object before he could make another. This knocked down the price to Maple's advantage.[25]

The supplier workshops in and around Tottenham Court Road could well have been affected in this way. But, in the 1930s, with Fascism raising its head in Britain, claims of sweating took an anti-Semitic turn with assertions in some quarters that Jewish employers were responsible for sweating in the furniture trade – such allegations were also often made concerning the clothing trade. The Board of Deputies and other Jewish organisations worked to counter these accusations, with *The Jewish Chronicle* of 5 February 1937 publishing a long piece, 'Jews and Labour Conditions: The Furniture Trade'. The findings of the report were that sweating by all employers, Jews and non-Jews, occurred in 'the absence of legal, minimum regulations, such as had been laid down by Trade Boards in other trades'. The conclusion was that fair industrial practice through regulation would not only help workers in the furniture and other trades but would also help to eliminate the conditions that were fostering Fascism.

Further regulation was on the way, arriving with the start of the Second World War. Unions and employers agreed on a Trade Board to fix wages, starting in March 1940. It set minimum rates at 1s 7d per hour for skilled men and 1s 3d for unskilled men. Women, on the other hand, received only 11d and 9d for skilled and unskilled work respectively.

After the Second World War there was an improvement in wages across the board. A National Labour Agreement of 1946 raised the men's London hourly rate to 2s 6½d. The women's rate was pegged at 75 per cent of the men's rate. Seemingly, there was full acceptance by the unions of this continued underpaying of the female workforce. Also, 1946 saw all furniture workers given the right to two weeks' holiday with pay. Some workers had received no paid holiday before, although some firms gave one week with pay. Wages rose quickly through the 1950s so that a weekly wage of around £5 grew to around £9 by 1958. However, rising inflation during these years eroded the value of wages.

The trend towards mechanisation in the furniture industry was evident, even before the turn of the twentieth century. Professor W. Cawthorne Unwin's address to the students of the Trades Training School in Great Titchfield Street, recorded in the Annual Report of 1900, declared, 'The specialisation of the workshop is carried so far that a workman may be kept for years at work of one particular kind, involving only a fraction of the knowledge and skill required in his trade.'

These mass-production methods were at first resisted by many of the small workshops in the Tottenham Court Road area. Their owners chose to follow the traditional techniques of manufacture that were appreciated by the relatively small number of customers who could afford to buy their goods. However, the new industrial developments impacting on the furniture trade became almost impossible to resist from the 1930s as consumer demand at the cheaper end of the market continued to expand and price pressures on small manufacturers grew. The 'volume' trade spread during the 1930s northeastwards from the East End to Tottenham, Edmonton and Walthamstow, where large factories sprang up.

Standardisation in furniture production reduced prices for the manufacturer and the customer but diminished the craftsman's art, leading to an erosion of skills. A student at the Trades Training School might have been learning advanced techniques in cabinet making or wood carving in the years before the Second World War, but outside the school he probably had little chance to practise them at his workbench.

The Second World War itself had a dire impact on traditional techniques of furniture craftsmanship; just one of the many smaller consequences of the war. The scarcity of materials, due to the lack of imports and resources being diverted to war production, meant that any new furniture could only be of the plainest design. It was produced in the least expensive way by mass production, using as few materials as possible. The government brought in controls on furniture production in the form of Utility furniture, based on principles of design put forward by the Council for Art & Industry. Furniture was to be 'well proportioned, simple, sensible, functional, good quality and reasonably priced, with no ornament'.[26]

Utility furniture could be made by unskilled labour. This was essential when most craftsmen and women were away in the forces or helping with the war effort in the munitions factories and shipbuilders. The dismay of many master furniture makers at this wartime situation is expressed by Maurice Clarke, of the firm J. Clarke, a High Wycombe firm of traditional makers:

> There was a very small [timber] allocation and of course you hadn't got the men ... We had to use [unskilled] people and help do half the work for them and be behind them all the time. *There was no design then.* [Attfield's emphasis] That's why we have no skilled labour now. Because the Utility confined you to the very cheapest of straight things. Three designs of dining chairs, that's all we were allowed to make.[27]

Utility furniture production continued well after the war. A letter to the *Picture Post* from 'G.P.H.' of Ilford, Essex, on 2 December 1950, gives an insight into both the Utility Scheme and the tax schemes that were accused of squashing any revival of the old industry:

> The need for the Utility Scheme in Furniture seems to have long passed ... The crippling incidence of purchase tax on furniture that is of a little better quality than the Utility Scheme permits, kills the market for such goods and

completely stifles development in design and workmanship. Even worse, the present production of Utility furniture is depriving the furniture manufacturers of all facilities for training their workmen in the craftsmanship for which the British furniture industry was so famous in the past. No man who has entered the industry since 1939 has had any opportunity of learning to make, or even of seeing, furniture of what used to be the traditionally British quality.

Unions pointed to the large rises in productivity brought about by wholesale mechanisation, which increased employers' profits while mechanisation had a detrimental effect on workers. The Communist Party's campaigning booklet, *Furniture – Production and Wages* (1959), claimed, 'The speed-up with the new techniques has brought greater exhaustion with each day's work. No industry has such an open-and-shut case for an immediate reduction in the working week.'

Max Cohen, a carpenter and cabinetmaker who joined the Communist Party as a young man and became a writer in his later years, gives a scathing, though amusing, account of his war experiences as a carpenter in Blitz-hit London, in *What Nobody Told the Foreman* (1953). Cohen and others like him suffered a lack of employment during the phoney war because no new building projects were started. Carpentry and cabinet making were regarded as reserved occupations, but craftsmen weren't yet called on for war work as the crisis hadn't yet materialised. However, when bombing started, and London was repeatedly hit by serious damage, the situation rapidly altered, and Cohen's services were snapped up by potential employers. Sometimes these 'contractors' had no legitimate claim to be doing building work of any sort but were simply out to make money, taking advantage of the lack of government control over repair work in the bomb-blasted city. Cohen writes trenchantly:

> [A]ll this was being run, not as a kind of Civil Defence operation, but on the good old lines of private profit. Thus, in addition to bona fide building firms, any half-wit or rogue could (and a number of them did) contract to do the work. The usual terms offered by a grateful nation still applied – all costs, plus ten per cent profit, guaranteed.[28]

Cohen recounts:

> My first interview for a job took place in a partly destroyed house in an area that was like a village devastated in the front line of battle. In an otherwise bare room, four of the most uninspiring beings I had ever set eyes on were sprawled in uncouth attitudes around a table. These four gentry were the

perfect prototype of those who were coming to be popularly known as 'black-marketeers'. As I gazed at them through the fog of cigarette smoke, I was quite convinced that these men had no professional connection with the building trade – or had never had until very recently indeed.[29]

Having refused to work on this particular job, Cohen was then employed on the testing task of repairing a railway bridge in winter, under the threat of frequent daytime air raids. He then found work in an aerodrome and was eventually called up, becoming a gunner and continuing to use his carpentry skills. There was an official enquiry held to investigate the wartime building and civil engineering industry, after strong public criticism of its operations, but the Commission refrained from condemning it, to the disgust of Cohen and, no doubt, many others in the trade.

The disruption and de-skilling caused by the war intensified a trend of decline that was already at work, eliminating many of London's remaining small craft furniture workshops. Hall's industry area map for 1951 shows only fifteen furniture workshops of all types in Fitzrovia, against nearly 100 work-shops in 1901, although the two sawmills remained. Two or three workshops hung on in Bloomsbury and perhaps another dozen businesses were still oper-ating north of Euston Road.

Pat Kirkham's 1978 paper for *Furniture History*, 'Recollections of Furniture Makers: Labour History, Oral History and Furniture Studies', includes an interview with two retired cabinetmakers. The paper commemorates trade skills that by then had all but disappeared:

Q. Can you remember any particular jobs?
A. Making a cabriole leg. It took the best part of two hours from start to finish, after it had just been roughly milled. You had to spoke shave it down and get right down to the foot. Then you had to make a set.
Q. Could you tell me about the machines you used as a cabinet maker over the years?
A. Not a lot … hand sanding machines – something and nothing. Power drills but otherwise nothing. I never worked on any machine.[30]

The traditional skills never completely died out. The Trades Training School, renamed the Building Crafts College, stayed at 153–155 Great Titchfield Street until 2001, when it moved to Stratford in East London, an area with which the Carpenters' Company has a long connection. The old skills are still taught, and small firms of independent furniture makers still exist in London to practise them, but the craft-based furniture industry on the Other Side of Oxford Street has vanished.

A Question of Taste

On 2 April 1921 the *Times* claimed, 'Furniture is the first idea that the name of Tottenham-court-road evokes.' However, the Other Side of Oxford Street had a perceived shiftiness about it which transferred itself to people's views of its furniture trade. Even as its high-quality cabinet making flourished and its retail department stores were reaching their apex, there were murmurs and outright sneers about both the standard and the design of its goods.

In April 1897, *The Artist* journal approvingly quoted Mrs Marriott Watson saying, in *The Art of the House*, 'Some of the most illustrious writers of today inhabit rooms and houses that, decoratively speaking, are a slur upon civilisation'. The journal article suggested that this 'slur' upon good taste emanated from Tottenham Court Road and its department stores, linking it snobbishly with the increasing popularity of the hire-purchase system – a complaint about 'the wrong type' of consumer that was to occur with the car trade. Taste wise, Tottenham Court Road was a 'notorious thoroughfare' for domestic furnishings, according to *The Artist*. Only one moderately priced bedroom suite on display at Heal's had escaped the journal's censure, with the suite's simplicity and comparative modernity winning its reluctant approval. Sir James Yoxall, in his book on antiques published some years later, *More about Collecting* (1913), warned readers about the 'black-oak dining-room and hall suites made for Tottenham Court Road smallish shops, in a travesty of Jacobean', saying, 'the merest chip with a knife will reveal the soft white wood underneath the stain'.[31] Cecil Vyse, in E.M. Forster's *Room with a View* (1908), likewise sneers at 'the trail of Tottenham Court Road' being upon a room that could otherwise have been 'successful'.[32]

Several threads appear to be tangled in these critiques of Tottenham Court Road furniture. Clearly, cost and class are both involved. The department stores are accused of making their goods too affordable through the hire-purchase system. Added to this, stores like Heal's and Maple's were producing their designs in a range of materials to suit the pockets of different buyers. Making good design accessible, though approved by *The Artist* journal where buyers displayed the 'correct' sense of taste, appeared objectionable to certain elite consumers and commentators who seemed to prefer that it should be available only to the wealthy. Others refused to concede that Fitzrovia's furniture stores could ever be home to good furniture design, conflating standards of design and price. Charles Eastlake, an architect and designer, complained in 1864, when Maple's and Heal's were already well-known names, 'People of ordinary means are compelled either to adopt the cheap vulgarities of Tottenham Court Road or to incur the ruinous expense of having furniture made to order'.[33] Eastlake estimates the cost of commissioned furniture to be 6 guineas a chair, perhaps one month's wages for a workman, but still rejects the department stores disdainfully, recognising no viable alternative for the customer of taste.

Cheapness is also associated with fakes, as in Yoxall's words about white wood showing beneath the suspicious black-oak Jacobean suites of Tottenham Court Road. The white wood suggests the low-cost deal furniture that was bought by the poorer classes, hastily fashioned into a piece associated with expensive hardwood – so hastily that 'the merest chip with the knife' will reveal the deceit. A point is being made here about a cheap item being dressed up as an expensive one. No doubt this was not unknown in the workshops of Fitzrovia, but, as we've discovered, Fitzrovia's trade reputation by the turn of the twentieth century was for 'high-class ready-made' furniture in Hall's classification. So why attack Tottenham Court Road in particular for poor-quality 'fake' furniture?

One rationale for the argument about fakery could have been that the department stores didn't only use local suppliers but had a much wider supply network that in some cases included London's East End workshops. Shoreditch and Hackney, by and large, turned out factory-made goods which were well below traditional 'West End' quality. This 'cheap' East End label could have stuck, even when the East End workshops were producing much better-quality pieces for the stores.

Maple's was one store that used East End suppliers. John Blundell Maple's long obituary in *The Times* of 25 November 1903, perhaps surprisingly for an obituary, raised the embarrassing questioning of Maple, some years before, by the Royal Commission on Sweating, when he was accused of sweating East End workers. Maple was cleared of this accusation but had to defend himself against adverse public opinion about the quality of his goods. Maple had said, 'What does it matter whether we make the goods, or whether we only guarantee them? In either case our responsibility is the same.'

In the light of these links, some consumers and arbiters of taste might have associated East End tat with the department stores and believed that their claims to sell high-class goods were false. John Blundell Maple had been confident that the Maple's brand was by that time strong enough to overcome the taint of the East End workshops in middle-class minds, but perhaps Sir James Yoxall's words about cheap furniture masquerading as expensive pieces gained some force from associations like these.

However, there was another important dimension to the critiques of the Tottenham Court Road furniture trade. Yoxall's words were all the sharper because the look of its cheaply made goods had harked back to the Jacobean style of design. He was implying that there was a deception involved in a new piece of furniture being made in an antique style. This implication also seems to be present in *The Artist*'s praise of the Heal's bedroom suite that evoked 'the new movement' in design rather than antique designs. In other words, antique reproduction furniture was 'inauthentic' and therefore to be despised.

Yet, at the same time, the late nineteenth and early twentieth centuries were seeing a big turn in taste towards the old styles. The fascination with genuine antiques, first ignited in aristocratic collectors of the eighteenth and nineteenth centuries by their Grand Tours of Europe, had transmuted and broadened across the social classes into a liking for period styles as a way of creating a pleasant domestic interior. According to Deborah Cohen, 'In the years between the whimsical stolidity of Victoriana and the advent of tubular steel furniture, the newest thing was the antique.'[34]

Magazines and journals appeared, catering for antique hunters – *The Connoisseur* was the earliest in 1900. Deborah Cohen felt that antique styles were perhaps an antidote to the modernity and 'endless reinvention' of the Edwardian period, while *The Times* of 15 May 1914 thought that middle-class consumers saw antique-style furniture as being 'pleasing to the eye without mortification of the body' and 'comfortable without being dull'.[35]

Exclusive shops selling authentic antique pieces had existed for some time, in areas such as Mayfair that were inhabited by the social elite, but by the late nineteenth century the top department stores like Heal's were selling, besides a selection of genuine antiques for their most discriminating customers, large numbers of furniture pieces that were coming to be called 'reproduction' items rather than humble copies. At this time, Fitzrovia's workshops appear to have been largely engaged in producing, not forgeries that falsely claimed to be from an earlier age, but 'fakes' in the sense of open imitations of old pieces, to cater for a strong consumer demand.

Acquiring real antiques wasn't easy. Antiquarians needed money, dedication, knowledge and discernment to seek out genuine pieces. And to possess antiques conferred a high social status. As Deborah Cohen explains:

> To cherish antiques was to proclaim a taste that required cultivation beyond the means of the vast majority. For those who embraced them, antiques offered a form of distinction, cultural capital all the more precious for the fact that it retained exclusivity in an increasingly homogenous world ...

the possessors of fine specimens were frankly to be admired, a markedly undemocratic sentiment in an era that witnessed Lloyd George's attack on inherited privilege and unearned income.[36]

If owning real antiques brought status and admiration, possessing only copies brought, at best, faint demeaning praise from the knowledgeable. Value judgements were often made about these reproduction pieces by experts and writers about art and design, many of whom disliked their perceived lack of originality. Writing tolerantly of ordinary purchasers' lack of discernment, *The Times* explains:

> Naturally enough the ordinary purchaser has not the rare instinct of the collector, nor the means to gratify a collector's desires if he had them. He is not concerned to place its true artistic value on a Jacobean masterpiece. Nor is he, as a rule, a curio hunter, bent upon the search for stools or tables apocryphally associated with the romantic persons of Elizabeth and Charles II. So long as his furniture has the inspiration of the seventeenth century he cares not that it was built in the twentieth [15 May 1914].

The Times, while positing 'the solid fact of an advance in the public taste', follows up, 'We may perhaps deplore the fact that the new spirit in decoration is reproductive rather than creative. But the latter quality we cannot command. We can but await its return.'

Alison Adburgham allocates responsibility for 'the lack of good modern design in the shops' to the wealthy consumers who helped to form taste (writing in the 1970s, she seems to be commenting on that period as well as the earlier period). She blames:

> The elitist attitude adopted by the distinguished designers of the day towards retail trade. They sought private commissions rather than retail outlets. Alas that most potential patrons of the decorative arts were of the *nouveaux riches* and the newly ennobled, who wanted to acquire stately country and town-house backgrounds. Not sure enough of their own taste to commission modern designers, they felt safe in putting themselves into the hands of the experts employed by old-established firms. These, they knew, could be relied upon to conjure up appropriate ancestral surroundings, and commit no anachronistic howlers.[37]

Adburgham is writing here as a proponent of modern design (she was a social historian and a fashion writer) and, although she fully allows the good quality of the top-drawer furniture produced by Heal's and the West End stores like Liberty's and Waring & Gillows, her distaste for what she seems to see as an unsophisticated, perhaps childish overreliance on the past comes through in the above article for the *Architectural Review*.

Of course, fake so-called 'genuine antiques' also formed a part of the market. Antique shops were thriving and spreading to areas outside Mayfair and Bond Street. By the 1920s they were popping up in Tottenham Court Road and the surrounding streets. The 1920 *Post Office Directory* for Tottenham Court Road lists only one 'Fine Art Dealer', Louis Wolff & Co., at No. 245. But by 1940 the *Directory* lists six firms besides Wolff: another art dealer, Jacob Mendelson; an 'antique dealer', George Knight Henn, and three businesses calling themselves 'antique furniture dealers' as well as the 'Old English Furniture Galleries' next door to Louis Wolff.

One of these businesses was Davis & Sons Ltd, mentioned earlier as having changed its listing from 'house furnisher' in 1920 to 'antique furniture dealer' by 1930. This firm's history can be traced, and it is obvious that it was a producer of antique reproduction furniture rather than a purveyor of original antiques, and probably never made any claim to sell antique furniture in its proper sense. Davis' furniture is now old enough to be fairly sold as antique on its own merit, as we saw above.

The other 'antique furniture dealers' mentioned could have sold actual antiques. Or, they could have been businesses like Davis & Sons, who were equally open about making reproductions, as the majority of workshops in the locality were doing at this time. However, we can see how the change in Davis' business description from 'house furnisher' to 'antique furniture dealer', no doubt triggered by the growing interest in antique-style furniture — as also in antiques themselves — marked a woolliness about the word 'antique' that helped those who truly wanted to deceive. Deborah Cohen describes how, at this time, 'Unscrupulous dealers "aged" furniture with fake wormholes, burns, or more creatively still, by encouraging rabbits to scamper across their surfaces'.[38]

The antique shops in Mayfair couldn't have been immune to the passing of fakes and undoubtedly Tottenham Court Road was home to many fakes also — if not to rabbits. And writers homed in on this aspect of the Other Side of Oxford Street, both exploiting and adding to the street's pre-existing shady reputation. Adburgham notes, 'At the less reputable end of the furniture trade, it was inevitable that the fashion for antiques led to the art, or craft, of creating fake antiques. For these, there were plenty of retail outlets on the shady side of Tottenham Court Road …'.[39]

All the debates around authenticity in age, design and manufacture combined with old and persistent narratives of a reputation-stained Tottenham Court Road to generate an air of doubt about its furniture trade, even when much good, perhaps excellent, work was being done. Adburgham's 'shady side' of the street sums up, not merely the two-sidedness but the multi-sidedness of the neighbourhood. After all, when shade shifts throughout the day, who knows exactly where the shady side is − where does it begin and end?

Fitzrovia's Japanese Lampshade Makers

Into this story of Fitzrovia's furniture trade dropped a small group of lampshade makers from Japan − people I didn't expect to find among the predominantly European nationalities that made their homes on the Other Side of Oxford Street. One of these makers appeared earlier than the others: Seiji Kaneko, a decorative artist, was listed in 1928 at 92 Charlotte Street, an address where a lampshade maker, Sam Brown & Co., had been listed. It's not clear that Seiji Kaneko was a lampshade painter, but it is likely, given that a cluster of Japanese lampshade makers was soon to spring up in the area and that he appeared at a lampshade maker's address. Kaneko stayed in Charlotte Street until 1965. He disappeared − perhaps interned − during the Second World War but had returned by 1950, next door to S. Kobayashi, a lampshade maker who appeared in 1948. The Japanese lampshade workers joined a cluster of similar British-owned businesses in Fitzrovia. Remnants of the trade are still visible in old business signs to be found in Whitfield Street.

By 1950, several other Japanese lampshade makers were dotted around the neighbourhood. N. Mayeda was at 20 Howland Street, while 143 Cleveland Street hosted Soneya lampshade makers. Alfred Place, just behind Tottenham Court Road on the Bloomsbury side, had Chiba Kaichi. The best-established local business was probably T.K. Nakamura, at 43 Howland Street, who perhaps also employed a lampshade wire worker, Nagatomi, at No. 27. Nakamura moved out of Howland Street to New Cavendish Street in 1958, operating his business from there until 1965. Takaki Kanji's Modern Lampshades was located in Bloomsbury at 73–75 Kenton Street, and then became Japan Express, continuing to make lampshades until 1983.

Why were Japanese lampshade makers here at this period? And how do they fit into the story of domestic furnishings on the Other Side of Oxford Street? One answer is that Edwardian Londoners were interested in Japanese decorative goods and furniture. The fashion had started in the late nine-

teenth century, fostered by retailers like Arthur Lasenby Liberty, who was
'in the avant-garde with the vogue for everything Japanese'.[40] This interest
was enhanced by the Japan–British Exhibition of 1910 at White City which
brought a little group of specially hired craftsmen and experts to London.
More than 500 passports were issued in 1910 to these Japanese visitors, some
of whom reputedly stayed on in the city afterwards. The Exhibition was
sponsored by the Japanese government at huge cost to improve trade and
diplomatic relationships with Great Britain, to raise the prestige of Japan
and to showcase high-class Japanese products. An essay by Shabbar Sagarwala
describes the background to the Exhibition:

> At the time of the Exhibition in 1910, Britain had been inundated with
> cheap, mass-produced arts and crafts made for the export market from Japan.
> The impression of Japanese products as having lower quality at this time was
> perhaps made worse by the fusion of traditional arts with the Japonica style
> demanded by the British public, leading to progressively cruder and less
> authentic products. The Exhibition was an opportunity to reverse this trend
> and present the British public with high quality, genuine artistic works in
> the form of fine arts, architecture and entire village environments. A holistic
> and sometimes life-size representation could give visitors first-hand experi-
> ence to study the construction of traditional buildings, intricately detailed
> by Japanese craftsmen.[41]

It seemed possible at first that the Howland Street lampshade makers were
among these craftsmen and would therefore have been creators of fine art
furnishings. But they were making paper shades, and sources on the Japan–
British Exhibition make no mention of paper lampshades, except in passing,
as simple lanterns lighting the gardens. Only bronze standard lamps are in the
exhibition itself, forming part of the décor in 'a reproduction of a room in
the Imperial Palace at Tokio', according to the *Daily Express* of 16 May 1910
covering the exhibition.

I was intrigued by the idea that the fine craftsmen involved in the Japan–
British Exhibition, or perhaps their descendants, were the ones working in
Fitzrovia thirty or forty years later, but there seems to be no link between the
two groups. Fine workmanship did appear to exist among London's Japanese
lampshade makers: at Modern Lampshades of Bloomsbury, Takaki Kanji
'was forever proud of his lampshades being purchased by Queen Elizabeth,
the Queen Mother'.[42] Is there perhaps a chance that Kanji came over for
the Exhibition? Unfortunately, no proof can so far be found. In any case, in

Fitzrovia the story seems very different and, like so much in this locality, it involved movement, serendipity and, appropriately, a little shadiness.

According to Keiko Itoh, who has researched the pre-war Japanese community, many of the lampshade workers were ex-seamen with no previous experience of lampshade making, who had fallen into the trade simply because they needed a job. The Japanese economy was doing very badly in the first decades of the twentieth century and was severely hit by the First World War besides. The country suffered famines and rice riots, as well as a devastating earthquake in 1923 in which nearly 150,000 were killed and many displaced. In this extremely difficult period for Japan many emigrated. The great majority moved to surrounding countries such as Korea and Taiwan, and significant numbers to the USA, but a few ended up in London looking for work. Itoh says:

> Just why the Japanese found a niche in lampshade making is difficult to pinpoint. Perhaps the earlier pioneers entered the trade because of its association with Japan's traditional craft of lantern making, and others simply followed … Yet, up until lampshade-making became mechanised and mass produced, the Japanese seem to have carved out a certain portion of British lampshade production …[43]

Japanese workers like these, many of them married to British women, mostly remained in Britain when the Second World War started, though some Japanese immigrants returned to Japan. Some who stayed became naturalised; others were interned, though most Japanese internees were eventually released well before the end of the war. Those who had been seamen were classed as prisoners of war since, if they had gone back to Japan, they could have helped to fight against Britain. They were sent to Knapdale prisoner-of-war camp in Scotland, but most had been released by the end of 1943. Some were repatriated, and some returned to their British homes. It's likely that many of the Fitzrovia lampshade makers were internees, as they almost all vanished from the *Directory* during the war years and reappeared afterwards, back working in the same trade.

Several lampshade makers worked for T.K. Nakamura at 43 Howland Street after the war. They were not exclusively Japanese: a Briton worked there also, John Neill. Neill had married Agnes Urashima whose father, Urashima Masato, had taken a job with Nakamura after being released from internment, asking Neill to join him. In this tiny and mostly male first-generation Japanese community, intermarriage was common. Neill reveals that the wire workers who worked for the firm all had English wives.

It seems as if life at Nakamura's was hard. From John Neill's account, this branch of lampshade making seems to have carried on sweating of a type that had always existed in corners of the neighbourhood and that was unfairly connected with the whole of the local furniture trade. And sweating it truly was. Neill says:

> Pop [Urashima Masato] was crippling himself, because when he was doing these lampshades … We call it the barbolla. We'd put plaster around the bottom of the shade and round the top, designs of ladies and things like that. He'd done that but then he'd have to have a fire on all the time to dry it. Of course his back used to be very hot all the time and he eventually started leaning over. And he had to mix plaster of Paris with Arabic glue. And that glue is very thick … And I'm mixing for him, you know. They were really slaves to be honest … I couldn't make lampshades! It would take me all night to make thirty-six, just the small ones, which we called candle clips … I made thirty-six for ten shillings.[44]

Nakamura, however, did give his workers a party every New Year, which sound like lively affairs:

> That's when they all got drunk … There was the bream, the fish, all wrapped up in parcels. We all had Japanese food. And you couldn't buy rice then. We had imitation rice. So he's having a big party each New Year. He used to sing an English song.[45]

The workers could also socialise at a club nearby. Moya Tani, the daughter of Tani Yukio, a judo instructor and a 'former music hall attraction', remembers, 'There was a Japanese club at Tottenham Court Road … and they started to teach Japanese, and I started going. It was a social club. Not the big one for bankers and whatnot.'[46] The 'big one for bankers' must have been the Japanese Society in the 'proper' West End that was the social centre for the more affluent middle-class members of the community.

To judge from the evidence of the Japanese lampshade industry in Fitzrovia, cheap and cheerful was the rule, and trained craftsmen and women were the exception. Everyone in the trade appeared to have found themselves there by accident: Nakamura himself had no long-term experience of lampshade production before he set up his workshop but had been a butcher for the shipping industry in Cardiff Docks in the 1930s before he moved to London. He must have spotted a minute gap in the home-furnishings market and taken his chance, joined by fellow countrymen with few skills who were finding it hard, in a post-war climate unfavourable to the Japanese ex-enemy, to get a job. British workers who married into Japanese families must have fallen into the trade in similar ways to John Neill.

Sometimes lampshade makers fell out of lampshade making in equally unexpected ways: a worker for Nakamura, Kenji Takaki, became an actor, taking small roles in well-known films such as *A Town Like Alice* (1956) and *The Long and the Short and the Tall* (1961). Diverse, unpredictable and tangential, Japanese lampshade making was almost a caricature of life on the Other Side of Oxford Street – but an appealing one.

Furniture making was rooted in the life of Fitzrovia for about 200 years and, as we have discovered, the industry grew up imbued with the protean characteristics attributed to the area itself from its beginnings. Changing tastes in furnishing during the late nineteenth and early twentieth centuries provoked debates about modernity and antiquity, authenticity and fakery, that resulted in the 'fake' label often being affixed to Tottenham Court Road furniture, for reasons apparently having much to do with snobbery. The local industry's integrity was persistently doubted and sneered at, even as customers flocked to its big outlets and most authorities acknowledged the influence of its taste formers like Ambrose Heal.

Only remnants of the handcrafted furniture trade were to be found by the 1950s. Nakamura's Howland Street workshop, where hard-pressed workers wrestled with paper, wire, plaster of Paris and copious amounts of glue, was the quirky, poor and unskilled relation of the traditional craft workshop. The following chapter will examine another many-sided craft trade and one that that came to dominate Fitzrovia for sixty years of the twentieth century: the clothing trade.

5

Fitzrovia's 'Half-Hidden' Clothing Industry

Fitzrovia, right next door to Oxford Street's booming fashion and department stores, was by 1900 becoming a production hub of women's outerwear. The character of the neighbourhood became increasingly defined by the 'mantle trade', as it was known in the industry: women's tailored costumes, dresses and blouses. The neighbourhood's industrial landscape altered from specialising in carpentered fittings and furniture to clothing manufacture over a period of only twenty or thirty years.

As an enduring home for immigrants, Fitzrovia embraced new arrivals who brought innovations and adaptations that had already helped the clothing industry to thrive in London's East End, transforming it into a mass-market industry since the mid-nineteenth century. Drawn by the surging clothing trade in Fitzrovia, a large and thriving Jewish community, including my maternal grandparents and their children, grew up there during the first half of the twentieth century. Jewish entrepreneurs were largely responsible for Fitzrovia becoming the manufacturing heart of women's fashion making.

Fitzrovia's clothing trade was a leading example of synergy between place and industry. Fitzrovia's small, adaptable commercial spaces were ideally suited to an industry that had always been flexible in its demands for space, and Fitzrovia's capacity for transformation had dramatic qualities. J.E. Martin refers to the theatre in evoking Fitzrovia as a place where 'the mantle and costume trade … live in an atmosphere of uncertainty, summarised as "tomorrow another style, tomorrow another production set-up".'[1]

The stage metaphor could be applied in several ways to the clothing trade here. Christopher Breward talks of the trade's backstage nature, calling it 'the half-hidden trade' because it was often carried on in small workshops, away from the public gaze.[2] Fitzrovia's 'half-hidden' clothing industry, tucked into its

innumerable housing warrens and often filling the gaps between other businesses like the local car industry, evokes invisibility and therefore also workers'
powerlessness and lack of voice. But it also supports the idea of Fitzrovia as a
home for 'otherness' and innovation, as we'll see in this chapter.

The West End Clothing Trade on the Move

The ready-to-wear trade spread to Fitzrovia from Soho, where the traditional
West End tailoring trade was based. By the beginning of the twentieth century
it had overflowed the boundary of Oxford Street and pushed the manufacturing centre of women's ready-to-wear northwards, attracting many Jewish
incomers. It was probably this change that eventually created the perception
among the Jews of both Fitzrovia and Soho that there was a separate community of Jews on 'the Other Side' of Oxford Street that was, in subtle but
unmistakeable ways, different from that on their own side. The title of this
book borrows from this piece of Jewish myth-making about their locale.

It's fascinating to see how local changes founded on the economic and spatial
needs of an industry can also change the cultural perception of its inhabitants;
and perhaps this concept of 'otherness' involving two adjacent communities,
practically identical yet distinct from each other in the minds of its members,
is one of the most intriguing examples of this process. And there were, besides,
small but real differences in Jewish life north and south of Oxford Street to give
some force to these feelings of separateness. For my mother's cousin, Henry
Harris, the distinction was felt in the rituals accompanying bar mitzvahs: he
remembers being surprised by the Soho tradition of throwing raisins at the bar
mitzvah boy, a custom he'd never experienced before.

A handicraft clothing industry had been long established in Soho, serving the 'Court trade' with expensive bespoke clothing since the eighteenth
century. However, even before 1900, an increasingly dominant branch of the
industry was ready-made garments which sold in huge volumes in the stores of
Oxford Street. By the turn of the century, the ready-made trade – what some
called the 'rag trade' – had begun a rapid advance into Fitzrovia in the drive
to stock the thriving department stores. Indeed, the area around Tottenham
Court Road began to be known as 'North Soho', reflecting the clothing
trade's spread and redirection from its Soho origins. The trade enabled, and
was spurred on by, a greatly increased demand from working people for new
clothing, as opposed to the second-hand garments of the original 'rag trade'
that was all that ordinary people had been able to afford before. So, a picture

emerges, from the late nineteenth century, of a snowballing garment industry in Fitzrovia, pursued on varying scales but often in small workshops serving larger suppliers, with ever more tailors and dressmakers being crammed into the narrow streets north of Oxford Street, serving the insatiable consumer.

The Oxford Street stores, often developing from drapery shops established in the nineteenth century, became increasingly important after the turn of the twentieth century. Bourne & Hollingsworth opened in 1902, and John Lewis, founded in 1864, had expanded considerably by 1900. The opening of Selfridges in 1909 gave the stores a leading competitor in Harry Gordon Selfridge, whose flair and acumen transformed the sector. Debenham & Freebody and Marshall & Snelgrove merged in 1919 to offer another imposing retail presence on Oxford Street. To add to these general department stores, Peter Robinson, the clothing store founded in 1833, was by the 1900s an important retailer occupying most of the corner block bounded by Oxford Street, Upper Regent Street, Great Castle Street, and Great Portland Street. All these stores sold large volumes of clothing, focusing on women's and children's clothes.

With this great cluster of large stores in the locality of Oxford Circus, there were many clothing workers in and around Great Portland Street, even though at the same time this was also the home of the new car trade. Tailors here often occupied the same buildings as did the car firms, their workshops tucked away on the upper floors, above the car showrooms. This patch of Fitzrovia also housed the department store factories, like Peter Robinson's factory behind the main store in Little Portland Street.

It was from this hub at Oxford Circus and Great Portland Street that the industry began to radiate throughout Fitzrovia, helped by the opening of the Central and Northern Tube Lines at the beginning of the century. The trade, and its workers, was on the move.

In 1900, Howland Street, the unobtrusive side street off Tottenham Court Road where my mother's family of tailors would later settle, had only four directory-listed businesses connected with making clothes, all of them dressmaking and ladies' tailoring establishments. At that time, the artisanal trades dominated the area: furnishing craft trades, or manual trades such as plumbing, house building, decorating and painting. But this was quickly to change.

The heart of the Fitzrovia clothing trade was Great Titchfield Street, which ran north–south across Howland Street and finished at Oxford Street. In 1911 Isaac Zalkin, then a young married man of 28 and father to a toddler, Harry, was already working as a tailor at 162 Great Titchfield Street, along with his 22-year-old tailor brother, Simson Zalkin. My maternal grandmother, Annie

Harris, as she was before marrying, was close by at 1 Little Titchfield Street, as was her elder sister, Deborah, both registered as tailoresses. Isaac Coshever, the man Annie married in 1912, was a men's tailor of some skill and versatility. In later life, he made my mother's wedding outfit, a bottle-green skirt and jacket that she proudly showed off in her wedding photographs.

By the time my mother was a toddler in 1930, Great Titchfield Street had at least fifty-two businesses devoted to clothing and related trades, with ladies' clothing becoming ever more dominant the closer the proximity to Oxford Street. The furnishing trades were in full retreat. Howland Street now featured fourteen tailors' or dressmakers' workshops as well as related businesses like an embroiderer and a hat blocker. This figure was likely to have been an underestimate as not all of the tiniest one-room workshops would have been officially listed.

The number of listed workshops on the street increased by one in 1936: the tailoring workshop of my great uncle, Isaac Zalkin, appears in the directory from that year at 41 Howland Street, almost opposite the house where my mother lived with her family. My mother remembered being given the job, as a child, of picking up stray pins from her Uncle Isaac's workshop floor at the end of the working day, looking forward to receiving some small treat as a reward. In Cleveland Street also, says local resident Nellie Muller, 'There was the rag trade all along … it was a big rag trade along there'.[3] Nellie may be using 'rag trade' in its newer sense here, to refer to the making and selling of new but inexpensive ready-made clothing rather than to the traditional 'rag trade' in old clothing that it had replaced.

P.G. Hall's 1951 distribution map of the mantle trade in his *Industries of London* is a good indicator of the strength of the Fitzrovia mantle-making industry by the end of the period. It shows dense clusters of workshops in the streets directly above the northern edge of Oxford Street; a change from Hall's 1861 map, where the clusters are thicker in Soho. Hall himself confirms this in his text, saying that the trade 'was concentrated by 1951 in the streets immediately north and east of Oxford Circus, bounded approximately by Regent Street (above Oxford Circus), Mortimer Street, Newman Street and Oxford Street; here, in 1951, most of the firms describing themselves as "gown makers" were found'.[4]

This migrating trade was strongly linked to Fitzrovia's history of foreign migration. The Jewish migrations into London of the 1880s and 1890s brought many skilled tailors to the city, while others were quick to learn the trade from their compatriots in their new country of residence. They required perhaps only a few weeks' training in basic processes and a few tools of the trade to set up in the ready-made sector. Some Jewish tailors had already set-tled in the West End during the nineteenth century, mainly in Soho, where Jews formed a close community with its own shops and its synagogues. The extension of the ladies' clothing trade northwards from Soho subsequently brought an increasing number of Jews into Fitzrovia, so that by the 1930s they formed a substantial part of the local community north of Oxford Street. Their workshops were seldom seen by shoppers in the West End. Operating in spaces sometimes as small as one or two rooms, the clothing trade could occupy quite narrow niches in the geographical and industrial fabric of the area, such as the upper floors of buildings used by other trades or even the bedrooms of family homes. This meant that it could spread quickly, unimpeded by a need for dedicated industrial workspace.

Because of these modest and flexible space requirements, the clothing trade could be thought of as only partially visible: the 'half-hidden trade' referred to by Breward. This invisibility even seems to extend to some of the industry's historical records. For example, it was hard to find detailed information about the clothing factories belonging to the Oxford Street department stores, even though many of the stores possessed their own workrooms and factories. And it also applied to people's working lives: the women's mantle trade was largely carried on by female 'hands' (the disembodied 'hands' is suggestive), mostly non-unionised and paid much less than men, whose voices in the industry too frequently went unheard. It is difficult for present-day researchers even to find out about department store factory workers' conditions and experiences, while the stores' retail staffs are comparatively well documented.

The 'invisible' quality of clothing manufacture in Fitzrovia fits in with the theatrical aspects of the fashion trade noted above. Writing about Oxford Street, Christopher Breward evokes a magical scene created by the enormous glass shop fronts crammed full of wonders, contrasting it with the 'backstage' production area of Fitzrovia streets tucked behind it out of sight:

> While the great department stores lining post-war Oxford Street displayed an ever-changing array of fashionable commodities that were seemingly con-jured out of thin air, in their hinterland along the backstreets of Marylebone and Soho lay the premises of the tailors, wholesalers and agents whose activi-ties made the magic possible.[5]

Breward is influenced by Erving Goffman's idea of institutions, in this case stores, engaging in presentational behaviour, a type of theatrical performance. Different regions within the building have a 'front stage', the shop floor and

shop windows, and 'back stage' regions such as adjacent workshops and clothing factories, both vital in generating the illusions that encourage the shopper
to spend money on fashion. Breward talks of localities such as Fitzrovia being
places where 'the territories of the client and the manufacturer met in the
evolving pattern of street and building-use, inscribing a sense of local character
… on the landscape'.[6] These words pick up on Fitzrovia's characteristic fluid-
ity, its ability to accommodate change and foster innovation. Describing the
characteristics of the local clothing industry that eventually produced the styles
of 'Swinging London' in the 1960s and 1970s, Breward turns back towards the
beginning of the century to show 'a landscape open to the changes' sweeping
across it as industries and working communities grew and changed.[7] He speaks
of post-war 'Marylebone' – often a synonym for Fitzrovia – as a centre of the
clothing trade, describing the locality as it appeared by 1960:

> The streets were full of company agents, textile merchants, ladies' dress, coat,
> skirt and trouser manufacturers and the precisely termed 'wholesale dress-
> makers', who relied less on the exclusive buying power of Regent Street
> emporia and the sartorial mores of Society, but were more concerned with
> maintaining their competitiveness through flexible production lines, the
> forging of strong national distribution networks and an engagement with
> international export drives.[8]

Breward colourfully evokes a dense local clothing network which eventually
started to disrupt the traditional clothing trade by showcasing street fashion
created by small independent firms. He describes how the working-class
localities around Oxford Street contributed to a new affordable vision of fashionable London that intrigued the whole world in the 1960s. Some traces
of that world are still visible today. His words are further illustrated by the
Peter Jones Chronicle, a staff magazine, in an article on 31 July 1959, describing
the scene around the Jonelle factory in Great Titchfield Street, where 'great
rainbow-coloured armfuls of finished garments are hurried out of hundreds
of buildings and across the pavements into … little vans' for distribution across
the country (Peter Jones was part of the John Lewis chain of stores).

Returning to 1900, what social and industrial changes had brought about
this magical, half-hidden world, and how did its denizens experience it? In the
1890s, Beatrice Potter (later Beatrice Webb) had described the appearance of:

> … a new province of production, inhabited by a peculiar people, working
> under a new system, with new instruments, and yet separated by a narrow

and constantly shifting boundary from the sphere of employment of an old-established native industry.[9]

This 'new province of production' was the manufacture of new ready-made clothing by makers like the Moses brothers of Aldgate. They were Jews – Potter's 'peculiar people' – who were bringing in the subdivisional method of manufacture that was revolutionising the industry, even affecting traditional handicraft tailoring.[10]

Jews had originally established themselves in old clothes, dealing on the eastern fringes of the old City of London as far back as the eighteenth century, and nineteenth-century entrepreneurs like the Moses brothers brought about the development of the wholesale ready-to-wear clothing industry in the East End. They introduced some key innovations into the trade by creating a system of production for ready-to-wear clothing that maximised volume and kept down costs. Workshops under this system were run along subdivisional lines, where most workers carried out just one repetitive operation. Workshops tended to specialise in one aspect of manufacture, dealing with one specific process such as 'finishing', e.g. hemming, buttonholes and buttons.

Along with subdivision went subcontraction, involving firms contracting work out to a chain of other workshops. This change was taking place from the mid-nineteenth century when inventions like the sewing machine and the bandsaw for cutting many layers of cloth were making mass production a reality. To this was added the emergence of the wholesaler, who ordered large volumes of clothes which were bulk produced in stock sizes.

A few decades later came the growth of the ready-to-wear industry in the West End. By the 1880s, these industrial changes were having an impact on the West End women's outerwear trade. Clothes of reasonable quality were becoming affordable for almost everyone. By 1902, the Chief Inspector of Factories' Annual Report was commenting on how people of the working and middle classes were dressing in ready-made clothes supplied by factory organisation.

The expansion of the clothing industry was subsequently aided by major political and social developments. Margaret Wray points out that during and after the First World War, women's fashions across the social classes became much simpler than before. This development was due largely to women's active participation in working life during men's absence at the front. The industry responded to the demand for new styles of clothing from women living more emancipated lives, with clothing that was more suited to mass production.

From early in the twentieth century, it was already being noted that Fitzrovia was becoming a centre for women's outerwear through its link with Oxford

Street, and, moreover, was producing clothing of good quality. A factory inspector, Miss Slocock, in the 1910 Annual Inspector's Report, commented on an established industry when she said:

> A steady increase is noticeable in the number of workshops making really high-class readymade dresses and blouses. The area immediately around and north of Oxford Circus is a favourable one for this class of work, and there is a tendency for City and East End firms to open a West End branch factory or workshop in this locality where they are in close communication with Oxford Street, one of the most important shopping centres of the Metropolis [page 112].

The inspector's observation that East End firms were opening branches north of Oxford Street shows the growth, interconnection and geographical spread of the trade within London; and it also provides a clue to how the Jewish population might have arrived in such numbers in Fitzrovia.

The Whitechapel area was usually the arrival point for the thousands of Jews from Europe who were finding their way to England at the turn of the twentieth century. It's likely that this interconnection between the East End and West End clothing trade – the trade of choice for numerous Jewish arrivals – encouraged a move westward for some, rather than that the somewhat smaller Soho Jewish population suddenly exploded to populate Fitzrovia. It could be that a movement of recently arrived Jews to Fitzrovia at least partly explains why this group was seen as 'other' by the older Soho community and vice versa.

V.D. Lipman, in his *Social History of the Jews in England 1850–1950* (1954), explained some of the reasons for Jewish immigrants taking up this trade in large numbers. He said they had sometimes worked as tailors before their arrival and many fellow Jews worked in the same trade and could help newcomers. Tailoring was also small-scale and flexible, offering plenty of opportunities for work and some control over one's working hours, as well as the chance to open one's own workshop after gaining experience and funds. Lipman also commented about Jews' supposed physical suitability for 'lighter' tailoring work – presumably this didn't apply to pressers, who were expected to constantly handle heavy irons weighing up to 14lb in the men's tailoring workshops! Added to the reasons given by Lipman are that tools of the trade were fairly cheap and easy for the new worker to acquire, and training periods – when little, if any, pay could be expected – lasted only a matter of a few weeks for an ordinary hand in a workshop run along subdivisional lines.

The 'narrow and constantly shifting boundary' that Beatrice Potter suggests, between the work and methods of the traditional English tailors and those of the Jewish incomers, grew even narrower and shiftier once the Jewish tailors had moved west. The boundary even narrowed for the top-quality men's tailoring based in the West End. At first, the old-established tailoring firms were reluctant to employ Jewish workers but, before long, the Savile Row firms were contracting some of their work out to the most skilled of the Jewish tailors. By now, some of these tailors had moved north as well as south of Oxford Street – however, men's tailors were in a minority in Fitzrovia since traditional high-class men's tailoring mostly remained in Soho. The discreet way in which the elite masters of the Savile Row trade used the skills of the newcomers gives another turn to the 'hidden' landscape of the Fitzrovia clothing trade.

The top end of the men's clothing trade generally stayed in Soho, but the growth in the women's mantle trade almost doubled the numbers employed north of Oxford Street from 5,308 in 1861, to 9,126 in 1951. These numbers surpassed the corresponding figures for the Borough of Westminster which contained the Soho hub of clothing production and which had topped the table in 1861.

S.P. Dobbs provides a very good explanation of what is meant by the 'mantle trade':

> [I]n the wholesale [trade] there is a clear distinction between 'Clothing', which in this connotation means men's outer garments, and 'Mantles', which means women's outer garments. Only in rare cases will the same firm engage in the manufacture of both men's and women's clothes … There are one or two important points of difference … there is the question of design. In the men's trade fashions change but slowly, and designing accordingly occupies a place of secondary importance. In the women's trade they change with bewildering rapidity and the designer is the most important person in the whole organization … bulk orders feature far less prominently in the mantle than in the clothing trade … broadly speaking, the materials used in the mantle trade are lighter than in the case of men's clothing, and accordingly a slightly different type of machine and a worker with a different type of skill is required. There is also less scope for elaborate sub-division of processes … Finally, the mantle trade differs from the men's trade, in that an even larger proportion of women is employed – though normally the foremen, pressers and cutters are men.[11]

Although Dobbs draws the distinction between the (women's) mantle trade and the (men's) clothing trade, 'clothing trade' is sometimes used in a looser sense by writers to refer to the whole garment industry, as I have often done in this chapter.

Factory production was an integral part of men's tailoring by the time of the First World War, but it was not so in tailored womenswear or dressmaking – the mainstays of Fitzrovia – until the late 1920s and 1930s. Until that time, the women's trade depended largely on outworkers, mostly women and mostly working in their own homes. However, bulk methods of production were also found in the small workshops in the form of subdivisional labour and subcontracting. Anne Kershen says the practice of subcontracting continued until 1939.[12]

Some technical innovations were specifically aimed at small workrooms: an early innovation was the Eastman cutter, a hand tool that could be used in any size of workspace. In the subcontracting system, the cloth for the garments would often be ready-cut by the wholesalers so that homeworkers needed only a treadle sewing machine, which was often hired from their employer.

The subdivisional and subcontracting system was widely practised by the growing number of Jewish tailors, and Jewish immigrant workers increasingly occupied the back streets of Fitzrovia, the hub of the women's mantle trade. The mantle trade employed many women, with Jewish men tending to work in tailoring and footwear rather than in dressmaking. In 1914, a huge 90 per cent of the parents of Jewish children at Upper Marylebone Street School described themselves as tailors, according to Gerry Black.[13] S.P. Dobbs, writing in 1928, says, 'On the other side of Oxford Street, countless busy Jews and Jewesses in sub-contractors' workshops, [are] working steadily on less artistic but more up-to-date lines [than their Soho handcraft counterparts].'[14] Many others worked in associated businesses such as millinery, boot and shoe making, trimmings and embroidery. On 22 January 1937 the *Jewish Chronicle* said, 'The Jewish tailor … has become the sub-contractor par excellence.'

Returning to the backstage, half-concealed nature of the clothing trade in Fitzrovia, or 'North Soho', it's not difficult to see how subcontracting, where orders were passed along a chain of workshops so that the instigator of the order didn't always know who was fulfilling that order, could foster a sense of concealment and, at its worst, could lead to sweating. The clothing trade was indeed often associated with low wages, cramped working conditions, long hours in the busy seasons which followed the fashion calendar – the spring months were always very busy as summer fashions were produced – and unemployment or short-time working in the slack seasons, which transformed good in-season weekly earnings into poor earnings across the whole year.

Jewish workers and employers were quite often blamed for creating or intensifying sweating, notably in the East End, but also in the West End. They were sometimes accused of acting as 'shock–absorbers of a fluctuating industry' in taking on large volumes of work at very short notice when non–Jewish workshops were unable to do so and thereby encouraging extremes of season-ality.[15] They were also accused, as immigrants have long been, of undercutting wages. Accusations like this were still being made well into the 1930s, when the *Jewish Chronicle* in 1932 and 1937 mounted vigorous campaigns to refute them, publishing detailed reports showing that sweating affected some sections of the industry irrespective of whether those involved were Jews or non-Jews.

Campaigns against the sweating system had earlier led to a select Parliamentary Committee investigation and to the setting up of trade boards for men's tailoring in 1909, for wholesale mantles and costumes in 1919 and for dressmaking and women's light clothing in 1920. The trade boards reg-ulated the industry by fixing minimum wages, although some unregulated workshops continued to operate.

Increased wages, workshop legislation and competition from the factories eventually led to a decline in small workshops. Even in the women's trade, S.P. Dobbs, by 1928, could go as far as saying that 'the mantle and dress factories are driving the small dressmaker out of existence' – although he qualifies this by saying the change is more noticeable in Leeds and other northern towns with large clothing industries.[16] In Fitzrovia, Dobbs' findings are supported by the 1930 MOH report for Marylebone, saying that there were fewer listed outworkers in the borough than before – the figure for 1930 was 183 con-tractors and 992 workers, falling by 1950 to 135 contractors and 211 workers. Given the sustained importance of the local mantle trade in 1950 this must mean that large employers had become more dominant than small ones, not that the size of the trade had shrunk. Indeed, the trade had grown by then rather than declined.

Women's outerwear production prospered generally during the Second World War as government controls rationalised and simplified production and cut manufacturers' costs. The Utility scheme, introduced from the end of 1941, reduced pre-war problems caused by seasonality, such as 'runs' of cloth-ing being produced which went out of fashion almost immediately so that wholesalers' stock remained unsold. Utility restrictions cut out the trimmings on clothing and emphasised simple, classic styles that didn't quickly date.

Along with these austerity regulations came clothes rationing from June 1941. Each adult was allocated sixty-six coupons in the first year of the scheme – reduced to only forty-eight the second year – to exchange for clothing. A coat could use up to thirty coupons, while a child's vest cost one coupon. Rationing meant that customers had to buy mainly necessities and couldn't follow fashion as they had before the war, so they tended to appreciate the return to style basics brought in by the Utility scheme.

However, people still found ways to be stylish. When Trudie Flinder of Hanson Street came home on weekend leave, her army clothing received an instant makeover:

I went home proudly in my uniform, and I walked through the door to be faced by about five family stunned faces as I walked in complete with a hat on and everything, and sort of threw my best salute, and my dad walked round me like he's never seen such a thing before and he said, 'Take off the jacket,' he said. I took off the jacket and he turned it inside out and he said, 'When have you got to go back to camp?' I said, 'On Monday morning', so he … looked at my brothers and he said, 'We'll have to take it to pieces and … and re-stitch it', which they did … They all stopped whatever they were going to do after Shabbos was done … my brother took it to pieces, my brother Ben, he was always very creative, my dad recut it, they redid it, they fitted it, they pressed it, and it looked better than any officer's uniform, seriously, I cannot tell you. And I went back to camp, and as I walked through the gates it felt so different … And the first person I met was probably my CO or something and I saluted, and I saw her following me with her eyes with a very puzzled look, as if to say, 'I wonder where she got that uniform from.'[17]

Uncluttered styles and mass-production methods, which raised average clothing standards, created a social evening out during and after the Second World War that was enhanced by the government Utility scheme aimed at making material and human resources go further. Margaret Wray says:

In the post-war period, class distinctions in clothing have tended to disappear. Clothing purchases for many consumers, particularly those in the 15–30 age groups who now earn good wages in offices and factories, are no longer regulated by basic necessity, while the middle classes generally have had to lower their pre-war standards.[18]

By 1950, the Apparel & Fashion Industry Association could say, 'Everything points to a higher basic level of demand for clothing … Redistribution of incomes, widening of outlooks, social advance, and the impact of "civilisation" generally, have all increased the potential demand for good clothing and have heightened and quickened consumer choice.'[19]

So the ground was prepared for the great burgeoning of the fashion industry that was such an important part of the exciting 1960s' cultural scene to which Christopher Breward pays homage. Although Carnaby Street in Soho was known as the epicentre of 'Swinging London's' fashion scene, Fitzrovia's buzzing and colourful streets were home to much of London's street fashion for women, its industry sustained by the hidden hands of its hard-pressed workers.

Clothing Workers on the Other Side of Oxford Street

The flow of clothing businesses and clothing workers into Fitzrovia transformed not only the industrial landscape of the neighbourhood but the texture of its everyday life. There had long been a Jewish presence on the Other Side of Oxford Street, but a strong Jewish community now grew up, becoming perhaps the dominant community in the area, present not only in its numerous tucked-away clothing workshops but in the many small local shops selling dresses, hats and shoes, the small food shops and cafes reflecting communal tastes and in the thriving synagogues and clubs like the beloved Boys' Club in Fitzroy Square.

Many local people's home lives were governed by their parents' work in the clothing trade, which they themselves often entered as they grew up. Their entry into the clothing trade sometimes began well before leaving school, meaning that even some school-age children were pretty much hidden away:

> After school you had your tea, went to *cheder* [Hebrew school], came home at about seven, and your father made you go into his workshop and help him for an hour or two before going to bed ... I was interested in painting ... but my father said, 'A painter, you'll never make a living.' So I became a tailor and started with my father. That's what happened in those days. I finished up with my own business in Savile Row.[20]

In some families' living quarters the bedrooms, living rooms and corridors were used as work spaces or storage spaces for finished garments. 'My father had his workshop in the flat in which we lived. I can remember from the age of three all the greatcoats being made up and piled in the passage and me sleeping on them in the afternoon.'[21]

Many poorer children, Jewish and Gentile, went into the trade, with girls having to pick up experience through several low-paid 'learner' jobs as there were no formal apprenticeships for women.[22] A local learner could easily start in one of the small workshops doing menial jobs to begin with. Clementina Black sketches a likely employment picture for young girls:

> The small man's workshop will seldom employ a great number of hands, but will pretty certainly include a man machinist, a man presser, two journeywomen (one who sews, and one who makes button-holes), and a girl who 'goes to shop,' that is, fetches and carries back work. This humble subordinate also runs on errands, and if she is quick, and understands her own interests, her aim – often successful – will be to 'pick up' the trade.[23]

Even at a comparatively early date, Frances Hicks, the Secretary of the Women's Trade Union Association, who was reporting on dressmakers and tailoresses for Galton's *Workers on their Industries* (1896), gives a good idea of the pull of Oxford Street for clothing workers. She describes it as a powerful draw for those who have learnt their trade and wish to branch out:

> An apprentice or improver is generally very glad to leave off work and try her hand in the West End. If she has made good use of her time, and applies for work at the right season, that is at the end of March or the beginning of April, she can almost certainly get taken on as a season hand at one of the large dressmaking firms in the neighbourhood of Oxford Street, starting at wages of about 8s per week.[24]

Hicks' comments reveal how the growing clothing industry could act as a broadener of horizons, but also a source of temptation, for poorer girls who might well in the previous generation have gone into domestic service, where miniscule wages, lack of independence, little leisure time and servility were almost all they could expect:

> It is here that the girl's eyes are opened to the ways of the world. The beautiful materials lavishly used, of which she hardly knew the existence before, completely dazzle her. The gossip that she hears of the private affairs of the grand customers, told by the knowing ones with all the hints and suggestions that are supposed to be understood, at first shocks the girl coming into it ... This is a time that tests a girl's character very severely. There is a greater

amount of a kind of freedom in this life, for, except in the matter of wages, every one is on terms of perfect equality.[25]

However, that simple 'matter of wages' was crucial to economic survival: the poor and irregular wages of women contributed greatly to the clothing trade as a whole being marked as a 'sweated trade'. As we've seen, in the earlier decades of the century sweating was a problem across the industry, impacting worst on the women who formed the bulk of the workforce in the mantle trade. To highlight conditions in the clothing industry, which hadn't been widely under-stood by the middle and upper social classes that were buying the end product, the Sweated Industries' Exhibition was held in May 1906 at the Queen's Hall, Langham Place, around the corner from some of the most densely packed Fitzrovia clothing workshops. Mary Neal, founder of the West London Mission's Club for Working Girls in Cleveland Street, wrote in the exhibition catalogue of her girls' working experiences in the clothing trade, highlighting the impact of seasonality on workers and the health effects of sweating:

> From the workers point of view the fact that dressmaking is a season trade is its greatest drawback … This means that it is quite usual for a girl to be on short time or out of work altogether for several months of the year … Last week I had occasion to ask a very good dressmaker what she earned. '£1 a week,' was her reply. 'Do you have much slack time?' I asked. 'Yes; I don't suppose I average more than 14/– a week all the year round.' … The trade is not a healthy one, the constant sitting and stooping over the work soon means bent backs and anaemic blood. The longest hours come in the hottest time of the year; there are few dressmakers who have spent a June day otherwise than in a heated and stuffy workroom.

Mary Neal was careful to point out that the girls she had spoken to were by no means the worst off in terms of sweating. The West End workrooms employing these members of her club were of the better sort, and much worse conditions and pay were often to be found in the smaller workshops.

Waistcoat making was one of the best tailoring trades for women at the beginning of the century. It paid the experienced worker 35–50s a week in busy times and offered regular work even in slack times. Another benefit, according to Clementina Black, was that it was one of the few tailoring trades to offer women apprenticeships. Waistcoat making took between one and three years to learn from a master tailor on payment of a premium of £1–£5. Apprentices were paid no more than a few shillings' wage.

However, waistcoat making was an elite speciality in the clothing trade. The great majority of female workers in the clothing trade were machinists in ready-to-wear clothing, with large numbers working in Fitzrovia's mantle trade. Female machinists in the mantle trade were at the turn of the century being paid 18–30s a week, a good wage for women at the time. However, Frances Hicks, commenting on the physical strain of the work, says, 'This comparatively high wage attracts many to the work, but very few women can stand more than four or five years constant employment in this branch without their health being ruined.'[26]

Even though 14-year-old school leavers often went straight into the trade, some training was available for girls through the trade schools. The nearest trade school for a girl from Fitzrovia was in Paddington. 'At such schools,' explains the 1936 Ministry of Labour pamphlet on *The Needle Trades*, 'you will be given instruction … according to sound trade methods.' The pamphlet lays out the main processes involved in ready-to-wear dressmaking: designing, cutting, machining and finishing. The courses lasted for two or three years, provided some general education as well as training, and were intended for girls wanting to go into the 'bespoke' trade rather than ready-to-wear, which taught school leavers on the job. There were fees of between 15s and £2 – a substantial sum when girls' weekly wages were usually less than 15s – but scholarships were available. The trade schools also provided evening classes. Department stores with their own dressmaking and tailoring workrooms also took on trainees.

Minimum trade board rates for young learners in the 1930s were still extremely low. Beginners earned 5s or 6s a week in the first year, 8–10s in the second year and 25–30s at the end of the training period for a forty-eight-hour week. Small wages like this for youths weren't unusual in other trades as well, as in the furniture industry. According to *The Needle Trades*, an experienced machinist at this period could earn 35s a week and up to £3 in the busy season, although the effect of seasonality was still considerable. The *Labour* journal recorded unemployment rates for 'insured persons' of 17.1 per cent in 1932, dropping to 11.3 per cent in 1937, then rising again the following year to 14.1 per cent (November 1938).

Rates of pay rose fast during the Second World War so that by January 1944 *The Garment Worker* was claiming that pay was at least 32 per cent higher than before the war. Nevertheless, the rise in wages was less than in many other trades. In the ready-made and wholesale bespoke trade, average weekly earnings in January 1944 were 110s 10d for men and 52s 9d for women. As in other trades, rates for women that were roughly half the men's rate were not only tolerated but thought to be right, even by trade unionists. The widespread belief was that a woman's wage was always only supplementing the male breadwinner's earnings. At this time, average earnings for both sexes in the clothing industry were lower than the average for all industries, so the comparatively good rates of pay for women in the clothing industry weren't sustained.

Girls could aspire to become fitters, designers or cutters, with many of these respected figures in the trade earning more than £5 a week. A top designer could earn much more. Designers were often skilled cutters and sometimes designed not by sketching but by cutting and draping the cloth. The designer supervised the pattern making and the cutting of the 'model garment' or 'toile', which was made by the best of the firm's dressmakers and shown at dress shows or taken round to retail firms by travelling salespeople.

However, women's aspirations very often remained simply dreams, as women were few in the most prestigious, skilled and well-paid jobs in the trade. Designers were almost always men. Female cutters in men's tailoring were rarely found and not encouraged, although they were sometimes employed in womenswear. During the Second World War, the male-dominated tailoring unions were quick to raise concerns about women being brought in by employers that were short of labour to do the 'man's job' of cutting. Trade union officials and members were requested to report and record every case of women being employed in this way. My mother's eldest sister, Cissie, a skilled cutter of women's garments, was in the 1960s finally given the job of cutting men's jackets. Her elevation in status aroused comment within the family, even at that comparatively late date.

Trade unionism was never very strong in the clothing industry. The structure of the industry, where small workshops were numerous and former workers commonly set up their own small businesses, possibly hampered trade union organisation since clothing workers arguably lacked a sense of themselves as a body of *workers* compared with those in other industries. Few women belonged to a union and the male tailors were often more concerned to protect their occupations from encroachment by women than to welcome them into 'their' unions.

Even prominent early-twentieth-century figures in the women's trade union movement, like Frances Hicks, the Secretary of the Women's Trade Union Association, saw married women's work – especially home work – as a source of unfair competition and undercutting of wages that harmed male workers. Hicks argued for the advantages of restricting married women's employment as a by-product of controlling or reducing home workshops. Her justifiable arguments about the unhealthy nature of home workshops and the ill effects on general wages unfortunately reinforced the primacy of the male breadwinner, rather than addressing the employers' duty to pay and treat all workers fairly.

The weakness of the union movement in the industry meant that many efforts at unionisation were short-lived, but six large trade unions joined forces in 1915 to create the long-lasting Tailors and Garment Workers' Union. This became the National Union of Tailors and Garment Workers (NUTGW) in 1931, absorbing the craft-based Amalgamated Society of Tailors during the Depression years at a time of high unemployment in the trade. A separate Jewish union, the United Ladies' Tailors' Trade Union, under the threat of Fascism at home and abroad, amalgamated with the NUTGW in 1938.

There were few strikes in the clothing industry. However, as we will see in Chapter 6, in April 1912 a successful strike of West End tailors took place for better pay and conditions, called by the London Society of Tailors. The West End tailors were supported by East End tailors – even those who weren't unionised – who successfully resisted being used to break the West End strike.

By 1940 the union journal, *The Tailor and Garment Worker*, shows that the union was primarily concerned with negotiating paid holidays for outworkers, winning national pay increases (it achieved a 2s increase for all clothing workers in 1940), and trying (unsuccessfully) to get equal pay for women temporarily doing 'men's work'. As we've seen, the union also wanted to restrict the 'men's work' done by women and got an agreement to that effect. So, women's contribution to the clothing industry continued, even in the mid-twentieth century, to be undervalued even by other workers, and their voices to be only faintly heard.

Behind the Scenes at the Department Stores

Looking at the manufacturing side of department store clothing in Fitzrovia increases the impression that the clothing industry was, in many respects, a 'hidden' industry whose workers were the invisible faces and voices of fashion. Although they were large-scale employers, the in-store factories on the Other Side of Oxford Street are hard to find out about in detail. Stores like Selfridges and John Lewis have considerable archives, and books have been written about the most celebrated founding figures, such as John Spedan Lewis and Harry Gordon Selfridge.[27] Indeed, there has recently (2013–16) been a much-watched television drama series based on Selfridge's career. There is also a substantial amount of information in the archives about the stores' ordinary sales employees. Yet, information about the experiences of the clothing factory workers in the same stores is scarce. Even the department stores' staff journals primarily concern the sales and management teams and have had to be combed through for fragments of information about the pay, conditions, attitudes and morale of the in-store garment makers. An archivist at the John Lewis Heritage Centre at Cookham, Berkshire, told me that, to her knowledge, no enquiries have ever been previously received about life in the John Lewis clothing workrooms, while many have asked about the retail side of the business.

The absence of information about the department store workrooms seems even stranger when we bear in mind that the Oxford Street department stores concentrated on selling clothing, and the store workrooms were becoming more important elements of the trade as the century progressed. The in-store clothing factories were part of a trend that saw the decline of the wholesaler or industry middleman. Margaret Wray, in her 1957 survey of the women's outerwear trade, found that by the 1940s about two-thirds of the trade was direct from manufacturer to retailer. Wray concisely explains the history of the synergy between the department stores and ready-to-wear clothes:

> The increased supplies of ready-made outerwear fitted readily into department store methods of selling; the stocking of a wide range of attractive goods, the provision of many amenities to make shopping expeditions pleasant and comfortable and the use of extensive advertising to attract large numbers of customers to their centrally situated premises … their expert choice of stocks and their specialised methods of display combined to make ready-to-wear outerwear more attractive generally than bespoke products.[28]

So, department stores and multiple stores (where several different stores are owned by the same parent company) became even more important features of London's clothing industry in the twentieth century. Department stores like Bourne & Hollingsworth 'sold' gentility: like the furniture stores in Tottenham Court Road, they 'deliberately targeted a certain "ordinary" middle-class clientele, making a virtue of its familiarity, homeliness and safety'.[29] They also possessed a certain grandeur and high levels of customer service. Some stores, like John Lewis, increasingly made a virtue of appealing to middle-class customers on low budgets. When John Lewis was able to expand along Oxford Street, thanks to taking over T.J. Harries in 1928, John Spedan Lewis declared in the staff *Gazette* of 22 September 1928, 'We ought, I think, to go for the real "new poor", that is to say for those who have to satisfy cultivated tastes upon a very small income'. Lewis defines this very small income as 'some hundreds' a year, therefore it would still have been appreciably higher than the average working-class income.

But it wasn't very long before working-class women and girls, exploiting their improved purchasing power, were claiming some of the Oxford Street gloss, even if they could only afford to buy few of the fashions. Sally Alexander describes how shopping 'was a ritual, a tribute to a special occasion, and one willingly saved up for. Window-shopping, on the other hand, was a more regular enjoyment, like the cinema or dancing.'[30] Alexander speaks about the influence of films and film stars on the self-image of girls in the 1920s and 1930s and how this translated for some young working-class women into a greater preoccupation with the glamour of fashion, catered for by the store windows of Oxford Street. If they were skilful, these young women might be able to make their own fashionable clothes or, if they were lucky, they knew someone who could do it for them:

> We'd get them to make us a hat, and it was really something unusual, or they would make our dresses for us, and they could make the dresses for a mere 10 shillings … One would buy a black suit with a check colour, and then you would get a white flat hat with a black-and-white ribbon round it, match it all up. And you'd have your white gloves and your black-and-white shoes, or your black shoes … But you only wore them on Sundays to start off with … and you only went out shopping just before Whitsun and just before Christmas – twice a year …[31]

The department stores were sustained by their alluring clothing departments, and what sustained those clothing departments were the thousands of hard-working garment workers north of Oxford Street. Some stores offered accommodation to their employees: Bourne & Hollingsworth had, by 1912, opened a staff hostel in Store Street, off Tottenham Court Road, and another in Gower Street in Bloomsbury.

Some stores never opened their own factories. Marks & Spencer didn't do so, for example, but John Lewis, Peter Robinson, Debenham & Freebody and Bourne & Hollingsworth all opened in-store production facilities, as did C&A on the south side of Oxford Street. John Lewis began in-store factory production in their Oxford Street premises after taking over the T.J. Harries workrooms in 1928.

In-store factories meant that the stores could offer a bit more variety in clothing than the more standardised garments produced by large manufacturers and could suit their own individual customers better. Department store factories also tended to produce clothing that was a little better in quality than standard ready-to-wear. During and just after the Second World War, department store production increased, mainly to overcome supply difficulties and high manufacturer's prices at this time, although later it fell back again as relationships with the big manufacturers improved post-war.

Local resident Noel Ambrose made outerwear for Selfridges:

> I worked in the rag trade. I was a waterproof garment maker by trade, but I went into the women's dresses the last few years. The last 50 years I worked for Selfridges, my wife worked for Selfridges for 46 years ... I used to make riding coats; you know the heavy duty double textured riding coats. With a special solution and they used to seal the seams with a tape. You used to have special blocks and all that to put things on and you could throw a bucket of water on them and you wouldn't get wet.[32]

Alice Anson was born in Vienna in 1924 and escaped the Nazis in 1938 on the *Kindertransport* to England. She was apprenticed as a dressmaker at Debenham & Freebody in 1939 and was paid 10s a week. After paying her fares to work she had 2s 6d to spend. Luckily, she boarded with a family for free, so had no other expenses. Alice started in a section which made dresses as well as carrying out repairs, with dress fittings taking place in the same workroom. The first months of her four-year apprenticeship were wearisome:

> I was unlucky because I started off learning how to make shoulder straps and shoulder pads ... and in between I had to run about with dresses and I had to fit one, and if it rained I had to go all the way underneath [the shop] and up again, and ... they kept me running for nine months which was way above the thing, so whether it was my background that did it or not I don't know.

Apprentices usually spent only the first few months doing these odd jobs. When Alice mentions her 'background' holding her back she probably means that she experienced discrimination because she was Jewish. At least one senior member of staff at her workplace was Anti-Semitic, she believed.[33] Alice started at Debenham & Freebody at around the same time as the Second World War began and describes how the firm switched over to mass war production. We can assume that the store was a designated firm under wartime government orders:

> We did uniforms ... I was on the machine and I had to make straps for the belts ... You have these little loops on the belts and I had to make so many hundreds a day, first inside stitching then you turned them inside out, then you passed them to the button-hole maker ... it wasn't quite the thing I wanted ...[34]

After leaving Debenham & Freebody, Alice worked for a dressmaker's firm near Harrods and then found a job making premium hot water bottle covers for a firm in Bond Street. She earned £5 a week for making these coveted items which cost 5 guineas each.

After the Second World War, John Lewis opened a Workroom Junior School for training school leavers. They learnt 'the elements of tailoring and dressmaking for from three to six months', with ten trainees accepted during the first year, later to be raised to twenty, according to an internal memo of 17 December 1946. Along with the technical schools that, by this time, were offering classes for those entering the clothing industry, the department stores were aiming to make up for the lack of formal apprenticeships in ready-to-wear with a training in at least the basics of the trade.

One of the very few records I managed to find at the John Lewis Heritage Centre that deals directly with the life of the department store workrooms is a feature from the in-house journal, the *Peter Jones Chronicle*, of 31 July 1959. Entitled 'A Peep Behind the Jonelle Scenes', emphasising the backstage theme, this article is a whimsical survey of the backroom world and personnel of Elsley Court in Great Titchfield Street. Goods were produced there under the Jonelle label and it was run by Taylor & Penton, which was part of the John Lewis Partnership. This piece was written by 'Phoenix' and begins by evoking high fashion theatre, the 'glamorously staged ... presentation of a top Dress Designer's "Collection".' It then makes the connection between this world and what it calls the Elsley Court 'workaday world', a connection found through the calico toile which is the basic model for a fashion line and from which variations will be created by the store's own designers during the season. Each toile bought from a designer for the Jonelle fashion range cost the store 150 guineas on average. The smaller firms in Oxford Street sometimes made their way in the trade by using 'pirated' toiles, 'purveyed by sinister little men with "connections" in Paris', according to Eric Newby, who was brought up in the trade.[35]

Elsley Court, Phoenix says, is 'one of those places where ... high fashion is brought down to earth', conjuring up the street scene:

The streets there are filled with squat little vans fitted with rails to carry the dresses. All day long, while racks and great rainbow-coloured armfuls of finished garments are hurried out of hundreds of buildings and across the pavements into the little vans, the throb of sewing machines is as ceaseless as the thunder of traffic in nearby Regent Street and Oxford Street.

The factory at Elsley Court was a sizeable one, employing 100 'partners' as John Lewis employees were called, since they were entitled to shares in the business. The article introduces some of the key staff and their roles, with a few details about their background or out-of-work interests added for colour: Mr Ellis, the manager, who has designed some of the 'precision gadgets' that quicken the processes, and times them with a stopwatch; Miss Furlong, a cutter, 'a keen member of the John Lewis Netball Team'; Miss Egan, a senior passer, who shows the interviewer a pigeon's nest on the window ledge keenly watched by the workroom staff; and Mrs Seaward, the forewoman of the Finishing Department, who has fitted costumes on the cast of *The Rape of Lucrece* at Glyndebourne. Under the subheading 'Cosmopolitan', Phoenix emphasises the diversity of the workforce. The article brings in, among others, a machinist, Mrs Cobham, who was 'made to work during the war in the Krupps munitions factory'; Mrs Zagorska, an actress in Poland before the war, whose husband was a Resistance leader; and Mrs Borucka, who was sent with her family to Siberia and returned home by ox-sleigh.

Elsley Court wasn't the John Lewis Partnership's only workroom. The others included Phoenix Yard near Oxford Street. It's likely that the 'Phoenix' who wrote the article quoted above was a staff member based there. John Lewis and Peter Jones each had several workrooms, not only for clothing but also for furnishings. John Lewis' clothing workrooms employed 505 female and forty male staff. The male staff were likely to be in senior roles such as workroom manager and cutter.

It's evident that the workrooms were very important features of the Partnership. Yet, with the one exception of the staff magazine piece by Phoenix, it seems that the workroom staff were barely on the store's radar as being a part of its success story. An effort is clearly made by Phoenix, at the relatively late date of 1959, to inform other store staff about Elsley Court's backstage scenes and lives, and to include the workroom employees as partners who are worthy of attention. But, the hint of exotica about the piece is telling – these workroom staff appear, as a rule, to be 'silent partners'.

44–46 Howland Street in the 1900s. My mother's family lived in a similar house at 48–50 Howland Street of which no photograph exists. (Camden Local Studies and Archives Centre: photograph by Erik Ros)

My great-grandfather, Gershon Simkovitch (later Harris), with two of his daughters, Debbie and Mary. (Personal photograph reproduced by Erik Ros)

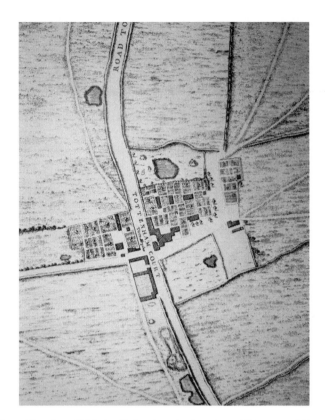

Roque's Map of London, 1746, detail showing the junction of Hampstead Road and Tottenham Court Road narrowed by a turnpike. (Camden Local Studies and Archives Centre: photograph by Erik Ros)

Street car dealers on 'Setty Corner' near the Warren Street car market. (Getty Images)

The Middlesex Infirmary in the 1930s, housed in the former Strand Union Workhouse buildings in Cleveland Street. (Reproduced with permission from UCLH Arts & Heritage, UCLH NHS Foundation Trust)

The Middlesex Hospital in 1935 after reconstruction. (Reproduced with permission from UCLH Arts and Heritage, UCLH NHS Foundation Trust)

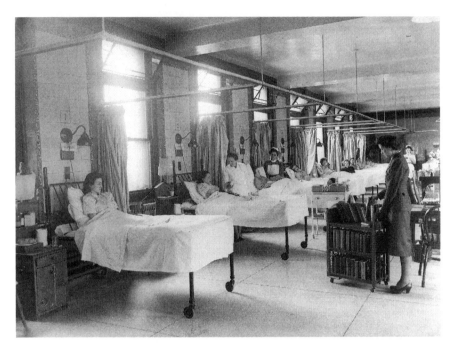

A Middlesex Hospital ward in the 1950s (Reproduced with permission from UCLH Arts and Heritage, UCLH NHS Foundation Trust)

Trades Training College in Great Titchfield Street established by the Carpenter's Company in 1893. (Reproduced with kind permission of the Carpenters' Company)

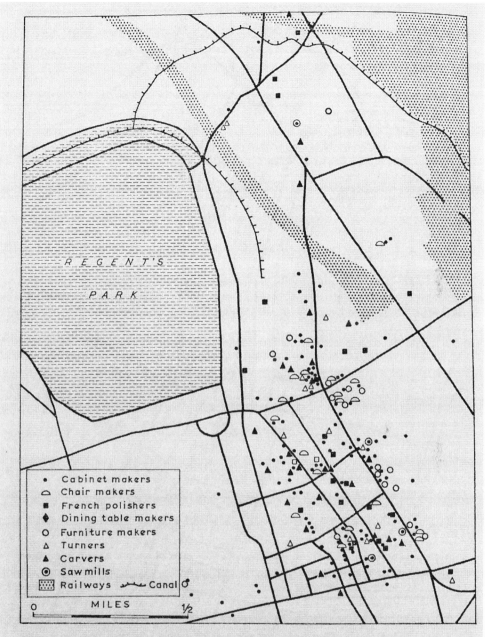

Fig. 16. Furniture: Tottenham Court Road–Camden Town, 1901
(Source: Directories)

Area map of the West End furniture industry 1901, from P.G. Hall's *Industries of London since 1861*
(1962).

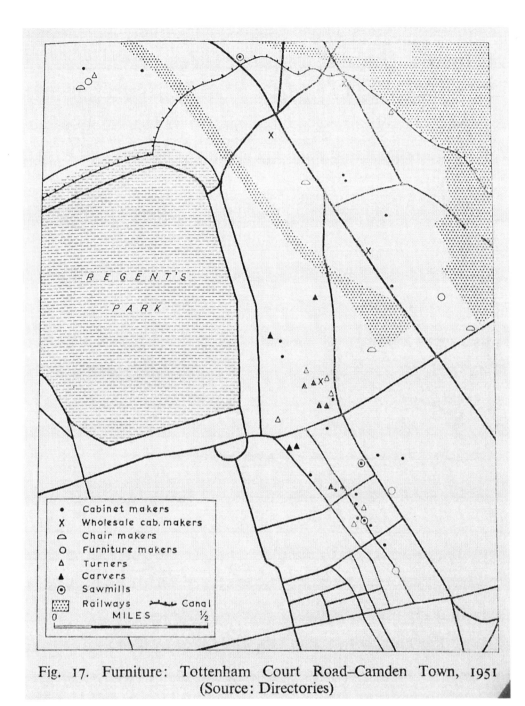

Fig. 17. Furniture: Tottenham Court Road–Camden Town, 1951
(Source: Directories)

Area map of the West End furniture industry 1951, from P.G. Hall's *Industries of London since 1861* (1962).

Façade of Heal's, 2018. (Erik Ros)

Lampshade maker's sign at 48 Whitfield Street, 2018. (Erik Ros)

Wedding photograph of my parents, Paul Strzeja and Rebecca Coshever, showing my mother's tailored suit made by my grandfather. (Personal photograph reproduced by Erik Ros)

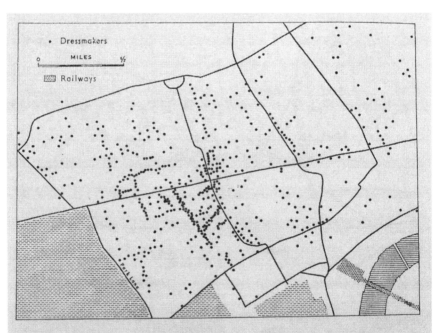

Fig. 11. Women's outerwear: West End, 1861 (Source: Directories. No undertakings mapped west of Edgware Road or north of Marylebone Road)

Area map of the West End women's outerwear industry 1861, from P.G. Hall's *Industries of London since 1861* (1962).

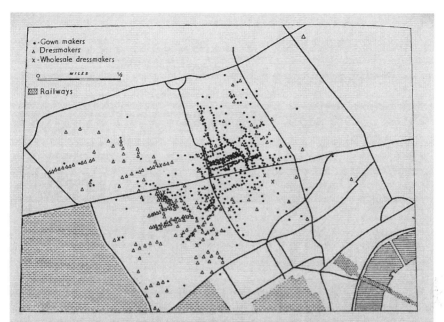

Fig. 12. Women's outerwear: West End, 1951 (Source: Directories. No undertakings mapped west of Edgware Road or north of Marylebone Road)

Area map of the West End women's outerwear industry 1951, from P.G. Hall's *Industries of London since 1861* (1962).

A domestic tailoring workshop in the early twentieth century. (Reproduced with kind permission of the Jewish Museum, London)

A clothing shop in Great Titchfield Street, 2018. (Erik Ros)

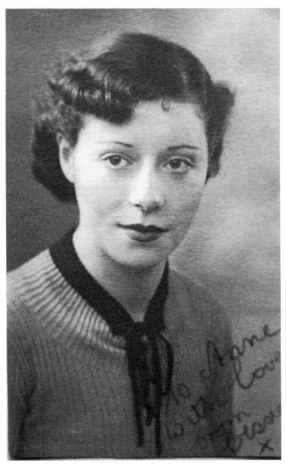

My Aunt Cecelia, a skilled tailor and cutter, shown in the 1930s. (Personal photograph reproduced by Erik Ros)

John Lewis' silk room, 1930s. (With kind permission of John Lewis' Heritage Centre)

John Lewis, Oxford Street, 1939. (With kind permission of John Lewis' Heritage Centre)

Madhan Lal Dhingra, the Indian Nationalist who assassinated Sir William Hutt Curzon Wyllie on 1 July 1909. (Wikimedia Commons, enhanced by Erik Ros)

Venezuelan Consulate at 56 Grafton Way, 2018. (Erik Ros)

Interior of
Oxford Music
Hall. (Wikimedia
Commons)

La Continentale
Cinema in
Tottenham
Court Road
in the 1970s.
(Fitzrovia
Neighbourhood
Association
Archive)

Dancers at the Paramount Ballroom in Tottenham Court Road, 1949. (Getty Images)

West Central
Jewish Lads' Club
at 38 Fitzroy
Square, 1933.
(Reproduced with
kind permission
of the Jewish
Museum, London)

West Central Jewish Girls' Club members dressed up for a dramatic performance, 1910. (Reproduced with kind permission of the Jewish Museum, London)

The Percy Restaurant in Percy Street, 1904. (Camden Local Studies and Archives Centre: photograph by Erik Ros)

The Fitzroy Tavern, Charlotte Street, 2018. (Erik Ros)

Interior of the Lyons' Corner House at Coventry Street, 1942. (Wikimedia Commons)

The impression of a divide between retail staff and factory staff is heightened by the information about in-house factories gathered from the John Lewis *Gazette*. Hints are dropped that the factory staff lag somewhat behind the sales staff when it comes to facilities and other conditions of work. An item from 17 November 1928 – just after the takeover of the Harries factory – highlights inadequate dining arrangements for John Lewis' new factory staff, who have separate dining rooms from the sales staff. This issue draws comment from John Spedan Lewis:

> It seems to me that, if we cannot provide, at present, dining room accommodation for all of these [factory] Partners, it would be better to stipulate definitely that some of them shall go out for their meals, rather than that, by trying to crowd into too small a room, they shall spoil it for everyone.

J.S. Lewis doesn't appear to tackle urgently the issue of inadequate dining space for the factory staff, seeming to regard these staff as getting in the way of the other staff. He casually proffers an unsatisfactory temporary solution, begging the question of whether an identical problem involving sales staff would have been a higher priority.

Lewis did take up staff issues in factory workrooms, even if the resulting actions lagged behind events. In a memo of 9 June 1934, nearly six years after acquiring the Harries workrooms, he tells his chief financial advisor:

> Workrooms are commonly furnished almost exactly as if the workers were cattle or chickens.
>
> In the treatment of the windows, ceilings, walls and floors and in the choice of the furniture there is no consideration at all for anything except bodily health and the efficiency of the work.

Lewis suggests that the management should decorate and furnish the workrooms as 'intelligent, well-to-do people' would do if they had to work in them. He suggests linoleum, pictures on the walls, decorative curtains, flowers and attractive, comfortable furniture. He asks for this to be carried out in one workroom as an experiment, to be repeated if the changes are well received by staff. Lewis also wants to introduce music into the workroom by way of gramophone or wireless concerts, or to have literary works read aloud to staff. Six years after batting away the question of dining rooms, he also states that he wants to see good dining facilities for workroom staff, as well as good medical facilities. But, again, these delayed plans raise questions about the extent to which the welfare of workroom staff was an afterthought. John Lewis has always been famous for caring for its staff, but the implication here is that, in the past, it didn't quite care equally for everyone.

Holiday pay and sick pay were other areas of less than equitable treatment by the firm towards workroom staff. The issue generated a long dispute within the company's committee. It seemed finally to have been resolved by June 1948, when the company conference decided that factory staff should get holiday and sick pay on an equal basis to other staff, with the cost being charged to the firm centrally instead of being taken out of the workrooms budget, as had been tried before that time. John Lewis did tend to pay its factory staff more than the relevant applicable trade board rate, although their pay was still less than equivalent sales staff.

All told, there are clear indications of a gap between factory and sales staff, with factory workers at the John Lewis Partnership appearing to occupy a lower-ranked category than their retail colleagues. We can suspect that this was the case as far as other large West End retailers were concerned, given the general invisibility of their factory staff and also since John Lewis was seen to be a model employer.

Was the 'hidden' nature of clothing manufacture north of Oxford Street connected to discrimination? We need to look harder at the factors that tended to make it an invisible trade, and how this, in turn, was linked to Fitzrovia's sense of place.

The Hidden Side of Oxford Street?

'Phoenix's' reference to the staging of fashion once more evokes the front and back stage areas of fashion production and consumption and suggests that their geographical locations took on a distinctive character created by these networks of activities. Breward makes a valuable point about Fitzrovia and the clothing trade, which the research for this book has proved about other trades and activities – Fitzrovia made its booming trades happen by the way in which its small-scale, tightly knit geography and industrial structures encouraged meetings and connections between producers, retailers and consumers. It threw people together and struck sparks of creativity.

However, we can also appreciate that there were negative effects of a back-stage 'invisible' Fitzrovia upon its working people, which have been overlooked by Breward. The theatrical fashion magic that he writes about was created by human beings who, far from having supernatural powers, were relatively lacking in power and were less well regarded than those on the retail stage: the customers and the retail staff who supported them.

What caused the disadvantage attached to the 'hidden' clothing trade? One issue that clearly emerges is social class and how this was interwoven with the geography of the city as well as the structure of the clothing industry. Class associations even affected the prestige of Oxford Street itself. Its eastern end, in between Oxford Circus and Tottenham Court Road and nearest to Fitzrovia, was regarded as being less prestigious than its western end between Oxford Circus and Marble Arch.

It's been shown by Sonia Ashmore and others that Bourne & Hollingsworth, which moved east of Oxford Circus to 116–118 Oxford Street in 1902, eventually declined partly because it was perceived as being at 'the "wrong" end of Oxford Street', away from the 'front stage' of West End fashion.[36] Ashmore explains that, before Selfridges opened in 1909 and began to attract genteel customers westwards along Oxford Street, there had been a similar mix of businesses along the whole street, but Bourne & Hollingsworth's relocation to the eastern end of the street – at the southern boundary of Fitzrovia instead of western Marylebone – was a major wrong step, because that site was soon to be designated an unfashionable backstage area by the wealthy and well-to-do consumers whose tastes drove the culture of fashion. Provision for the wealthy elite was concentrated in Mayfair and the Piccadilly area. As Breward points out, 'The sites of fashion "manufacturing, distribution, ordering and retail" were located across the West End in a clear pattern, and their dispersal neatly reflected the long-standing social gradations of the district in obvious ways.'[37]

Bourne & Hollingsworth was in fact the only major department store on Oxford Street to be located east of Oxford Circus (Peter Robinson was at the east side of Oxford Circus but was not strictly speaking a department store). The damage to Bourne & Hollingsworth started with its mislocation, continued with fierce competition from Selfridges after 1909 and was exacerbated, from the 1930s, by a proliferation at the eastern end of Oxford Street of popular chain stores catering for working-class 'new consumers' – Drages furniture store, C&A Modes, and Dorothy Perkins. Ashmore says that it was bad decisions over the sale of company property that led Bourne & Hollingsworth to its final decline and closure in the 1980s, but it had already become less noticed and had failed to thrive in the same way as the department stores to its west.

It is obvious that the Oxford Street stores strongly appreciated the force of the stage metaphor. They took great pains, especially after Selfridges transformed the shopping experience, to put the customer on a glorious stage set with sumptuous displays of goods, grandiose décor and elegant restaurants, cafes and restrooms. Bringing any signs of the making process to customers' notice would have spoiled the illusion.

Yet, the desire to emphasise the glamour of fashionable clothes doesn't completely explain the near total invisibility of Fitzrovia's clothes makers. The tailors of Savile Row and the Court dressmakers attracted top-drawer customers to premises in Bond Street, Bruton Street or Conduit Street, and these wealthy patrons were open about which makers they patronised. So why were the stores so silent about their own workers' contribution to clothes making?

A clue might lie in the nature of the clothes-making process and its connection with social class and Fitzrovia. As we know, Fitzrovia, throughout the first half of the twentieth century, was primarily a working-class area with large pockets of poverty. It also possessed a reputation for disrespectability that was very hard to dislodge, as we saw in regard to the furniture trade. Added to this, Fitzrovia had become a centre for ready-made, although good-quality, outerwear. It was therefore associated with clothing for the masses, not for the elite. It's hard to ignore the snobbish sneer about Fitzrovia and its inhabitants in Dobbs' description of the 'countless busy Jews and Jewesses in sub-contractors' workshops [who are] working steadily on less artistic but more up-to-date lines' than the handicraft tailors in Soho, south of Oxford Street.[38] And Fitzrovia's untrustworthy reputation also stained its clothing industry. Just as Tottenham Court Road's furniture trade tended to be sneered at, so did the tailored ready-mades of Fitzrovia.

The fact that the 'disreputable' area north of Oxford Street was also a production hub of ready-made women's clothing, linking with consumer perceptions and prejudices about fashion and taste, might suggest a set of reasons why Oxford Street department stores possessing their own clothing factories kept so quiet about their existence. Department stores such as John Lewis did have workrooms for hand-produced goods. However, the majority of clothing workrooms employed the same bulk production techniques as were to be found across most of the clothing industry and were common in Fitzrovia. It could have been the association with the mass production of clothing and the lower-class status attached to this activity that made the department stores stay so silent on the topic of their factories. The Oxford Street stores might have had even stronger reasons for not mentioning their factories, given their location in undesirable Fitzrovia, the unglamorous hub of ready-mades.

Class discrimination probably also partly explains the obscurity and less-favourable treatment of in-store factory employees compared with other groups of employees within the department stores. Poorer children, by and large, were the ones who entered the clothing trade in Fitzrovia, although to work in a department store workroom would likely have been a step up in status and pay compared with working in a small workshop. Within the store, as we have seen, there was a divide in social status between workroom staff and sales staff, as well as a difference in the type of activity performed. Most workroom staff members were essentially manual workers, whereas the sales people were white-collar staff, and this distinction was expressed in rates of pay and other conditions of service.

A small degree of movement between categories was sometimes permitted: in John Lewis, small numbers of workroom staff were trained to work on the shop floor at the busiest times, like before Christmas, and the staff *Gazette* of 15 December 1934 praises the success of this initiative. But, overall, there were occupational and social barriers between manual and non-manual workers in the clothing trade. This must have been an important factor in the 'hidden' quality of the clothing makers, since, until recently, the experiences of those lower down in the social scale have been less well recorded.

Female workers were another factor in the hidden, backstage world of clothing production. It's no secret that women's experiences have also – again until recently – been less noticed than men's. Adding in the effects of class, the voices of working-class women were very seldom heard, and the clothing industry was no exception. In womenswear, the great majority of workers were women and girls, who were mostly not unionised and so lacking a voice as workers. Another layer can therefore be added to the narrative of a 'hidden' and even voiceless workforce.

However, yet another factor was in play. As we know, many of the clothing workers were first- or second-generation immigrants, with the small workshops in the neighbourhood being the province mainly of Jewish owners and workers. No doubt the factories behind Oxford Street also employed many recent arrivals to the country, as did the Jonelle workrooms at Elsley Court in Great Titchfield Street. For every immigrant who managed to open a dress shop and show a presence in the bustling Fitzrovia garment trade, there were dozens or scores more concealed behind it, trying to get a start in life for themselves and their families. Fitzrovia in the 1900s had been an area known for the non-enforcement of the workshop laws on health and safety, no doubt due to the difficulty of finding out where the workshops were.[39] These workers, almost all of them non-unionised, would 'finish work at 9.30 p.m., maybe 10 o'clock, and fall asleep at the table while ... having supper. Then ... get up again at two o'clock in the morning in order to get the work ready'.[40] This was the harshest side of the 'hidden' trade on the Other Side of Oxford Street.

There is good reason to believe that multiple discrimination on grounds of class, gender and ethnic background was at work in Fitzrovia's clothing trade. The 'invisibility' of workers was, in some important respects, expressing the prejudices against them. At the same time, Christopher Breward talks about the 'porosity' of the clothing trade – its openness to immigrants and entrepreneurs – which, he believes, was important in creating 'Swinging London' in the 1960s. I would add that it was the porosity of Fitzrovia – its ability to find space for and to absorb new movements of many kinds – that, as with the furniture trade a century or two earlier, enabled the trade in women's outerwear to be so successful and long lasting. It wasn't until the 1970s and the beginning of the globalisation of the trade that it began to disappear. The trade flowed north of Oxford Street as strongly as it did because the trade's adaptable structures allowed the use of varying types and sizes of physical location, which Fitzrovia was able to accommodate.

The changeful nature of Fitzrovia – its capacity to absorb new peoples and to find space for new activities – does seem to borrow from the theatre's protean essence. And, like the theatre, it's associated with a play on boundaries, both spatial and imagined. We can see how the Jewish story about the 'Other Side' of Oxford Street, with its mirrored populations, could also shake up the theatre model of front stage and backstage, if we take front stage to be the 'proper' West End south of Oxford Street and backstage to be Fitzrovia. And, if backstage and front stage have fluctuated to make the hidden become visible, it's only fitting – it is in this perpetual uncertainty that Fitzrovia has been born and reborn.

Fitzrovia's Radicals

Radical Beginnings

Fitzrovia's anti-authoritarian roots extend far back in time, to the licentious Tottenham Fairs held in the fields of Tottenhall Manor in the seventeenth and eighteenth centuries. The New (Euston) Road, built in 1756, bisected Tottenham Fields but could neither impose control on London's rampant growth nor change Tottenham Court Road and Fitzrovia enough to bring the area into full middle-class urban respectability. Its population had anti-Establishment political tendencies, too. By the 1880s Fitzrovia was 'one of the recognised British centres of anarchism and the international Communist movement'.[1]

Why was Fitzrovia such a centre for radicals and radical politics? Some of the reasons lie far back in its relationship with the city. Like Clerkenwell, a mile or so to its east, Fitzrovia had had a long association with radicalism. In *London: The Biography*, the inveterate London historian Peter Ackroyd explored Clerkenwell's mysterious tendency to retain radical associations over hundreds of years, speculating that it had to do with its being a 'shadowland' outside the old City of London.[2] Clerkenwell was 'beyond the bars' of the City of London from its medieval beginnings: it was outside the city's jurisdiction, and therefore a place where 'outlaws' could thrive.[3] But Fitzrovia, emerging at a later point in the city's history than Clerkenwell, began in a different way. It evolved just *inside* the city boundary, newly defined by the Euston Road. Yet Fitzrovia from its beginnings mounted an outsider challenge to the mainstream political and social ideas of late eighteenth-century London. 'Fitzrovia evolved in ways very different to those envisaged by its original architects,' says Hugh David, and his comment seems suggestive of the anarchic, insurrectionary spirit that flourished there 150 years later, around 1900.[4]

This radical spirit was partly due to Fitzrovia being a strong artisan base from its inception. Apart from Fitzroy Square, its streets had been laid out on a small and somewhat haphazard scale, unlike the big London squares nearby. It was built over with low to middle-grade houses attracting many artisans: furniture makers, carpenters, French polishers, gilders and other highly skilled workers. These artisans, the so-called 'aristocracy of labour', without their own property or a vote but better paid, better educated and with more leisure time than other workers, tended to favour social change. They proved receptive to new political ideas like anarchism, and among these radically inclined artisans were substantial numbers of foreign workers coming from countries with strong anarchist or socialist traditions, such as Italy, Germany, France and later Russia. The openness to foreign immigration so characteristic of Fitzrovia from its beginnings meant that, from early on in its history, new political and social ideas easily circulated and spread. Fitzrovia's 'outlaws' didn't live outside the city like Clerkenwell's but were often foreign 'outsiders' who, in some cases, were also escaping their home countries' legal system and found a home within the body of London.

Fitzrovia's early anarchism persisted. Clive Bloom says, in *Violent London*, 'Anarchism, intellectually appealing to the artisan class of the late eighteenth century and Regency period, continued to have great appeal in the mid-nineteenth century when self-help individualism and cooperative organization united various utopian schemes and pastoral visions.'[5] The desire for representation and radical reform, channelled in a variety of directions, notably Chartism with its People's Charter calling for manhood suffrage, was a strong force among sections of the working class. Added to this, conditions in England were in flux: there were economic slumps in the 1870s and 1890–93. At the same time, trade unionism was becoming established and growing after the Master and Servant Act of 1867, and the Workman Act and Conspiracy & Protection of Property Act of 1875. Reformist and non-violent radicalism spread among the working class. And London was the biggest radical centre, joined by cities such as Leeds and Manchester.

The outgrowth of these radical visions was clearly visible in nineteenth-century Fitzrovia. By this time, Fitzrovia had long been a centre of attraction for political dissenters. From 1805–07, the activist William Godwin, husband of the early feminist Mary Wollstonecraft and father of *Frankenstein* author, Mary Shelley, ran a radical bookshop there. Situated in Hanway Street, a small street curving between Tottenham Court Road and Oxford Street, it traded

as the Juvenile Library, but attracted politically minded adults.[6] Hugh David
says of Godwin:

> Ostensibly a dealer in children's books, under the counter he peddled more
> radical wares, not the least of which were his own expositions of a brand of
> Utopian socialism which had received its clearest expression in the writings
> of two French philosophers of the Enlightenment, Pierre Joseph Proudhon
> and Jean Jacques Rousseau.[7]

These writings challenged the basic economic relationship between employers and workers and gave rise to organisations that aimed to implement these
ideas. Some were based in Fitzrovia. In 1833, the social reformer Robert
Owen opened the short-lived National Equitable Labour Exchange at
4 Charlotte Street, where it had moved from Gray's Inn Road. The exchange
offered workers a fairer return for their labour by giving them the chance to
exchange products they had made for 'labour notes', representing hours of
work, which they then used to 'buy' other products. Women's work was still
valued at a lower rate than men's, however. The exchange was unsuccessful and
closed in 1834 after disputes arose over the worth of the goods.

Another local institution, the Capital & Labour Association's shop at 110–
113, Tottenham Court Road, represented a later attempt to share the profits
of labour more equitably. It was established in the 1870s and replicated in
other parts of London. The association was based on the ideas and practices
of Edme-Jean Leclaire in France, who in the 1840s had set up a Mutual Aid
Society for his workers based on profit sharing. He later persuaded them to put
their yearly bonuses into a joint pension scheme.

There were dozens of British firms that practised profit sharing by the 1890s,
with some also running partnership schemes with workers. John Stuart Mill
became a strong supporter, as did the economist and MP Henry Fawcett; and
Sedley Taylor, a good friend of Fawcett, wrote several essays on the topic to
encourage more participation in Britain. The growing Workers' Co-operative
Movement was no doubt influenced by these ideas, and the Capital and Labour
Association itself lasted for some time: the Tottenham Court Road shop was
there until 1909. In 1840, Owen had also established the Scientific & Literary
Institute in Whitfield Street, a venue for political discussion and union meet-
ings and a centre of radical activity used by the Chartists in the 1840s.

It's not difficult to see, then, that the ground had been well prepared for the
upsurge of radicalism Fitzrovia experienced forty or fifty years later, when the
European anarchists arrived in the area. First Italians, then Germans, French

and Russians, mingled together to eat, drink and argue in numberless small, stuffy back rooms off Tottenham Court Road. Fitzrovia was primed to attract migrating political activists from across Europe who needed refuge from states that were clamping down on sometimes violent political activism. It possessed cheap housing, plentiful, if often low-paid, employment through its nearness to the West End, and a dense and diverse working-class population with many European communities already established within it. Many of these radicals embraced anarchism and communism, but others were of a different stripe, including Nationalists and Fascists.

There were occasionally those who successfully used violent means in pursuing their aims. Indian Nationalist Madan Lal Dhingra, a student of University College in Gower Street, assassinated a representative of the British Raj, Sir William Curzon Wyllie, after honing his shooting skills at a shooting gallery in Tottenham Court Road. That event in 1909 was an outburst of a violent insurrectionary spirit in early twentieth-century London, but not many Britons joined the violent revolutionists among the foreign radicals and such revolutionists were, in any case, a minority.

Government and police authorities were always vigilant in keeping track of foreign radicals. Prominent Italian anarchists residing in London, like Errico Malatesta, were closely watched at the request of the Italian government, who feared him, while the nationalists of India House in Hampstead could never meet without a police spy being present. As we will see, the British authorities weren't above employing agents provocateurs in the quest to extinguish the anarchist and communist strands in British-based radical activity, notably in the events that closed Fitzrovia's anarchist Autonomie Club in 1894.

The neighbourhood's radical associations were strengthened by the proximity of Bloomsbury, steeped in its own tradition of nonconformity and lying only steps away to the east of Tottenham Court Road. Bloomsbury was home to the forerunner of the Fabian Society, the Fellowship of the New Life. The Fabian Society itself, an influential reformist group of early socialists, was based in Osnaburgh Street, opposite Great Portland Street Station on the north side of Euston Road.

The suffragette Emmeline Pankhurst lived at 8 Russell Square in Bloomsbury during the 1880s and early 1890s with her young daughters, Sylvia and Christabel. Pankhurst busily entertained 'Socialists, Fabians, Anarchists, Suffragists, Free Thinkers, Radicals and Humanitarians of all schools', according to Sylvia Pankhurst.[8] Their visitors included Errico Malatesta, Dadabhai Naoroji, the first Indian MP, William Morris, Annie Besant, and the anarchist Louise Michel of the Paris Commune, 'the *petroleuse*', according to her enemies. Michel was described by Sylvia Pankhurst as 'a tiny old woman in a brown cloak, intensely lean, with gleaming eyes and swarthy skin, the most wrinkled you ever saw, which made me think of the twisted seams in the bark of an ancient chestnut tree'.[9]

The connections between Fitzrovia and Bloomsbury were symbolised by the Bloomsbury set, who resided at Gordon Square before moving to Fitzroy Street and Fitzroy Square. With its centres of higher education and research that were the colleges of the University of London, and that focal point of learning, the British Museum, the Bloomsbury 'Other Side' to Fitzrovia was bound to be a draw and an additional influence on Fitzrovia radicals and intellectuals.

Bloomsbury was far from being the only connection for Fitzrovia's political radicals, who had links across the city. There was a powerful activist stream between north London and Fitzrovia. Madhan Lal Dhingra and others established a web of connections that included India House in Highgate, University College and Fairyland, the whimsically named Tottenham Court Road amusement arcade and shooting gallery. Twenty years later, the St Pancras Communist Party was active on both sides of Euston Road, its organisation following the lines of the St Pancras borough boundaries that stretched northwards from Fitzrovia to Kentish Town, Camden Town, Belsize Park, Hampstead and Highgate. And currents of radicalism flowed just as strongly back and forth across Fitzrovia's southern boundary, with political activists living, working and freely intermingling across both sides of Oxford Street.

Some writers on London have prioritised Soho over Fitzrovia when it comes to mapping London's radicalism. Judith R. Walkowitz, writing in *Nights Out* about the cosmopolitanism and radicalism of Soho, talks about a radical 'overflow of Soho' developing in Fitzrovia after 1870 as political émigrés increased in numbers and looked to stay near established national communities with their associated shops, cafes and clubs. Walkowitz, therefore, speaks as if the main radical current flowed through Soho.[10] However, the number of radical institutions and groupings around Tottenham Court Road shows that there was at least an equally important flow of radicals and radical ideas from Fitzrovia southwards across Oxford Street into Soho. The very active groups of German radicals, for example, were based in Fitzrovia, not Soho.

Here is more evidence that the 'Other Side' of Oxford Street accommodated multiple perspectives. Altogether, Fitzrovia in the twentieth century played a key part in invigorating the political life of London and – with its many foreign activists continually in motion between countries – the international political scene.

Anarchism in Fitzrovia

Italian anarchists were the first group of European anarchists to arrive in London. Leaving their homelands due to harsh economic times, Italians in London had been steadily increasing in number since the middle of the nineteenth century. They settled, to begin with, in the Clerkenwell area of Holborn but, from the 1870s, rapidly spread out to Westminster, St Pancras and St Marylebone, Fitzrovia's ruling boroughs. They worked in restaurants, cafes and hotels, and as domestic servants, ice-cream sellers and street musicians. By 1911, Lucio Sponza's survey found 1,155 Italians in St Pancras and 513 in St Marylebone, besides 2,606 in Westminster, many of these in Soho.[11] The majority were economic migrants, but anarchists increasingly joined them as the nineteenth century progressed, escaping from the authorities at home.

Italian anarchists tended to live, work and meet both north and south of Oxford Street. They were objects of concern to the Italian Embassy, their comings and goings noted by the police. Giovanni Defendi, who fought with Garibaldi in France, lived at 17 Cleveland Street, while Francesco Ginnasi stayed in Bloomsbury at 53 Huntley Street, off Tottenham Court Road. Newly arrived immigrants often shared lodgings and worked near to where they lived. The leading Italian anarchist, Errico Malatesta, had arrived in London in 1881 and was mixing with others such as Defendi, Vito Solieri, and Aristide Ceccarelli.

It was primarily the Germans who gave Fitzrovia its radical flavour at this time. Some were refugees escaping the Anti-Socialist Laws in their home country. Some German craftsmen and small businessmen had lived in Fitzrovia for generations, but revolutionary times abroad and repressive legislation in Germany had caused an influx of activist refugees to add to the settled immigrant population. Rudolf Rocker, the German anarchist who was to devote many years to political activity in the East End, settled there when he first arrived in London in the 1890s.

Fitzrovia was the base for the 1881 International Revolutionary Socialist Congress, organised from a base at 41 Upper Rathbone Street; its organisers included Malatesta. The congress ended with a public meeting on 18 July 1881 at Cleveland Hall in Cleveland Street, which included speeches from Marie Le Compte, Louise Michel and the Russian anarchist Peter Kropotkin.[12] The Italian Consul reported to the Italian Ambassador on the congress on 19 July. Rudolf Rocker says, in *The London Years*, that the Italian government attached 'great significance ... to Malatesta's person' and he was consequently 'shadowed by Scotland Yard men, who followed every movement he made'.[13]

However, according to Rocker, 'It never stopped Malatesta disappearing from London without trace every time the waves of wrath and resentment rose high in Italy'.[14] Besides, Italian anarchist energies were primarily focused on the home country, where many were later to return.

During the 1880s and 1890s there was a proliferation, on both sides of Oxford Street, of clubs, meeting places and organisations dedicated to helping working men and their families. Pietro Di Paola notes, 'Clubs represented a vital support for refugees who landed in London after long and exhausting journeys. Indeed, it was in the clubs that refugees received first aid from their comrades: hospitality, some food, and precious advice.'[15] The Communist Refugees' Society, with links in Soho dating back to the 1870s, organised a soup kitchen in Fitzrovia, off Newman Street, offering meals for 2*d*. Meanwhile, the Unione Ticinese, a centre for workers from Ticino, was set up in 1874 by the restaurant owner Stefano Gatti and was based at the Schweitzerbund Swiss Club at 74 Charlotte Street. The Unione Ticinese, which still exists as an organisation, seemed to function purely as a social club and mutual aid organisation with no political role; at least, it never appears in connection with political activity. The Ticinese comprised a large group among the London Swiss community, mostly working in local cafes, restaurants and hotels, often as waiters, and their club remained at Charlotte Street for many decades. Enduring into the 1960s and 1970s and listed as the Swiss House Social Club and then the Suisse Chalet Club & Restaurant, it lasted until 1975, when the building passed into the hands of the BBC.

Political clubs were numerous, often combining social and political roles. The Club International des études sociales de Londres was set up in 1880 at the White Hart Pub at 9 Windmill Street, near Goodge Street. The Club International focused on the intellectual development of its members and regularly discussed social questions, publishing a monthly bulletin, *Le Travail*. It was a centre where anarchist and socialist radicals could meet and influence each other.

There were also Fitzrovian experiments in providing a radical education to children. The anarchist International School was set up in the 1890s at 19 Fitzroy Street. It was run by Louise Michel, that gleaming-eyed guest of the Pankhursts, who had been involved in the Paris Commune of 1871 and lived at 59 Charlotte Street. The school committee included Peter Kropotkin, Errico Malatesta and William Morris. They aimed to 'keep the children out of the religiously oriented state schools which, consciously or unconsciously, teach that the people are to be sacrificed to the power of the State and the profit of the privileged classes'.[16] The short-lived school taught French, German, English, music, drawing, sewing and engraving. It was closed when the police raided it in 1892 and found bombs in the basement. At the trials that followed this discovery, the anarchists claimed that the bombs had been planted by a police spy, Auguste Coulon, who was a teaching assistant at the school and who was also to feature in the 1894 Greenwich Park bombing described below.

Some years later in 1913, Lillian Evelyn, who had worked with Rudolf Rocker at the Jubilee Street Club in the East End, ran the Ferrer School at 99 Charlotte Street, modelled on the principles of Francisco Ferrer, a Catalan anarchist educationist who opposed compulsion in educational methods. The Italian anarchist group *Gruppo di Studi Sociali di Londra* also met at the same address. The Ferrer School probably didn't last long either, as the *Post Office Directory* of 1920 shows no sign of it.

In 1878, an international centre for activists, the Rose Street Club, had been founded in what is now Manette Street off Charing Cross Road, not far from the junction with Oxford Street. It was a meeting point close to Fitzrovia for German communists and anarchists, who had regularly met at different venues in London since 1840 under a variety of names, beginning as the German Democratic Society. The longest-lasting centre for these radicals was eventually to become known as the Communist Club. The Rose Street Club was also set up as a meeting place for refugees by Frank Kitz, a British anarchist dyer who became the editor of the anarchist paper *Freiheit*, and the German anarchist, John Neve. The building formerly housed the St James & Soho Working Men's Club.[17] Pietro Di Paola notes that the Rose Street Club 'was the central meeting point for revolutionary refugees in London'.[18]

However, relations among club members were sometimes turbulent. The Rose Street anarchists and Social-Democrats split on the question of supporting the German anarchist Johann Most over his arrest for upholding assassination as a political weapon in the pages of *Freiheit*. The anarchist section associated with Most stayed put in Rose Street, then in 1883 moved to St Stephen's Mews, Rathbone Place, where they founded the Anarchist Club.[19] Meanwhile, the ex-Rose Street Social-Democrats moved to 49 Tottenham Street, becoming the Second Section of the *Communistische Arbeiter Bildungs Verein* (CABV) – the Communist Workers' Educational Union, or simply the Communist Club (the 'Second Section' label was later dropped from the CABV). For some years, the Communist Club was an important venue for socialist lectures and events. Friedrich Engels, George Bernard Shaw, Keir Hardie and William Morris all spoke there. One of the most notable events was the sixth and final Annual Conference of the Socialist League, held at the club on 25 May 1890.

However, the Autonomie Club was, during this period, perhaps the most well known, not to say notorious, of these clubs. The club was founded in 1886 in Charlotte Street by Josef Peukert, a German anarchist, after his expulsion from another club in Whitfield Street off Tottenham Court Road. The Autonomie Club later moved to 6 Windmill Street, becoming a near neighbour of Club International. The group published an anarchist periodical, *Autonomie*, which they smuggled into Germany – although Rocker reports that the group 'hadn't received a penny' from Germany to do this and had had to pay the whole cost themselves.[20] The Autonomie group were responsible for Rocker's first short visit to London in 1893; the aim of the visit was to discuss how the group could continue smuggling literature over the German–Belgian border after the arrest of some of its members.

The Autonomie Club was soon afterwards to become notorious to the police and in the press as the supposed centre of bomb plots, and was the target of police raids and surveillance, which finished the club in 1894.

Anarchist and socialist clubs had been raided by the police before. The Anarchist Club in St Stephen's Mews was hit in 1885, with its members being attacked by the police and the public in an outbreak of anti-foreign violence related to suspicion of socialist propaganda. There were also raids on London clubs in 1892, in the wake of a suspected anarchist bombing campaign in Walsall. The anarchist International School was raided and closed at this time. However, the Autonomie Club raid is perhaps the best known. By the time Rocker settled in London in 1895, *Autonomie* had ceased publication and the Autonomie Club itself was no more.

The break-up of the Autonomie Club happened in the wake of a bomb explosion in Greenwich Park on 15 February 1894. The bombing was memorialised in Joseph Conrad's *The Secret Agent* (1907), which was serialised by the BBC in 2016. The only casualty was the man who was carrying the bomb, Martial Bourdin. This happened just a few days after a bomb had exploded at the Café Terminus in Paris in another anarchist action. Two years earlier, the supposed bombing campaign in Walsall had aroused public fear and outrage, though bombs had never been set off or even found there, and now, after the Paris bombing, public anxiety was high. On Bourdin's body at Greenwich Park was found a membership card for the Autonomie Club. This discovery led to police raids the next day on the club and Bourdin's lodgings at 18 Titchfield Street. In Bourdin's room, 'hidden at the bottom of a wardrobe under a pile of newspapers was a small flagon of sulphuric acid, identical in detail to the one reconstructed from fragments at the site of the explosion'.[21] Nothing was found at the club, which in any case was under police surveillance and would doubtless have been avoided by anyone planning attacks in the city.

Bourdin had been under observation before the explosion by the police double agent, Auguste Coulon, according to Coulon himself. To add to this, Bourdin, on the day the bomb exploded in the park, was reportedly with H.B. Samuels, an anarchist accused by other anarchists of being a police agent and an agent provocateur. Samuels had supposedly encouraged Bourdin to carry out the bombing 'as an experiment' to test new ingredients.[22]

So, the circumstances of the explosion were ambiguous, to say the least, but that didn't help the anarchists. Official and public hostility made it difficult for members to continue using the Autonomie Club. When a funeral procession was held for Bourdin on 23 February 1894, anarchist attenders faced an antagonistic crowd whose 'general mood ... was hostile and violent. In Fitzroy Square [where the procession was due to pause] there was sporadic fighting and six medical students were arrested. A group of men went to the Autonomie Club and stoned it, breaking several windows.'[23] The crowd pursued the coffin with violent intent as far north as St John's Wood, and at the cemetery the body was buried with no speeches or ceremony. Soon afterwards, the Autonomie group stopped publishing their paper, relinquished their club premises in Windmill Street, and were homeless and defunct.

The matter was discussed at length by the House of Lords while debating an Aliens Bill in July 1894. Although violent incidents had been tiny in number, their influence on the public had been great and the aftermath owed a lot to political expediency. The Aliens Bill called for government powers to be strengthened to restrict immigration, citing national security in an age of European insurrectionism, as well as the danger of British citizens being infected by diseases brought in by foreigners. These restrictions came into force with the Aliens Act, passed in 1905. The perception of Fitzrovia and Fitzrovians as a threat to the city was receiving yet another embellishment from the political establishment.

The Mystery of Grafton Hall

The Communist Club at 49 Tottenham Street remained open through the 1890s and until 1902, when it moved to 107 Charlotte Street. Meanwhile, another centre for Fitzrovia's radicals had grown up at Grafton Hall, at 55 Grafton Street, now Grafton Way. Some former members of the Autonomie group were regulars there and Grafton Hall evidently became a second home for many of Fitzrovia's radicals towards the end of the nineteenth century, as well as a general workers' social club. Rudolf Rocker describes a coming together of different German political groupings at Grafton Hall, so that by the time he returned to Fitzrovia in 1895, 'I found the German movement flourishing' with over 500 paying club members at the hall.[24] To add to the evidence of very high levels of foreign immigration into Fitzrovia, Rocker observes:

> When I came to London [in 1895] the whole district from Oxford Street to Euston Road, and from Tottenham Court Road to Cleveland Street was almost exclusively inhabited by Germans, French, Austrians and Swiss. The language spoken in the streets was more often German or French than English.[25]

Grafton Hall was a general club, where German workers ate and socialised, but it now also attracted what Rocker calls 'Social revolutionaries, and a few adherents of the young movement in Germany', who must have given the established club a new impetus.[26] Rocker soon became the club's librarian and the guardian of its valuable book collection, a job he very much enjoyed. According to him, 'The new Grafton Hall Club was the finest meeting place the foreign revolutionaries in London ever had.'[27] It had generous facilities:

> There was a large room on the ground floor, where the comrades who lived in the neighbourhood came every evening, for company, and for their evening meal. On Saturdays and Sundays it was packed with comrades from other parts of the huge city … The big, bright, comfortable library was at the back. The entire first floor was taken up by a spacious hall, which easily seated 500 people, and was often hired for meetings by groups of French, Italian and other foreign comrades. The office rooms and committee rooms were on the second floor.[28]

Given Grafton Hall's obvious importance as a meeting place for European radicals, and its relatively long history compared with many venues used by radical groups, it is surprising to find so few references to the place in sources dealing with the history of London radicalism. Grafton Hall undoubtedly hosted meetings of revolutionists from an early date in its history: its name crops up in 1881 as a meeting place for radicals, mentioned in a Parliamentary debate about whether any measures should be taken against the revolutionary sentiments expressed by Johann Most.[29] But apart from Rocker's testimony, it is hardly visible, either within written histories of Fitzrovia or of the radical movement.

It seems that the hall never attracted the notoriety of the Autonomie and Anarchist Clubs. Perhaps this was because it was a very busy place used for many different social purposes. In fact, Rocker complains about this, saying:

> A place like Grafton Hall was expensive to run, and those who were responsible for its upkeep could not be selective in their admission of members. They also hired the hall to all sorts of bodies; it was not always pleasant. Most of the revenue came from the bar, from selling beer, wine and other intoxicants.[30]

Rocker also concedes that many club members 'were not much interested in the movement as such; they contributed to the funds, but only when they were pressed by the comrades. They rarely came to the discussion evenings.'[31]

There are signs, though, that Grafton Hall did draw official attention, even if no proof exists that police were watching its comings and goings. An LCC archive file on the hall contains evidence of various safety inspections with unfavourable comments. A note dated 15 November 1886 to the Metropolitan Board of Works, apparently from a fire and safety inspector, Frederick Wallace (surname is partly illegible) says, 'I think the Hall is the worst place for getting out of I ever saw'.[32]

A glance at the council's architect's plan of Grafton Hall shows why Wallace was worried about it. Behind its street door is a very narrow corridor with a tiny porter's cubbyhole: a tightly enclosed space. Rather than running through the building, this short corridor terminates at a wall with two doors. One door leads to another corridor giving access to stairs, which run up to the main hall and down to the basement, where there is a skittle alley with a back exit in Hertford Place. The floor level of the main hall is several feet above street level. The other door in the wall leads to a small room and then to more stairs up to the hall and the bar. At the back of the hall, another set of stairs leads down to the basement. With its narrow entrance, blocking wall and back stairs and exit, one can see the attraction of such a place for activists on the alert for police raids, as well as how difficult it might be for large numbers of people to leave quickly in an emergency.

The popular press was excited by the atmosphere of clubs like these. According to *Tit Bits* of 7 May 1892, dramatically reporting on a similar, unnamed, venue:

> The door is opened by means of a wire running from a second door a few yards along [the] passage. This wire is operated by a swarthy-looking janitor

… This door-keeper knows by sight all the admitted members of the party
in London … This second door … does not look formidable, but it is for
all that. It is covered with green baize, and has a small slide let into a panel
through which the keeper can inspect anyone coming down the passage. The
door would take some time to force.[33]

The Grafton Hall Club, with its porter's cubbyhole, may well have had a
knowledgeable doorkeeper, perhaps even a 'suspicious' swarthy-looking foreigner in the *Tit Bits* mould. And it may have been under police supervision.
In any case, between April and June 1894 – only months after the Greenwich
Park bomb explosion and the raids on the Autonomie Club – Grafton Hall
was obviously under close inspection by the LCC, with continuing correspondence between the Superintending Architect's Department and the LCC
solicitor. This resulted in the issuing of a court summons against the proprietors for not having a certificate to put on public entertainments. The architect's
report to the court on 10 May notes:

The only entrance to the club premises & hall is by a door 4' wide in no. 55
Grafton Street. There is an exit into Hertford Place from the skittle alley in
the basement 2' 5" wide; the doors of this exit & of the entrance in Grafton
Street open inwards. The whole of the floors and partitions are of combus-
tible material … there are no fire extinguishing appliances on the premises.
The hall is heated by a coke stove … there is also a stove in the entrance
vestibule. The building does not in any way comply with the present regulations of the Council.[34]

The magistrate, however, lets the proprietors off with a fine of £3 plus £3 6s
costs and their promise not to use the hall again for public entertainments – a
promise they must have broken, according to Rudolf Rocker's comments in
1895 on the frequent hire of the hall. We can't know whether the LCC was
carrying out regular inspections of places of entertainment at this time, or
whether the police had suggested that Grafton Hall deserved special attention
(and possible closure?) for admittedly serious breaches of safety regulations.
In fact, the hall apparently didn't remain open much longer: its management
changed in 1896 and by 1897 it had vanished from the *Post Office Directory*.

The continuing Communist Club at 49 Tottenham Street moved to 107
Charlotte Street in 1902, but even though the club spent nearly twenty years
at 107 Charlotte Street this address doesn't appear in the *Post Office Directory*
of businesses and organisations. It's more than likely that, with the Boer War

going on in 1902 and in the jingoistic climate of those days, Communist Club members wouldn't wish to advertise their presence too openly for fear of attack. The Communist Club was situated behind a small German restaurant which club members had to walk through to reach the meeting room.

The difficult conditions in which the anarchists were operating in this period greatly hampered the movement. Police spies and political repression must have helped to deter all but the most committed activists. The British anarchist David Nicoll complained that the area around Fitzroy Square was full of 'vermin in the shape of spies', while the police would tell employers of their workers' radical views and often get them sacked.[35]

Besides, revolutionary anarchism never really took hold in Britain as it did in other parts of Europe. The Labour Representation Committee was established in 1900 to develop a Labour Party presence in Parliament, becoming the Labour Party in 1906 when it won twenty-nine seats. The socialist groups out of which the Labour Party was formed – the Social Democratic Federation (SDF), the Fabian Society and the Independent Labour Party (ILP) – disagreed over the nature of social reform, with the SDF arguing that the overthrow of capitalism was the only context for any short-term reforms while the ILP worked for social reform itself, even if it was piecemeal.[36] But the overall programme was substantially the same: the minimum wage, the eight-hour day, old age pensions and welfare and education reforms. The Labour Movement and trade unionism, not revolutionism, were the channels followed by almost all British workers.

The European anarchists made relatively few British converts. Many European anarchist leaders were expelled, while others left after the First World War to return to their home countries, where their activities in Britain had always been directed. Of the Italian anarchists, only the feared Malatesta wasn't allowed to go back.

Their departure was another reason for the deep, long-term decline in the British movement. The Boer War (1899–1902) aroused a reactionary patriotism which made public opinion even more hostile to the anarchists, who, by then, were already quiescent.

However, Fitzrovia's anarchist movement was not yet dead: a large anti-Boer War meeting was held at the Queen's Hall, Langham Place, in 1901. It was followed by fighting, after which the Queen's Hall and other halls were routinely closed to other similar meetings. The ongoing police suppression and the jingoism aroused by the Boer War, according to Quail, 'almost completely destroyed' the anarchist movement.[37] It says much for Fitzrovia's political environment that it was the only place in London, apart from Aldgate, where *Freedom* continued to be sold. However, in February 1906 the Jubilee Street Club opened in London's East End: an important anarchist centre where Rudolf Rocker worked for many years, running classes in history and sociology. The club provided classes in English for immigrants and a Sunday school for children.

In and around Fitzrovia, the 1900s also saw anarchist activism related to workers' employment. Many Italian workers in the West End were employed in catering but were subject to poor conditions, aggravated by specialist employment agencies that charged a fee to find work and didn't represent workers' interests.

An Italian anarchist, Bergia, who ran his own restaurant at 70 Cleveland Street, began to campaign against these agencies and for unionisation, opening a free employment agency there in 1905. Bergia also founded the *Revue: International Organ for the interests of all Employees in Hotels, Restaurants, Boarding-Houses, etc.*, with M. Clark, an English activist, and he accepted correspondence at his address for the Caterers' Employees Union. Over the next few years meetings were held in Fitzrovia, Soho and Clerkenwell for the abolition of registry offices and employment agencies and for one rest day a week.

There were also protests against the 'Tronc' system where employees' tips were pooled and shared out according to the whims of the employers, and workers were often deprived of their fair share. On 18 April 1909, the campaign held a big demonstration in Trafalgar Square organised by anarchists and socialists and attended by restaurant workers of all nationalities. There is no evidence, though, of this campaign changing the law or of major changes in employers' practices.

Madan Lal Dhingra, Fairyland and the Assassination of Lord Wyllie

In July 1909, public opinion was further inflamed against radicals of all shades and beliefs in perhaps the most momentous occurrence of this period: the fatal shooting by Madan Lal Dhingra of Sir William Curzon Wyllie, the aide-de-camp to Lord Morley, who was the Secretary of State for India. This political assassination involved an unlikely sounding location in Tottenham Court Road – Fairyland, a penny arcade owned by Henry Stanton Morley (no relation to Lord Morley!). Besides offering coin-in-the-slot machines, Fairyland also had an upstairs shooting gallery which served as a practice venue for Dhingra and other Indian nationalists before the assassination.

Henry Stanton Morley was called as a witness at Dhingra's trial later that month and testified that he regularly used the shooting range. Anarchists were again held to have played a role: one of the guns found on Dhingra was believed to have been supplied by anarchist sources in Paris.[38]

Dhingra was a student of engineering at University College, situated close to Tottenham Court Road in Gower Street. He had arrived in London in 1906 and become a fervent Indian nationalist under the influence of V.D. Savarkar, a leading member of the Highgate-based India House set of Indian nationals who advocated the violent overthrow of British rule in India. Using sources kept at the British Museum, Savarkar had written a book on the Indian Rebellion of 1857, published in 1908, in which he urged killing and sacrifice for 'Mother India'. British reprisals in India for revolutionary activities, such as the execution of Khudi Ram for bomb throwing in 1908, fed a narrative of patriots making sacrifices for a free motherland and increased the desire among Nationalists to retaliate in Britain.

As part of this campaign Dr Desai lectured on 'The Making of Bombs' at India House in June 1908. *The Indian Sociologist*, edited and published monthly by Shyamji Krishnavarma, who had established India House in 1905, also advocated the use of violence for political ends, and was read by members of India House. By April 1909, anti-British feeling was running extremely high at India House, and Dhingra, who had been living there, was asked by his parents, who were well connected and knew Lord Wyllie, to move somewhere else. He moved but remained very closely attached to Savarkar and the others at India House.

After practising shooting at Fairyland on 1 July, Dhingra attended the National Indian Association's evening gathering at Imperial College at which official guests were present. At around 11 p.m., when guests were leaving, he fired four shots at Wyllie's face and head, also unintentionally shooting Dr Lalcaca, who had tried to help Wyllie and who later died from his injuries. It was reported that Dhingra was urged to shoot Wyllie by a fellow nationalist, Koregaonkar, who was with him and was supposed to have told him, 'Well, go on! What are you doing?' immediately beforehand.[39] Dhingra tried to shoot himself at the scene but failed when he accidentally put his gun's safety catch on and couldn't fire.

V.N. Datta, in *Madan Lal Dhingra and the Revolutionary Movement*, suggests that Dhingra's real aim had been to kill Lord Morley, the Secretary of State for India, or Lord Curzon, only shooting Wyllie when he realised that he had no chance of reaching these important figures.[40] Dhingra's attack was intended to be followed by others. According to the India Office's 'Memorandum on the Anti-British Agitation Among Natives of India in England', 'In the second

week of July there was some talk amongst Savarkar's set of further assassina-
tions … and attempts were still being made to incite M.P. Tirumala Chari to
sacrifice himself in this way.'[41]

Dhingra made no attempt to save himself at his trial, making it clear that he
had every intention of killing Wyllie. Henry Stanton Morley said at the trial:

> About three months ago the prisoner commenced to frequent [Morley's]
> range for revolver practice; he attended two or three times a week, bringing
> his own revolver, an automatic Colt, and his own ammunition. He used to
> fire 12 shots on each visit. He took a lot of care in his shooting and acquired
> considerable proficiency. On July 1, about 5.30 p.m., he was at the range, and
> I saw him fire 12 shots at a target at a distance of 18 ft. [The target was shown
> to the jury; there were eleven hits.][42]

According to the *Times* of 24 July 1909, Dhingra 'asked no questions; he maintained a demeanour of studied indifference; he walked smiling from the dock'.
Dhingra was sentenced to death and hanged by Henry Albert Pierrepoint (the
father of Albert Pierrepoint, who succeeded him as England's executioner until
1956) on 17 August 1909. Some of the key members of the India House set
dispersed before the end of July, either to India or to Paris, although Savarkar
was later caught and sentenced to transportation for life to the Andaman
Islands. India House was closed and sold.

Henry Stanton Morley's Fairyland hadn't seen the last of its involvement
in political radicalism, however. In September 1909, the police were informed
by a Mrs Moore, a member of the Women's Freedom League who was also
a friend of Prime Minister Herbert Asquith's sister-in-law, that two suffragettes, fellow members of the league, had been using the shooting range. It
was rumoured that this was in preparation for the shooting of Asquith. Morley
was visited by the police and confirmed that the women had been seen at
the range and had been practising with a Browning pistol, but the suffragettes
made no more visits and if any such assassination plans had ever existed they
must have been shelved.[43] Fairyland remained open until the 1920s, although
Morley died in 1916.

The Anarchists and the Tailors' Strike

After the turbulent year of 1909, the anti-anarchist and anti-alien mood only
intensified with the Houndsditch murders in 1910: the fatal shooting of three

policemen followed by the siege of Sidney Street in Stepney when two of the murderers were shot and killed by police. Press scare stories linked this event with foreign revolutionaries, on scanty evidence. Rocker, now settled in the East End, reported that the *Daily Mail* and other papers were vilifying social clubs like his Jubilee Street Club and calling for all aliens to be deported. Even English socialists like Robert Blatchford, the editor of *Clarion*, were speaking out against aliens, although Rocker also says that sections of the British press gave the anarchists a fair hearing.[44]

It was also true that some activists, particularly the Russians, were planning violence. Rocker relates how he 'couldn't believe my ears' when a young Russian comrade, who had then thought better of it, told him that a small group he was part of had been planning to throw a bomb at the Lord Mayor's Show. Rocker went to the group and managed to dissuade them.[45] The anarchists were now under even greater pressure.

Nevertheless, by April 1912 the anarchist movement was still strong enough to support a successful strike of highly skilled West End tailors, called by the London Society of Tailors, for better pay and conditions. Some of these striking tailors could have lived and worked in Fitzrovia since, by then, the move of the industry north of Oxford Street was well under way. An important part of the struggle was to prevent the East End tailors, mostly Jews, from being used to break the West End strike. In this, the campaigners were successful, even though most of the strikers were not trade unionists.

According to Rocker, who was active in the strike organisation, 'The whole clothing industry in the East End was at a standstill.'[46] Rocker started a strike fund to help the non-union workers. The West End workers and employers reached an agreement after three weeks; the East End remained on strike and reached a successful settlement later. Rocker optimistically credits the strike with dealing 'the death-blow to the sweatshop system'.[47] This claim was exaggerated but West Enders and East Enders, Jews and non-Jews, had united to achieve a common goal. Rocker added, 'The English workers looked at the Jewish workers with quite different eyes after this victory.'[48]

But the final decline of the anarchist movement was imminent. The First World War saw mass internments of foreigners and foreign activists, many of whom returned to their home countries after the war. Then, with the formation of the Communist Party of Great Britain, the communist platform quickly came to dominate, and the anarchists were side-lined. As Clive Bloom puts it:

The complex and fluid relationships of a number of organizations whose Communist credentials were not Bolshevist were bulldozed into a mono-lithic unity by Maiden Lane [Communist Party headquarters]. For the middle forty years of the twentieth century anarchists were barely able to get quorate meetings as the CPGB battled Trotskyist recidivism.[49]

From the 1920s on, in Fitzrovia as elsewhere, the radical momentum passed to the Communist Party and sections of the Labour Movement and the trade unions.

Serving the Party: Communism in Fitzrovia

The Communist Party of Great Britain (CPGB), closely following the party line of the Soviet Union, was formed in 1920 from three groups: the British Socialist Party, which had evolved from the SDF; the Workers' Socialist Federation led by Sylvia Pankhurst; and the Scottish Socialist Labour Party. The ILP was excluded for not being a revolutionary party. The CPGB's position was that 'it is not possible to end capitalism and establish socialism in Britain by the election of a majority in the House of Commons ... a workers' revolu-tion can do it ... this over-throw must be a forceful one'.[50] Revolutionism distinguished the CPGB from the reformism of the ILP and the Labour Party, where the Fabians had now found a home.

The evolution of the CPGB meant the death of the old Communist Club at 107 Charlotte Street. Harold Edwards, the club secretary, says of the latter days of the club:

All kinds and sorts of people went to the Club, which was close to Howland Street on the west side of Charlotte Street. There was a dance-room and you could get very good and very cheap meals. A Czech would play the zither all the evening. It was run by a committee, who were almost all East European Jews, many of them tailors– I was one of the few with an English name. The members belonged to the British Socialist Party, Socialist Party of Great Britain (I cannot think how that was man-aged – they must have kept quiet about it!) Socialist Labour Party, Herald League, I.W.W.; and there were quite a number of anarchists, but it was not respectable enough for the I.L.P. It provided an international social place for revolutionaries. I was fourteen when the war broke out and had never known any foreigners, so it was a great thing for me to be able to meet people from all over Europe.[51]

According to Keith Scholey's essay on the Communist Club:

> In most sources it is stated that the Club was closed down after police raids in 1918. However … the SPGB [Socialist Party of Great Britain] was still holding meetings here in late 1919 (which were recorded in the minutes as taking place in the Communist Club). Weller gives the date of closure as 1920.[52]

By 1921, the Charlotte Street building was listed as housing the Young Musical Students' Society as well as a restaurant and an employment agency. However, Scholey says, 'The premises continued to be used as a meeting place until at least 1922', adding that it was destroyed by bombing during the 1940–41 Blitz.[53]

Edwards wonders what became of the club's 'marvellous library of German books' that Rudolf Rocker had treasured so much years before. 'It must have gone to Moscow in the end!', he speculates.[54] The Communist Club took with it a haven for supporters of pre-Bolshevist socialism and anarchism.

Fitzrovia's radical tradition took a new direction after the virtual demise of the anarchists. In St Pancras, Communists were influential in the Labour Party branch and in local trades councils.[55] In the local elections of 1928, 1931 and 1934, the CPGB stood candidates in a number of St Pancras wards, although none were elected. Labour gained St Pancras Council from the Municipal Reform (Conservative) Group only in 1945. In St Marylebone, the Municipal Reform Group and the Conservatives ran the council during the whole period from 1900–50. After Labour's 1924 ban on Communists standing as Labour candidates, great efforts were made by both parties to distinguish their programmes from each other's. At the same time, as in St Pancras, Communists were active in infiltrating Labour Party branches and trades unions, despite periodically being discovered and expelled.

During the General Strike of May 1926, when greatly reduced wages and worsened conditions of work for the miners sparked national action, local trades councils set up strike committees to co-ordinate action. St Pancras Trades Council joined other radical councils in calling these committees 'Councils of Action', because in 1920 the Labour Party and trade unions had set up such committees to resist British Government involvement in attacks on the new government of Soviet Russia.[56]

Ellena Burns, a St Pancras resident, was active in the St Pancras Communist Party and spent much of her time at the party offices in Chalk Farm Road organising discussion groups for strikers' wives. Ellena, whose husband, trade union historian Emile Burns, wrote a book about the general strike, recalls fifty years later in a local paper, 'We discussed how women could go about influencing events. I think the general strike was the first time we in the Communist Party were able to get women involved in political discussion.'[57]

Marylebone Town Hall was the area HQ for the organisation of services during the strike, with responsibility for a large area that included St Pancras as well as Marylebone. The Town Clerk was the Food Emergency Officer, helped by the MOH and the Sanitary Inspectors. The council was responsible for rationing coal, electricity and gas supplies, and for street cleaning, refuse removal and disposal during the emergency. Volunteers, paid and unpaid, carried out some essential services: in the Marylebone area, with almost all council workers on strike except for senior officers and technical staff in the Electricity Department, volunteer drivers were given jobs such as driving teachers and doctors to work and patients to and from hospital, distributing government notices, and running a transport service from Golders Green to Baker Street.

After eight days the strikers were holding firm, but on 12 May 1926, the strike was called off by the Trades Union Congress (TUC) General Council due to the reluctance of the TUC and some Labour Party leaders to continue a national strike. Some workers did try to continue the strike for a few more days but almost all council workers in Marylebone had returned to work by 19 May. However, Marylebone Council didn't automatically re-employ striking workers who hadn't returned to work by 13 May. Workers had to reapply for their jobs and at first were only given them on a temporary basis and at the senior departmental officer's discretion, with not everyone (though a majority) being accepted back.[58]

Irish Republicanism had been simmering for decades and later impinged on Fitzrovia when a bombing campaign, directed at getting British troops out of Ireland, came to the boil in 1939. Summer 1939 saw an intensive bombing campaign in central London preceded by explosions in February, in Tottenham Court Road and Leicester Square Tube stations. Many Londoners were wounded and one person was killed in these bombings, and sixty-two suspects were arrested in London. It also led to the Prevention of Terrorism Act of 1939.

In the 1930s Fitzrovia was home to a number of active Communists. Reuben Falber of Tottenham Street was active from around 1935 and had been familiar with communist ideas as a child. He says, 'The family had some friends who were the kind of old Bolshevik tribe. You know, I can recollect as a child the arguments about Trotsky and Lenin and so on.'[59] Falber describes how he first joined the Labour Party as a young man but soon realised that his views had a closer affinity to the CPGB, to the extent that he was taking Communist Party pamphlets along to Labour Party meetings and selling them. Of his political education as a Communist, he says:

> Well, you see, it opened up a whole new world to me. I'd had no education, I'd never done any studying of any kind, but I then began to study, I began to read Marx and the other prominent Marxist writers … I developed at least an elementary understanding of the process of history, I got new interests and I met people who I would never have met earlier in my life. I would get involved in discussion and argument with people who'd been to universities, who'd got academic qualifications, which of course was inconceivable to me before that. And when I got into brushes with the police at demonstrations, er, you know, I was able to stand up for myself.[60]

Something of the strength of the Communist Party in St Pancras can be seen in the comprehensive, well-produced and illustrated pamphlets detailing their local programme. Their 1936 *Plan for Life in St Pancras* urged a Labour Council to provide its workers with good housing and welfare, and to put 'Mothers and Children First!' by providing a full-time municipal midwives service, free meals and milk for mothers and children, and more infant welfare centres; though, as we've seen, St Pancras was already providing a more comprehensive service than many boroughs, including its neighbour, St Marylebone.

In 1945, the local Communist Party emphasis was somewhat different in the light of the wartime destruction of houses in the area. Their booklet, *St. Pancras: Homes or Slums?* sets out the problems caused by the demolition and lack of repairs to the thousands of bombed buildings, advocating a programme of repair, council requisition, slum clearance and rehousing. The 1945 elections resulted in a Labour majority on the council, and no Communist candidates stood in St Pancras in 1945, presumably so as not to split the Labour vote.

Covert Communist influence on the local Labour Party continued throughout the 1930s into wartime, despite Labour Party warnings to members about Communist infiltration, the listing of proscribed organisations and expulsion of Communists from the party. Charlotte Haldane describes, in her autobiography *Truth Will Out* (1949), how, soon after the Second World War began, she, as a Communist sympathiser, was instructed by Harry Pollitt, a leading CPGB member, to put herself forward for co-option into the South-West St Pancras

Labour Party, which covered a chunk of Fitzrovia.[61] At that time, elections had been suspended for the duration of the war and when places became vacant another member of the same party could simply step in. Charlotte Haldane was married to the well-known biologist J.B.S. Haldane, who supported the Communist Party and wrote for the *Daily Worker*. His high profile made him a prized associate of the party.

Charlotte, who was living in Fitzroy Road, writes that the South-West St Pancras Labour Party was:

> … a small group, but even here there was a strong [Communist] Party frac-tion, of which I was, of course, a member also. In due course the fraction got through my nomination to the Borough Council. I became a member of the Labour Group on the Council on January 17th, 1940 … On May 1st, 1940, I was appointed a member of the St. Pancras Borough Council Air Raid Precautions Emergency Committee.[62]

As we saw in Chapter 2, the Communist Party played an active role in the agitation and actions over public access to deep shelters after the German air raids began in 1940. Haldane herself states, 'The Communist Party started a loud campaign, in the *Daily Worker*, and on its political platforms, for deep air-raid shelters.'[63] Her opinion was that the Communists had placed her on the St Pancras ARP Committee because of her husband's prestige as a scien-tist and his having published a book on air-raid precautions (ARP), based on the Spanish experience, although his book dealt with poisonous gases rather than explosives.

Charlotte's personal experience was of being kept out of Communist Party discussions and decisions on the shelter campaign, while her husband was at the centre of them. Yet, she became dedicated to doing council ARP work. She collaborated amicably with the St Pancras Borough Engineer, Clement Bainbridge, the only person locally who, she felt, had a good grasp of the issues and problems, even though he was disliked by her fellow Communists. Charlotte continued pressing throughout the Blitz for shelter improvements. She left the Communist Party, and her husband, in 1942.

During and after the war, the local Communist Party declined as substan-tial numbers of members left the CPGB after disillusionment with Stalinism set in. The invasion of Hungary in 1956 gave impetus to many more depar-tures. One leaver was Raphael Samuel, who had joined the St Pancras branch at a young age, having been born into a Communist family. Samuel later became a writer and historian. In *The Lost World of British Communism*

(2006), he evocatively describes the ethos and daily work of the branch as he experienced it as a schoolboy and a young man in the 1940s and 1950s. He stresses the quasi-religious aspect of party membership: the spiritual battle with unbelievers, the belief in 'awakening' and the call to sacrifice. The Jewish Samuel points out:

> For my mother's generation Communism, though not intended as such, was a way of being English, a bridge by which the children of the ghetto entered the national culture. It was also … a break from hereditary upbringing, as my mother put it, 'to emancipate ourselves from the narrowness of a religious environment'.[64]

It seems as if, for Samuel, and perhaps others like Reuben Falber also, the CPGB was a radical alternative to the anglicising young people's clubs attended by generations of Jews.

In the 1950s, there were still a number of societies like the British–Soviet Friendship Society, designed to encourage good comradeship with the Soviet Union: a late cultural flowering of Soviet Communism that Samuel must have known about, with its film shows and festivals based in Fitzrovia at the Scala Theatre in Charlotte Street.

Socialist ideas weren't confined to the CPGB in St Pancras. In the late 1950s, a significant group within the ruling Labour council was strongly socialist and dominated some of the council's wards, though they were faced by strong opposition from within the Labour Group on the council and the wider Labour Party, who accused them of being Communists. During this period, the council cut rents and created a big slum clearance and house-building programme for its tenants. It voted against having a Civil Defence programme and refused to allocate five 'grace and favour' council seats to Conservative opposition members, abandoning what had been the custom under previous councils.

The socialist group, headed by John Lawrence, decided to fly the red flag from St Pancras Town Hall on May Day 1958 in support of international workers, an action that brought matters to a head. John Lawrence and other members were eventually expelled from the Labour Party, although 5,000 local Labour members signed a petition supporting them. In the May 1959 elections, the Conservatives overturned the Labour council majority in St Pancras. John Lawrence and six other members of the former leftist Labour grouping joined the Communist Party.

The Conservatives were shortly afterwards to introduce means-tested rent rises that provoked intense local opposition, leading to a rent strike that became a byword for community politics and a landmark in London's history.[65]

Fascism, Anti-Semitism and Anti-Fascism

Political radicalism on the Other Side of Oxford Street did not emerge exclusively from the Left but from the far Right, also. In the 1930s, Fascism sprouted and developed among certain first and second-generation migrant communities in Fitzrovia, although perhaps to a lesser degree there than in some other localities in London.

By the time of the Second World War, Jews were a predominant group in Fitzrovia. Having migrated into the rich ethnic mix of Fitzrovia and being a much smaller group than in the East End, these Jews were far less exposed to anti-Semitism than the East End Jews. However, as the 1930s progressed, strong forces threatened Jews, not only in Germany and other European states, but also at home in London and other British cities. The German communities who were settled both north and south of Oxford Street contained a number of Fascists, whose known meeting place was Schmidt's Restaurant at 33–37 Charlotte Street.

The Italians living in Fitzrovia, Soho and Clerkenwell (about 15,000 in 1931), like their compatriots elsewhere in Britain, were encouraged by the Italian government to embrace Fascism, although there's not much evidence that large numbers did so. The Italian Fascist base was nearby at the Club Cooperativo in Greek Street, Soho, moving with other Italian associations to a new building in Charing Cross Road in 1937. However, the biggest Fascist movement in London was Oswald Mosley's British Union of Fascists (BUF), which operated mostly in the East End but had several offices in the West End. The nearest to Fitzrovia was probably the Women's Section office at 233 Regent Street, run by Lady Makgill; in 1934 this office moved to 12 Lower Grosvenor Place near Victoria Station.[66]

Jews living in Fitzrovia and the West End, like many other Londoners, were mainly concerned with avoiding 'trouble' and going about their daily business without interference. In my own family of Fitzrovia tailors, this was the ruling view, according to my mother's cousin Henry, a small boy in the 1930s. The people he knew were 'humble and timid people', he says, not well informed about the current situation and not prone to getting into fights with anyone.

But by 1936, the feelings of unease and fearfulness at what was going on in Nazi Germany and at home had built up into a powerful sense of threat that was causing constant pressure on the Board of Deputies to take action.

A Jewish Defence Campaign set up by the Board of Deputies was announced in the *Jewish Chronicle* on 24 July 1936, less than three months before the Mosleyites tried to march in Cable Street. The Defence Campaign aimed to oppose the denigration of and attacks on Jews by reasoned arguments against anti-Semitism and the presentation of the positive contribution Jews were making to British society. The Jewish People's Council against Fascism and Anti-Semitism was also formed at this time. The council took action on the streets and engaged in anti-defamation work that exposed the political motives of the Fascists. It worked closely with the National Council for Civil Liberties, organising joint conferences and having their speakers on the same platform at meetings. Other defence organisations were formed at around the same time, including a Jewish ex-servicemen's organisation that soon had more than 1,000 members.

In the 1937 London local elections the BUF fielded candidates, including in St Pancras' Ward 1 which comprised parts of Highgate and Hampstead. Hampstead Heath, a couple of miles north of Tottenham Court Road, was a regular spot for the Mosleyites' open-air meetings – and for those wishing to heckle and oppose them. However, in St Pancras and St Marylebone no Fascists were elected as councillors.

Some local residents resisted the BUF, and sometimes ended up in court. The *Times* of 25 June 1937 reports that a fitter's mate and St Pancras resident, William Joseph Fairman, had been fined 40*s* for 'using insulting words and behaviour' by shouting 'Smash Fascism! Down with the Fascists!' at a group of BUF marchers from Shoreditch and Stepney who were marching through St Pancras opposed by 'about 1,000 St Pancras residents'. Fairman had been found with 'Communist literature and application forms'. He must have been among many Communists who opposed the BUF locally.

The policing of demonstrations and protests could be harsh. When PC David John policed the East End Fascist marches, according to his son, Simon John, 'They were told by senior offices [sic] no arrests. Communist, Fascist, etc. I think you just whacked them'.

Anti-Fascist protests continued unabated until the banning of the BUF at the outbreak of the war and the internment of its key figures, including Mosley. But, after the war in the late 1940s, there were attempts by Mosley and others to revive the British Fascist movement. Markets, including Soho's Berwick Street Market, were targeted for the distribution of Fascist literature, although Hackney was the area of London most affected by the Mosleyites. Several other Fascist groups were operating at that time: perhaps as many as fourteen groups in London, many based in West London.

This drive was vigorously countered by various groups who, by 1950, had aided in ending the Union Movement (UM), as Mosley's new group was called. The 43 Group consisted of Jewish men and women, many of whom had served in the war and weren't prepared to see Fascism take root again in British soil. Their story is compellingly told by one of the 43 Group's key members, Morris Beckman, in his book, *The 43 Group* (1992). The 43 Group frequently met at a familiar rendezvous especially popular with Jewish people: Lyons' Corner House in Tottenham Court Road. Their office was in Panton Street, Soho.

A local lad, Sidney Spellman, was one of the 43 Group's members. Brought up in Hanson Street, he was an apprentice compositor in the print trade at the time of his involvement. Sidney writes in a letter quoted in *The 43 Group*:

My first involvement was attending fascist meetings Saturday afternoons at Notting Hill Gate. Victor Burgess [a well-known Fascist and anti-Semite who belonged to the pro-Mosley British Union of Freemen before joining the UM] spoke. ... The platform was often knocked over ... One meeting was the first night of the Succoth festival [a Jewish festival commemorating the Exodus from Egypt and taking place between late September and late October]. The fascists were about 2000 strong. They were protected by mounted and foot police who kept us apart. Next morning the *Daily Graphic* had a large front page picture showing me in the front row. I needed this to show my father why I had not been at synagogue the previous evening.[67]

The 43 Group's response to the Fascists was, 'We were born here! We fought for this country and were trained to kill the same type of bastard coming back out of the woodwork. They, too, must be attacked and destroyed. If you can't do it, we will!'[68] The group helped to beat the Mosleyites with continual pressure on the Fascists, often leading to violent confrontations at Fascist meetings; by working to gain support from people living in the most affected localities; and obtaining advance information on the movements and intentions of the UM through infiltrators.

By 1950 Oswald Mosley had conceded that efforts to keep the UM going had failed, moving to Ireland in 1951, then to Paris. Although Mosley later returned to Britain briefly and stood for Kensington North in the 1959 General Election, he failed to make an impact and returned to France. So, by

1950, those like Sidney Spellman who had fought to defeat post-war Fascism could feel that their job was almost completed.

The Radical Stream

The radical strand in Fitzrovia's life wasn't extinct after 1950, although it was diluted by post-war political, social and demographic changes that were beginning to transform the area. During the 1960s, after the jailing of Nelson Mandela and other activists, the command group of the African National Congress (ANC) in exile – Ronnie Kasrils, Yusuf Dadoo, Joe Slovo and Jack Hodgson – was headquartered at 39 Goodge Street in the office of Yusuf Dadoo and the exiled South African Communist Party. From there, at a time when the anti-Apartheid movement had been all but suppressed, they planned the smuggling into South Africa and broadcasting of taped messages against the Apartheid regime. They also arranged the distribution at rail and bus stations in South Africa of leaflets blown into the air from exploding buckets. London's ANC office was close by at 49–51 Rathbone Street, and the Anti-Apartheid Movement was based at 89 Charlotte Street, bombed out of a previous office at 200 Gower Street in 1961 by BOSS, the South African secret police.[69]

Bolivar Hall is still to be seen at 54–56 Grafton Way, close to where Grafton Hall, the Communist Club's 'finest meeting-place' in the 1890s, once stood at No. 55. Bolivar Hall is now the embassy of the revolutionary Bolivarian Republic of Venezuela, named after Simon Bolivar, its leading representative when it asserted Bolivia's independence from Spain in 1810. This is perhaps the last echo of Fitzrovia's radical history.

Radicalism on the Other Side of Oxford Street was rooted in its beginnings: in its attraction for the artisan and poorer classes and the growing immigrant communities to whom it provided cheap accommodation, jobs, a tolerant welcome among large numbers of other outsiders, and a haven from political persecution. Its network of clubs and meeting places provided safety, familiarity, comradeship and practical support to those who often desperately needed it. This pre-existing network drew successive generations of anarchist and Communist activists who enriched the radical stream.

The cosmopolitanism of this small corner of London, and its proximity to other areas like Bloomsbury where unorthodox ideas were being generated and circulated, created an intellectual greenhouse where political and philosophical ideas could be formulated, debated, and spread. Even after anarchist resistance faded, St Pancras was a vector for a stream of radicalism as the St Pancras Communist Party gave impetus to local politics. Poverty and economic inequality provided the motivating forces for action, fostering Fitzrovia's radical tradition.

Radicalism was a threat to the powerful; in the pronouncements on anarchists or Communists made by Parliament, the police and the press, we find many negative but familiar associations made between radicalism and foreigners, crime, invasion and contagion. But the story of outsider contagion has a twist here, because Fitzrovia, from its origins, resembled an 'outsider' pocket sewn into the very fabric of central London, seen by some as a dark space of unorthodoxy, disorder and potential violence. Its presence in the city caused disturbance; there were times when it alarmed the authorities, who feared that both London and Londoners had become uncontainable and its inhabitants were transgressing social and political boundaries, in the same way as the city itself had burst through the geographical boundary of the New Road. Fitzrovia's radical presence was a sign that London and its people were liable to break out unexpectedly against attempts at control.

Fitzrovia's Changing Entertainment Scene

The People at Leisure

The 1900s were exciting times for working people seeking entertainment in Fitzrovia, and for the enterprising individuals who provided it. Even 'leisure time' itself was a relatively new concept for working people in the twentieth century. Higher wages and shorter hours of work meant more time for amusement and relaxation, and new amusements sprang up to meet the demand. The period between the start of the twentieth century and its mid-point was one of rapid technological change that penetrated every facet of people's lives, and there are few better places to see this process at work than in the mass-entertainment industries.

Rapid transformation has been the theme whether we've been exploring the geographical spaces of Fitzrovia or its activity, and perhaps no area of daily experience reflected these transmogrifications better than the impact of the entertainment industry on the area. The new entertainment industries offered plenty of new business and employment opportunities, with Fitzrovia's entrepreneurial immigrants often the quickest to respond to them, as this chapter will show.

For working people, the biggest impact on leisure was caused by cinema. People responded enthusiastically to cinemas' low prices, varied output and conveniently timed, frequent programmes. The coming of the purpose-built cinema to Fitzrovia from 1909 saw venues proliferate in Tottenham Court Road for those who wanted to enjoy their spare time experiencing this new medium. The street had perhaps London's highest concentration of cinemas in the first decades of the century. London's budding film industry flourished just across Oxford Street in and around Wardour Street, Soho.

And even before the cinemas came, Tottenham Court Road hosted a cluster of penny arcades or 'automatic exhibitions', the precursors of amusement arcades, where some of the earliest experiments in the moving image proved to be an entertainment hit. While at home, radio broadcasting permanently changed people's lives from the 1920s, bringing huge volumes of entertainment indoors. From 1932, the BBC was a near neighbour at Broadcasting House in Langham Place and its broadcasting venues became scattered across Fitzrovia.

Fitzrovians had plenty of traditional musical and theatrical entertainments on their doorstep as well, although, reflecting the local lack of affluence, Tottenham Court Road possessed relatively few grand entertainment venues like those in Leicester Square. An exception was the Dominion Theatre, opened in 1929 at the corner of Tottenham Court Road and New Oxford Street. Its prime location is one explanation for its long-lasting success that has continued until the present day. Opposite the site of the Dominion, the age of music hall produced one highly popular, and magnificent, local venue: Oxford Hall. This house of entertainment and variety was built in 1861 and rebuilt on a much grander scale in 1893, attracting large audiences.[1] To add to these edifices were the more sedate Queen's Hall and St George's Hall, next door to each other in Langham Place on Fitzrovia's western boundary, almost opposite where Broadcasting House would stand. Queen's Hall was known as the home of the 'Proms', the Promenade concerts started by Henry Wood in 1895, while St George's hosted musical and variety acts.

However, Fitzrovia experienced failures in the creation of high-level performance halls, as we'll see in this chapter. The Scala Theatre in Charlotte Street, built in the eighteenth century, narrowly missed its chance at being fashionable, fell on very hard times, was lavishly rebuilt and reopened in 1905, but quickly failed once more as a stage theatre. Nonetheless, it experienced some interesting times when it became closely connected with the cinema, finding new ways in which to make ends meet. The tiny subterranean Grafton Theatre on Tottenham Court Road went the opposite way to the Scala by beginning as a cinema but changing to live theatre. It kept going until it was bombed in 1940. In ever-changing times, a varied offering was the means of survival for these local theatres. The transformations of the Scala and the Grafton are evidence of the continuing resourcefulness with which people's leisure demands were addressed on the Other Side of Oxford Street.

Young people in Fitzrovia during this period were catered for socially and educationally by clubs that tried both to extend and regulate their leisure activities. Sometimes these clubs could transform a child's life. The Jewish Lads' Club in Fitzroy Square and the West Central Jewish Girls' Club in Alfred Place,

Bloomsbury, stand out as providing a great formative influence; in the boys' case largely, though by no means exclusively, through sports. An important aim of these clubs was to Anglicise the children of first-generation immigrants by encouraging them to fit into the wider culture.

Social integration had an important class dimension as well. The young working poor were encouraged to join clubs that were intended not only to enrich their lives but also to alter their social perspective. In Fitzrovia, one such club was the Wesleyan West London Mission's Club for Working Girls in Cleveland Street. The ethos of these clubs wasn't always in tune with the amusements loved by the children, but both clubs and amusements were potentially important influences on local young people's lives.

This chapter will explore what changes the new entertainments brought to the working people of Fitzrovia and their children. It will try to show some of the ways in which Fitzrovia's population experienced social changes through consuming different forms of entertainment and it will explore how the people working in the entertainment industries on the Other Side of Oxford Street contributed to British identity.

Time Off

For many local children, their street provided most of their entertainment. Joyce Hooper of Hanson Street recalls that, as late as the 1950s:

> The children always used to be playing in the street, because you see there were no cars. When my eldest daughter was born, I used to … put her in the pram outside … The only thing I ever did was put a notice on, 'Please do not feed this child'.[2]

There was also plenty of open space nearby. Regents Park drew the local children: it provided a generous and beautiful space for walks, games, picnics or swimming. Every summer, my mother Becky and her older sisters Cissy and Esther used to take paper bags of peanuts there and sit on the grass enjoyably cracking peanut shells.

In May 1906, schoolchildren, including boys and girls in St Pancras, were asked to describe how they spent their leisure time on one particular weekend. The Deputy Warden of Toynbee Hall in East London, T.E. Harvey, wrote a report on this snapshot survey consisting of hundreds of essays. The children's family backgrounds ranged from very poor to 'comfortable artizan homes'.[3]

Mr Harvey's report shows how, for many older children in the first decades of the twentieth century, time at weekends was often largely taken up with work. Girls worked even harder than their brothers, mostly doing unpaid baby minding and domestic chores, while the boys worked outside and at least usually had some money to spend after their labours. Harvey concentrates mostly on the boys' accounts. He comments that the girls' essays are 'naturally somewhat less interesting', precisely because many of them were kept at home. He remarks also on 'the quieter character of their amusements'. Fifteen of the boys' essays are quoted in full, whereas only extracts of the girls' essays appear, so unfortunately we discover very little about how girls played, what tasks engaged their time at home or how they tackled the demanding job of looking after younger brothers and sisters.

If their leisure pastimes were similar to the games Sonia Birnbaum says she played in later years, they would have included skipping, ball, five stones or 'gobs', hoop and stick, or 'scraps' (probably meaning sticking themed pictures cut from magazines into a scrapbook) or sometimes just talking.

Some boys' days outside school hours, like many girls', seem completely taken up by work. One lad in the survey sells goods from a barrow at a market, then vends newspapers until late afternoon, finishing his exhausting day by helping his father to sell his goods until suppertime. He concludes his essay, 'We returned home and had a hearty supper, and retired to bed about ten o'clock.' Money earned on Saturdays is spent on treats like ice cream, as well as on going out. Others describe an intensely busy day that doesn't end till midnight.

After work the boys might go for a walk or a cart ride, play football, watch the local cricket club play or go to the park, perhaps for a swim. Few of these activities cost anything. Mr Harvey also lists the 'larger variety of games' played by lads from the more comfortable homes, apart from football and cricket, '"base-ball", release, egg-cap, swimming, "tibby-cat", bicycling, fishing, ping-pong, "knocking up catches", ludo and draughts'. 'Tibby-cat' is probably the same as tip-cat, where a short piece of wood tapered at the ends (the 'cat') is hit to a distance with a longer piece of wood like a baseball bat. 'Egg-cap' may have been cup-and-ball, where a wooden ball had to be caught on a wooden pin or shallow cup.

Some young people's hard-working days were rounded off with a late theatre or show. The splendiferous Oxford Hall pulled in top music-hall acts: Dan Leno could be seen for as little as a shilling while, in November 1904, bills advertised the hugely popular turns, George Robey, Harry Lauder and Harry Tate, for the same price. The Oxford, standing where Lyons' Corner House was later to be located, was an exceptionally fine venue in which to appreciate these acts. *The Sketch* of 15 February 1893 declared, '[T]he building glitters with gold, electric blue, and pale pink ... whilst coolness has been gained by use of the electric light.' 'Certainly now,' the writer continues, with some snobbery, 'the Oxford can hold its head up among the most gorgeous palaces of illegitimate drama'.

Those who loved music hall might also have visited Maskelyne's, officially named St George's Hall, standing in Langham Place on the north-western edge of Fitzrovia. St George's, built in 1867 as a concert hall, had by 1904 been taken into the hands of the Maskelyne family, John Nevil Maskelyne and his son, Nevil, who transformed it into a venue for performances of magic involving spectacular special effects and illusions. The magic programmes were filled out by noted musical performers such as Barclay Gammon, Nelson Jackson, Ernest Hastings and Harry Hemsley, whose 'turns' were the perfect length to amuse audiences while the stage was being set for the next magic act. They were often well known for performing comic and topical songs at the piano.

Barclay Gammon, a very large man with a 'breathless manner', gave a show in which he 'made satirical comments on the events of the day, played witty musical variations on well-known tunes, and accompanied himself in humorous songs, the points being delivered, as some journalist said, every one as a "hit to square leg"'.[4] Gammon, who worked on the railway for decades before becoming a celebrity, started his entertainment career at St George's Hall under John Nevil Maskelyne and David Devant, as he revealed in an interview for *Cassell's Magazine* in 1909: '... a week's engagement at the St George's Hall, more or less as a stop-gap during the preparation of a new illusion, brought me to my present dizzy eminence'.[5] Gammon was to become famous, going on a tour of Australia and New Zealand with the Maskelynes in 1909 and featuring in more than one Royal Variety Performance.

Even before the Maskelyne regime began, St George's Hall was known for nurturing the careers of piano entertainers, ancestors of Flanders & Swann and Kit & the Widow. From the 1870s, Thomas and Priscilla German Reed, who preceded the Maskelynes at St George's Hall, gave a start to performers like Richard Corney Grain and George Grossmith, who collaborated with W.S. Gilbert and wrote several characters for Gilbert & Sullivan operettas such as KoKo, the Lord High Executioner in *The Mikado*. This style of entertainment – a man singing witty songs at the piano – was highly popular in the last decades of the nineteenth century and the first couple of decades of the twentieth. Occasionally it was a woman at the piano: Margaret Cooper was another who got her break at St George's.

The magic performances for which Maskelyne's was best known included spectacles such as 'The Magic Kettle', the 'Burmese Gong', 'The Sylph' and

'Mental Magnetism'.[6] They naturally fascinated the youth of the neighbour-hood. Alec Flinder, who lived in Soho, was able to see shows there for free as his mother would advertise them outside the family barber's shop and receive tickets in return.[7]

The Queen's Hall, next door to Maskelyne's, catered for audiences who appreciated classical music. It was a large concert hall seating 2,500, which became the home of the Promenade concerts and the London Philharmonic Orchestra. The Queen's Hall was a prime concert venue for London until, along with Maskelyne's, it received a direct hit from a bomb in 1940. A deci-sion was eventually made not to rebuild it.[8] It was another source of free tickets for Alec Flinder, who discloses that he also 'bunked in' from time to time, once hearing Myra Hess playing the Schuman Piano Concerto, an event that was 'the beginning of my love for music'.[9]

New Illusions

The future of entertainment was about to hit Fitzrovia. David Nasaw, in *Going Out* (1993), describes the new penny arcades that made an appearance in New York and Chicago in 1903, then spread to London and other big cities. By around 1905 such an arcade had appeared in Fitzrovia: Fairyland, at 92 Tottenham Court Road, which would be used by the assassin Dhingra in 1909. The arcades combined older-style fairground amusements with new experimental mechanical entertainments:

> [T]here were punching bags ... shooting-gallery rifles; weights to pull; hammers to pound; stationary bicycles and hobby-horses. There were also automatic amusement machines that dispensed cards with your fortune, your horoscope, or your future wife's picture; metal embossers that spit out 'Your Name in Aluminium'; 'automatic' gum, candy and peanut machines; coin-in-the-slot phonographs ... and peep-show machines.[10]

Fairyland boasted free admission, advertised prominently on a notice shown in a photograph of the arcade. The picture shows the frontage of Fairyland open to the street, with two workmen poised on a plank between two high stepladders outside the building, either putting up a sign or carrying out maintenance work. A man inside the arcade, presumably the listed owner, Henry Stanton Morley, leans nonchalantly on a machine, visible through the ladders. Across the upper-storey windows in large capitals are the words, 'London's Premier

Revolver Gunshooting'. By 1920 there were three similar arcades listed on the west side of Tottenham Court Road.

Many arcades featured 'peep shows': thick rolls of still pictures on a spindle turned by a handle so that the images seemed to be in motion. They were a magnet for boys and young men. Their often racy subject matter would have been taboo at respectable venues, which were starting to exhibit short films as the novel medium of cinema rapidly developed. As early as 1906, in Harvey's report on children's leisure time, one boy's essay mentions watching 'Cinematagraph scenes'. At this date he must have been referring to seeing a picture show of a kind that preceded professional film shows. This particular show took place at the Leysian Mission, so it was probably educational and undoubtedly had thoroughly 'proper' subject matter.

However, the new entertainment venues, which were often open-fronted shops in busy streets, sometimes provoked complaints from watchful institutions like the West London Mission, whose boys' and girls' clubs tried to direct the activities of the young into proper channels. Complaints were aimed most of all at venues that hosted the early film shows, sometimes called 'penny gaffs' as they charged a penny to enter. From its beginnings, cinema was regarded with suspicion in some official quarters as being detrimental to the morality of young people. Strong disquiet was raised by cinematograph shows being held in dark, crowded rooms full of youths. There were allegations of indecent behaviour involving children at these places.

According to a study of early cinema by Jon Burrows, the only two penny gaffs near Fitzrovia were in Soho, at 6 Ingestre Place and 20 Frith Street.[11] Fairyland was the only entertainment arcade in Marylebone police subdivision in the 1900s, but it didn't appear to hold film shows using projection onto a screen so was not a penny gaff.

Misgivings about this new form of entertainment were strong enough to generate representations to the Secretary of State, which resulted in a series of police reports on venues putting on commercial film shows. In March 1909, the Commissioner of Police wrote to the Secretary of State:

> With regard to acts of indecency there is ample evidence that the places … afford exceptional facilities for offences of this kind … Several cases of acts of indecency by adults towards children have been reported to me, and I have reason to believe that the nature of the exhibitions and the surroundings generally are conducive to the commission of such acts with one another on the part of precocious children.[12]

The commissioner suggested seating girls separately from boys to mini-mise the dangers; he also highlighted the fire risk, which was very real in the era of flammable film stock. He concluded, 'The necessity of some form of control being introduced may be considered to require no fur-ther demonstration.'

The Police Superintendent of Marylebone Division, S.J. Bantick, said in his report of March 1909 on Fairyland, it was 'much patronised by children'. He stated:

> The place is an open-fronted shop, containing a number of small 'Phonograph' machines ... the latter being fitted with a number of slides of photographs etc., which on a handle being turned and a penny being placed in the slot, revolve and make what they call a cinematograph exhibition. There are also spinning machines, dancing balls, rifle range etc.[13]

Fairyland wasn't involved in any cases of child molestation. Bantick said, 'No lowering of lights takes place, and no suggestions of indecent handling of chil-dren have been made.' However, he said, 'A complaint was made a few months ago of girls from a neighbouring girls club gambling their money there' – an objection very likely made by the sisters running the West Central Mission's girls' club at Cleveland Hall.[14] Nevertheless, after legal advice, the police took the matter no further.

By December 1909 there were seventy nickelodeon-style cinema shows in London, taking place in small converted shops seating perhaps 100–200 people and charging only 1 or 2 pennies for admission. The Cinematograph Act of 1909 made provision for securing safety at film exhibition venues, but it also allowed local councils to impose 'reasonable' conditions on film show-ings, including on film content. This led the film industry, in 1913, to set up its own censorship body, the British Board of Film Censors, so it could avoid piecemeal cuts to films by different local authorities.[15]

Going to the Pictures

Cinema was about to take off and go professional. Cinema building increased rapidly so that, by the end of 1909, there were fifty-two dedicated cinemas in London, rocketing to 128 by the end of 1910.[16] Charging 3*d* or 6*d* to enter, they were more expensive than the makeshift penny shows in shop buildings but still within the means of most people. The earliest cinemas in Tottenham

Court Road were small halls, replacing former coffee rooms, tobacconists and a ham and beef dealer.

The first cinema to open in Tottenham Court Road was the Gaiety on 4 December 1909. Sited near the junction with Oxford Street at No. 22, the cinema's 240 seats were priced at 6d. The Gaiety was followed in February 1910 by the Grand Central Picture Theatre, two doors down at 24 Tottenham Court Road. The Grand Central had a pianist to accompany the films, and a sliding roof for coolness in summer.

Only a few days later, the cinema impresario, Montagu A. Pyke, opened another hall, Pyke House, around the corner at 19–23 Oxford Street. Seating 350 people, the well-appointed Pyke House featured 'elaborately carved figures in marble above the doors'.[17] The Corner Theatre, located below ground under a boot and shoe shop at 134a Tottenham Court Road, also began in 1910. It changed its name to the Grafton in 1911. The Court Electric Theatre, opened in 1911, was situated on what is now the foyer of the Dominion Theatre. In 1912 and 1913, there were two more additions: the large and elegant Majestic Picturedrome at 36 Tottenham Court Road and its sister theatre, the Carlton Theatre, at No. 30. The Dominion opened some years later, in 1929, and the Paramount Theatre, another grand 'West End' cinema theatre like the Dominion, didn't open until 1936. Most of the cinema halls were bunched close together at the south-western end of Tottenham Court Road, near Oxford Street.

The sound reasons for Tottenham Court Road being a prime cinema location were laid out in *How to Run a Picture Theatre: A Handbook for Proprietors, Managers and Exhibitors*, published by the *Kinematograph Weekly* around 1912. Its advice to prospective owners and managers makes it clear why this spot was favoured:

> ... a main business artery is to be preferred and care should be also taken to have the theatre on the right side of the street. It is strange, but nevertheless true, that twice as many persons frequent one side of a street as are to [be] found on the other side, and it is the side most used by pedestrians that is best fitted for the electric theatre ...
>
> It is well to consider also from whence your *clientele* is likely to be drawn when you have opened your theatre. It does not pay to expect one's patrons after the turmoil of the day to walk miles to the theatre. Therefore, the site should be as near as possible to the part most densely populated by the comfortably positioned artizan or middle classes, as they are the greatest supporters of the picture theatre.[18]

Tottenham Court Road, a major shopping street leading to perhaps *the* busiest London shopping street, Oxford Street, in a Fitzrovia rife with artisans and full of small business premises that could be bought or rented at reasonable rates, was a natural home for cinema. Its west side, the closest to Oxford Street, proved to be the ideal location. It attracted both entrepreneurs and audiences in droves.

The only purpose-built cinema in Fitzrovia not to occupy Tottenham Court Road was the Fitzroy Picture Palace (around 1912) at 64a Charlotte Street.[19] However, the Scala Theatre at the junction of Tottenham Street and Charlotte Street also had a screen career that supplemented its live performances. The Scala would acquire a special significance regarding the screening of cinema classics and international film, as we will see later.

In the first years of cinema, venues were constantly opening and shutting down as businessmen experimented in this new industry with varying success. Not all of the early local venues lasted very long. The Fitzroy Picture Palace in Charlotte Street closed in 1916. However, all the above-mentioned cinemas in Tottenham Court Road were still open in 1920, although sometimes under a different name, e.g. the Court Playhouse replaced the Court Electric Theatre and Pyke House was renamed the Phoenix. Many London music halls were converted into cinemas as cinema grew and music hall declined.[20]

Since children formed much of the cinema audience in the early days, the cinema owners had to price their shows accordingly. Typical prices were 3*d* for adults and 2*d* for children at regular showings, and 1*d* for the children's Saturday matinees.[21] The shows were extremely popular and affected other forms of recreation. Youth club membership suffered, at least temporarily. The Jewish Lads' Club's annual report for 1910 sombrely noted, '[T]he cause of the falling off in membership has doubtless been the large number of rival and, in some cases, unhealthy attractions, which have grown up in the neighbourhood in the last few years.' With 1909 and 1910 seeing the rapid emergence of the cinema hall, the nature of the 'unhealthy attraction' is clear. The annual report warns, 'To cope effectively … it will unfortunately be necessary to spend a large sum of money in brightening and warming the Club.' Brightness and heat, so often lacking at home as well as at the clubs, were obviously among the desirable features of the new entertainment.

Not all authorities deplored the showing of films, especially when programmes were arranged by reputable organisations in lecture halls and other 'respectable' venues, as still often happened in the early days. The Reverend J. Ernest Rattenbury, organiser of the West London Mission's Cleveland Street section, was a supporter. He said in the *Westminster Gazette*, 'On the whole, these shows are good and not bad' and he had attended a considerable number of film shows and 'only once seen anything that was offensive'.[22]

Many charitable groups arranged Sunday cinematograph showings. These Sunday shows were particularly tightly regulated by the LCC under the Cinematograph Act. Organisers had to obtain a licence and comply with provisos such as 'entertainments will be of a healthy and elevating character ... and not for private gain'.[23] The couple of pence charged for admission meant that these film shows were a very useful means of fundraising for the organisations involved.

Several short films made up a typical bill at this time. They often consisted of recordings of notable occasions such as state visits, exhibitions of scientific innovations or important sporting events. But they also included melodramas and cliffhanger serials like the American-made *The Adventures of Kathlyn* (1913) or *The Perils of Pauline* (1914), which sometimes excited adult disapproval. Stars of music hall began to appear in short films, performing the kind of sketch comedy that was familiar from the stage and influencing the development of early cinema.[24]

Alec Flinder, as a boy, often patronised his local cinemas including those in Tottenham Court Road. He made a regular once-weekly trip with his mother, Bessie:

> Monday night used to be her cinema night. So I can remember going to the cinema very very early on in the days of the silent films and I used to go with her ... As with every Jewish mother she never went out without taking us something to eat and she was very fond of oranges which she used to peel as she was sitting down. On one occasion I remember a chap behind me saying blimey the roof's leaking ... she had squeezed the orange and it had squirted right over and landed on his head ... we used to see Tom Mix, Fatty Arbuckle, Mary Pickford, all the old films ... the kids used to stand on the seats and wave like anything at all the cowboy films.[25]

It's hard to measure the direct influence of cinema on employment locally, as that level of detail on people's occupations is available only in the census and the most recent census publicly available is 1911, when the film and cinema exhibition industries had barely begun. However, the need for staff to sell tickets and refreshments must have caused at least a small spike in local job opportunities. Porters and drivers were also needed to deliver the reels of film, as well as technicians to run them.

It's also possible, using the *Post Office Directories*, to spot associated industries taking a foothold in Fitzrovia over the years. By 1920 there was an electrical lighting specialist, Mann, Egerton & Co. Ltd, at 177 Cleveland Street, who could have provided lighting for cinema halls and cinema frontages among other services. Manufacturers and merchants of electrical accessories in Charlotte Street and Cleveland Street also appeared in the 1920s. Perhaps firms like these contributed to the brightness and heat of the cinema complained of by the young people's clubs as taking away their members?

Other businesses, like those providing refreshment and accommodation, were also boosted by the film industry at this time. The Bedford Hotel in Tottenham Court Road advertised itself in the *Bioscope* as the best-located venue for film buyers visiting London. Pubs must have received a boost as well – in later years, the pubs frequented by BBC staff included the George in Great Portland St, the Yorkshire Grey in Langham Street, the Cock in Great Portland Street, the Stag's Head in New Cavendish Street, the Northumberland Arms (now Draft House) in Goodge Street, and the Dover Castle in Weymouth Mews, as well as the Wheatsheaf and the Fitzroy Tavern beloved by the Fitzrovia Set of artists and writers.

One resident associated with film does pop up in the 1911 census: Eugine Taupin, a French cinematograph theatre proprietor living at 11 Howland Street. Mr Taupin had perhaps prospered from his cinema, since according to the census he owned the house and also rented rooms to lodgers. We don't know, however, whether his cinema was in Fitzrovia or not.

A Fitzrovian cinema-goer in 1920, still the silent era in film making, could have seen notable British films like *Bleak House* directed by Maurice Elvey, *The Ever Open Door*, starring Hayford Hobbs, and *A Son of David*, starring Ronald Colman, as well as international productions like *The Golem*, made in Germany. And they could have thrilled to great American stars of cinema such as Charlie Chaplin, Mary Pickford and Buster Keaton. The coming of sound brought an even greater wave of cinema hits in the 1930s.

As the silent film era was coming to a close at the end of the 1920s, a new form of cinema started to become increasingly popular: the newsreel. Tottenham Court Road's Gaiety Theatre, 'Reputedly, the last cinema in London' to screen silent films, had closed by 1933 and reopened as the Sphere News Theatre – or, as my grandfather used to call it, 'the Sphera' – with a rolling one-hour newsreel show.[26] A photograph of the Sphere's exterior taken in 1934 shows a brightly neon-lit frontage in Art Deco style with a shining globe outlined by bold swirls of light and the words 'SPHERE NEWS' above it. The entrance prices, 7*d* and 1*s*, glowed inside large stars on either side of the neon globe.[27]

Newsreel theatres were small in number. There were only about twenty-two of them in the country by 1939 but sixteen of them were in London, where they undoubtedly made an impact.[28] The great advantage to customers, when catching up with the weekly or twice-weekly news, was that rolling programmes throughout the day and evening allowed them to pop in whenever there was an hour to spare.[29] The bustling Tottenham Court Road was ideal for attracting these transient customers.

Some people who didn't otherwise visit the cinema would go to a news theatre. J. Neill Brown notes, 'Most news cinema managers [are] very proud of the type of patron they cater for … the educated man who wants to get an even broader outlook on current events than he can get from the daily papers.'[30] Newsreel programmes, almost all produced by five big companies including Paramount News and Pathé News, tended to consist of 'about 15 to 18 minutes of news, a single reel travelogue, a general interest film of two reels, a cartoon (usually Disney), and sometimes a comedy'.[31]

Short newsreels were also shown in many general cinema theatres, as were weekly cine-magazines focusing on fashion, travel and the entertainment industry itself, with its stars and shows. And newsreels had the potential to influence a lot of people. By 1939, cinema admission figures had increased to a staggering 20–23 million a week – around half the UK population. Working-class customers attended most of all, as was confirmed by surveys such as the 1934 Social Survey of Merseyside. As Nicholas Pronay puts it, 'Working-men and their wives … were better placed to get the kind of product which they actually wanted in the local cinema than anywhere else. For once it was they who paid the pipers and were seen to be paying them too.'[32] Fitzrovia's families were well catered for when it came to news – and if they wished, they could also go to the Tatler and the G.B. Movietone Theatre, both sited across Oxford Street at the top of Charing Cross Road.

Newsreel theatres like the Sphere had a special role to play just before and during the Second World War. J. Neill Brown, writing in the spring of 1939, describes the sense of urgency at the worsening situation and the temporary relief given by the 1938 Munich Agreement, as conveyed in the newsreels, 'The crisis – the Premier goes to Godesberg – Parliament reassembles – BBC news bulletins in French, German, and Italian – last minute intervention – Munich – thankfulness of a world that can expect its Christmas in peace'. Brown concludes, 'The busiest cinemas in London during crisis week were the newsreel houses.'[33] During the war itself, the newsreels were a vital medium of information and propaganda, but sometimes the war brutally disrupted this flow of information: the Sphere closed in 1940 due to bomb damage and did not reopen.

The influential nature of the newsreels led to scrutiny after the war, if not while the conflict was on. J.B. Priestley, writing on 11 June 1948 in the left-wing *Daily Herald*, strongly criticised the monopoly exercised by newsreel companies like the American Paramount Picture Company and the British J. Arthur Rank. Priestley called for action to diversify ownership and urged that co-operative societies, trade unions and cultural associations should be encouraged and helped to produce their own newsreels and to distribute them widely. He said, 'It cannot be a matter of indifference how nearly thirty million of our people are offered the news in cinemas.'[34]

As a child in the late fifties, with my mother I have a memory of watching, in a small, seedy, smoky theatre in Tottenham Court Road, what had then evolved into a rolling programme of Disney cartoons with a Pathé newsreel attached. I can't remember the name of the cinema – perhaps it is even a phantom memory, given that hardly any small cinemas remained in Tottenham Court Road at that time, although the Berkeley may have been a candidate. Nevertheless, the impression is lodged in my brain: my tenuous personal link with the cinema tradition on the Other Side of Oxford Street.

Entrepreneurship in the film exhibition industry involved numerous foreigners and outsiders, as did London's early film production industry, centred on Soho's Cecil Court, or 'Flicker Alley', as it was known. Many immigrants were involved with cinema production, sales and exhibition: large numbers of them were American, some were French, and at least one Soho-based company, Nordisk, was owned by a Dane, Ole Olsen. Jewish film makers were a strong presence in the London industry, as they were in the USA.

Fitzrovia strongly reflected this trend of Jewish entrepreneurship. The first proprietors of the Grand Central in Tottenham Court Road were Walter Hyman and A.D. Rosenthal. From 1915, the Grand Central proprietors ran the Majestic and the Carlton as well. Later, the Carlton cinema passed to Eric Hakim's Cinema House – Hakim came from France and was of Armenian extraction. The Carlton was then owned by Ben Jay (Benjamin Jacobs) in the 1930s. The Odeon circuit came to prominence in the 1930s, its success driven by Oscar Deutsch. The Paramount in Tottenham Court Road became part of the Odeon circuit in 1942. Kenneth Rive, born in Germany and a child actor, founded Gala Films and in the 1950s took over the Berkeley (the old Carlton) and La Continentale (the old Majestic) for the showing of foreign films, often with an erotic flavour.[35]

As we've seen, Fitzrovia was a welcoming environment for immigrants engaged in new enterprises, never more so than when the media industries were being created. But the wider background featured prejudice and anti-

Semitism against the many foreigners in the film industry, as Edward Marshall observes in his essay, 'The Dark Alien Executive'.[36] The hostility sprang from varied causes, ranging from fears of job losses among British film technicians to the belief that 'aliens' would undermine British culture and values with their 'rootless cosmopolitanism', vulgarity and ignorance.

Marshall notes that Jewish directors and producers often responded to this display of prejudice by making films that closely reflected and enhanced 'Englishness', for example historical films such as *The Private Life of Henry VIII* (1933) and those featuring the English gentleman as a hero, like *The Scarlet Pimpernel* (1934). *The Scarlet Pimpernel* starred Leslie Howard, who for many Britons represented the classic English gentleman. (Howard was, in fact, born Leslie Howard Steiner to Hungarian and Jewish parents.)

The film industry in this period could be a leading medium of integration for immigrants to Britain, helping to create Britishness. Keen young cinema-goers like Alec Flinder could absorb a sense of Britishness from film, perhaps as much as from the Anglicising mission of the Jewish Lad's Club.

Life in Between: The Dominion, the 'Magical' Scala Theatre, and the Grafton

Fitzrovia's live theatres were fringe enterprises in several senses. Outside the West End proper, they tended always to struggle financially. Perhaps their greatest success was in simply surviving for many years, in an in-between state, moving between the showing of stage and screen performances as circumstances dictated. Fitzrovia's actors and managers showed typical resourcefulness in keeping their venues going under adverse conditions: a resourcefulness that was often needed on the Other Side of Oxford Street.

The Dominion was built in 1929 for live shows. Created on the grand scale in Portland stone, it rose on the site of Meux's Brewery, absorbing the old Court Cinema. The Dominion soon turned to cinema itself, featuring *The Phantom of the Opera* with Lon Chaney in 1930, then Chaplin's *City Lights* the following year. It continued to stage live shows but couldn't pay its way by doing this and was bought by part of the Gaumont-British chain for cinema exhibition from 1933. After closing between October 1940 and January 1941 in wartime, it continued to show films.

However, after the war it also staged some memorable live performances, such as a Judy Garland show in November 1957. After a new Todd AO system and stereophonic sound was installed, the spectacular movie, *South Pacific*, ran there for nearly four and a half years, not closing until September 1962. It was followed by the wildly popular 1960s film, *The Sound of Music*. Although it has had some difficult days, the theatre's excellent location and its large scale kept it successfully hosting long-running blockbuster live shows for decades, until the present day. It was, and is, Fitzrovia's dominant performance venue, enduring by means of moving between stage and screen.

The Scala Theatre, at the corner of Charlotte Street and Tottenham Street, had an even more varied, though not so stellar, history. Though founded for live performance, it was more noteworthy for its contribution to cinema: it was even said to be brushed by cinema magic. The journalist Lesley Blanch explained the Scala's special link to cinema in an article written in November 1945, when the theatre hosted the festival, 'Fifty Years of Cinema, 1895–1945', organised by the New London Film Society. Blanch wrote:

> I'm glad the Festival will be held at the Scala: there's something magical about the Charlotte Street theatre ... D. W. Griffith's masterpiece, *The Birth of a Nation*, had its original run there in 1915: so did the greatest Russian films, when, after years of political banning, they were first shown to an appreciative public ... To many film enthusiasts the Scala is a temple, sacred to the memory of unforgettable pictures. One director told me how he came out from seeing one of the first great Griffith pictures, and reeled down Charlotte Street, punch drunk by its impact.[37]

The site's chequered history as an entertainment venue began as far back as 1772, when the New Rooms was built for musical concerts on the corner of Tottenham Street and Charlotte Street. For years, the building retained its musical nature under different names, but in 1802, as the Cognoscenti Theatre, it was used by an exclusive theatre club, the Pic-Nics, whose membership included the Prince of Wales.[38] But this fashionable set quickly moved on, leaving the theatre to the indignity of being used as a circus. By the time Marie Wilton took it over in 1865 it was known as the Queen's Theatre, but was nicknamed 'The Dusthole'.[39]

When Wilton visited the Scala in 1865 – just like the cinema-goer sitting below Alec Flinder's mother decades later – she nearly fell foul of an orange. According to Wilton:

> Some of the occupants of the stalls ... were engaged between the acts in devouring oranges (their faces being buried in them) and drinking ginger beer ... A woman looked up to our box, and seeing us staring aghast I sup-

pose with an expression of horror upon my face, first of all 'took a sight' at us, and then shouted, 'Now then, you stuck up ones, come out of that, or I'll send this 'ere orange at your 'eads!'[40]

Under Wilton's management the theatre flourished, hosting celebrated actors such as Ellen Terry. But by the 1880s the building badly needed renovating. In 1903 it was bought by Distin Maddick, who extended the site and built what became the Scala, designed on a grand scale by Frank T. Verity. The architect's plans reveal how the old building was extended out onto the pavement and altered to accommodate a large high-ceilinged restaurant that expanded upwards through the storeys of the theatre.[41] Mander and Mitchenson say, 'The interior is unique, with its stairways from either side of the dress circle leading down to the stalls, passing under the boxes.'[42] The theatre's name, Scala, was derived from these grand stairways.

The Scala's first play was *The Conquerer* in September 1905, but the venue was not a success and, after the first few years, it only staged plays sporadically. However, in 1910, at the dawn of the cinema, the Scala branched out into film, installing a cinematograph box. As Lesley Blanch says, the theatre played a special role in early cinema history. The cinema pioneer, Charles Urban, premiered his experimental Kinemacolor productions there from 1911. By hiring the Scala, Urban avoided risking money on a new-build cinema in what was then an unproven medium, and gained a characterful building well suited to his large-scale and extravagant displays. Urban put on spectacular shows there, such as the film of the Delhi Durbar welcoming King George V as the Emperor of India, shown in February 1912:

[H]ere it was that Urban demonstrated his greatest triumph … the film [was] a phenomenal two and a half hours long. The Scala stage was turned into a mock-up of the Taj Mahal, with special lighting effects … a chorus of twenty-four, a twenty-piece fife and drum corps, and three bagpipes.[43]

Urban's films were hugely popular. The mix of cinematic and theatrical showbusiness sparkle must have been heady. He was attracting middle-class customers, too, who were willing to pay more, betting on the probability that, as a cinema trade paper put it, 'the "stalls" are interested in pictures if they are put before them under conditions to which they are accustomed' – i.e. in space and comfort.[44]

Theodore Brown, the inventor, also used the theatre in 1913 to show his Kinoplastikon films, an experimental form of screenless cinema from

Germany where lifelike images appeared via reflected mirror projection. The 'Pepper's Ghost' illusion that was to inspire Kinoplastikon was staged nearby at Maskelyne's in Langham Place. According to Luke McKernan, 'Kinoplastikon films were produced in a studio lined with black velvet (the actors had to be dressed entirely in white) on the roof of the Scala theatre.'[45]

The Bioscope of 8 May 1913 comments, 'The appearance of these amazing spirit creatures is curious. They resemble the figures of an ordinary cinematograph film, cut away from their original background with a pair of scissors, and set to caper and gesticulate.'

In the Scala's cinematic career, the 1920s were mostly memorable for the showing of the D.W. Griffith films that followed *Birth of a Nation*, *Orphans of the Storm* and *White Rose*. Sidney Spellman of Hanson Street also mentions seeing Yiddish films from Poland and America at the Scala at this time.

The Scala always had a very patchy record of staging live productions. Its theatrical highlights in the 1930s included several productions of Ralph Reader's *Gang Show*, which were based on amateur revues performed by Scout troops, and there were highly popular recurrent seasons of *Peter Pan* in the 1940s. In between it served miscellaneous purposes, even becoming an occasional overflow synagogue for the local Jewish population. According to former residents, the long-serving Rabbi Ferber, who took over as rabbi of the tiny Manette Street synagogue in Soho in 1916 – '[H]e was known as the "Bishop of the West End" and was very popular' – used to conduct services at the Scala on High Holy Days.[46]

But, in 1945, the Scala gained a new lease of movie life with 'Fifty Years of Cinema 1895–1945', the Sunday programme of international classics praised by Lesley Blanch. The opening film was Griffiths' *Birth of a Nation*, followed by greats such as Robert Weine's *The Cabinet of Dr Caligari*, Eisenstein's *Potemkin* and *The Passion of Joan of Arc* by Karl Dreyer.

Lesley Blanch revealed that screenings included full live orchestral accompaniment with a half-time break for the players. She reminisces, '"End of Part I!", Up went the lights, the orchestra stumped out for half a pint of bitter … and audiences scrambled madly across each other's knees to get seated again for Part II.'[47]

Ten years later, the Scala made more cinema history by hosting the first ever UK Festival of Indian film. Organised by the Asian Film Society in 1955, its opener was Sohrab Modi's *Queen of Jhansi*, a take on the Indian Mutiny, attended by Peter Ustinov and Ingrid Bergman. Each show included a dance performance by Sitara, 'The Kathak Queen'. Its most successful film, and the first to obtain a British distribution deal, was *Munna*. The film attracted mild praise from Prime Minister Nehru, who was quoted in the programme as saying, 'I liked this film and consider it good from many points of view'.[48] At a second festival in 1957, the Scala hosted Satyajit Ray's masterpiece, *Pather Panchali*, drawing large audiences. A number of other film societies used the theatre at this period and in 1953 there was a 'Festival of Soviet Films', arranged by the British–Soviet Friendship Society.

The success of the second Indian film festival prompted BBC television to make a half-hour documentary on Indian cinema, which, suggests Edward Hotspur Johnson in *Sight and Sound* Autumn 1988, was 'possibly the first western television programme' on the Indian film industry. The theatre continued to show Indian films regularly: one current Fitzrovia resident, Mohammed Moyen Uddin, remembers going to Sunday afternoon screenings.

The Scala's final memorable connection with cinema was in being used by the Beatles in 1964 to film musical scenes for their film, *A Hard Day's Night*. The theatre was finally demolished in 1969. This eccentric place might not have made much of a mark in live theatre, but instead it became a small but valuable part of British film history.

The Grafton – From Cinema to Theatre

Tucked away underneath Tottenham Court Road, on the corner with Warren Street, was the Grafton Theatre. Taking the opposite career path to the Scala, the Grafton began as a cinema then converted to live performance. The Grafton's trajectory as a performance venue was just as erratic as the Scala's, however, and just as much in keeping with Fitzrovia's turbulent character.

Called the Corner Theatre, it opened in November 1910, located underground beneath Kelsey's Boot Shop, in a basement that was formerly a wine cellar.[49] Its pay kiosk was squashed in at the back of the shop on the ground floor. In 1911, new owners renamed it the Grafton Cinema. But, in 1929, when sound films came in, the cinema converted to a small live theatre, seating 187 people.

The Grafton was first intended for showing new work by emerging playwrights. It opened in May 1930 with *The Searcher*, a play by the American writer and theatre manager, Velona Pilcher. But the play was badly reviewed by the *Times* and the Grafton's management quickly changed. In 1931, two well-known actors, Beatrix Thomson and Helena Pickard, ran it jointly. Thomson and Pickard advertised the tiny venue as hosting 'London's Most Intimate Shows' and, for a while, put on plays frequently. The theatre showed, among others, *Spring Awakening* by the German playwright Frank Wedekind, which had not previously been staged in England; *The Lilies of the Field* by John Hastings Turner, starring Pickard and Thomson as a clergyman's two daughters; and *I Want* by Constance Holme, in which a celestial photographer looks into the souls of the smart young people who comprise the Haut-Ton Tennis Club. Pickard or Thomson, or sometimes both, starred in these dramas. They also revived the old tearjerker, *East Lynne*, featuring Helena Pickard as the maritally straying Lady Isabel, who speaks the unforgettable words concerning her son, 'Dead, dead, dead – and never called me Mother'. The company's deliberately straight rendition of the melodrama brought out the unwitting humour of the piece, according to the critic of *The Star*, who called it 'very amusing'.

However, Pickard and Thomson were only at the Grafton during 1931. After they pulled out, its record of productions became much thinner under short-lived managements. Its few productions included occasional variety shows. In March 1932, a variety programme was staged at the Grafton by The Bright Young Things, a company backed by George Bernard Shaw, which aimed at reviving the variety tradition by recreating old music-hall songs, mimes and folk songs. Its 1932 programme included songs, sketches and a fencing display arranged by Miss Eleanor Macdonald.

In 1937, Lionel Westlake became manager, and in November that year he put on the young actor Kenneth More as the murderer Reggie Ardwick in a one-week run of *Hands Never Lie* by Olive Remple.[50] The following year, Westlake staged *Livingstone*, a play about the Victorian explorer by David MacKane. A programme for this play has pencil notes on the back, probably made during the performance by a theatre critic who dourly remarked, 'There is absolutely no play to be made out of the life of Livingstone ... the singular uninspired dialogue and indifferent acting ... did little to alleviate the almost continuous depression of the evening'.[51] The Westlake management was, understandably, another short-lived regime.

The Grafton had been without a manager and empty for nearly a year when David Farrar, a star of both film and stage, took it over in 1939, a day or two before war broke out. '[F]or some inexplicable reason,' he says in his autobiography, *No Royal Road*, 'we felt irresistibly attracted to it.'[52] Anne Carew, Farrar's secretary and a contributor to the book, writes that before closing in 1938, the theatre:

> ... degenerated in the theatrical scale, being used occasionally for trying out plays, and then when we contemplated taking it, it had a rather sordid reputation for giving tenth-rate revues and inducing most of its patrons to

spend their evenings in the bar, which was very large indeed and quite out of proportion to the size of the theatre.[53]

Carew calls the Grafton, '… a very risky proposition. The auditorium itself was dilapidated; there was no carpet on the stone floors, the theatre signs were broken, and lamps missing, the bar counter stained with the rims of thousands of glasses and burnt black with cigarette ends.' The theatre's roof leaked, and the facilities backstage were equally poor, except for a good switchboard and curtains.

One potential advantage of the theatre was that, located in the edge-lands of Fitzrovia, the Grafton was just outside the central West End zone within which all theatres had been ordered by the government to close due to the war. It could, therefore, have attracted thousands of extra customers. However, the West End theatres had already reopened by the time the Grafton was ready to open, probably because the phoney war and the absence of bombing raids led to a change of government policy; so Farrar and his company didn't benefit. Moreover, the front-of-house area had to be blacked out due to the war, with no lighting allowed outside for advertising the theatre. The crowning problem was that, quite understandably, no one would help to finance the theatre.

Despite these tremendous difficulties, Farrar, Carew and company went ahead with a do or die attitude. They seem to have made a good go of it even if, frighteningly to our ears, their sets were made largely by 'buying up all the second-hand asbestos we could find'![54]

The company managed to stage three plays with David Farrar playing the lead. The first, an American play, *The Firebrand*, lost money due to setting-up expenses but was successful with audiences. Unfortunately, only two critics attended the first night as a West End theatre was opening a play the same night. The next production, *Captain Banner* by George Preedy (aka Marjorie Bowen), told the story of Caroline Matilda, the sister of George III. The third play was the popular *The Wandering Jew*, in which Farrar reprised his already famous role as the Jew. *The Wandering Jew* portrayed an image of Jewishness that was more complex and sympathetic than past negative media stereotypes of Jews and had already been made as a film in 1933, produced by Julius Hagen during the rise of German Nazism.

David Farrar's 'manifesto', set out in his foreword to the first programme, states the company's belief that:

> … there is a public for plays which we regard as 'good theatre.' What consti-
> tutes 'good theatre' is difficult to qualify, but our own feelings in the matter
> lead us to a preference for plays soundly constructed as to story and plot,

which will entertain with beauty of language, form and colour … We do not seek to present 'new angles' on the theatre, and we abhor all endeavours to strip the mystery from the legitimate stage.

The close of the theatre's short stage history, then, saw it embracing solidly traditional plays rather than experimental works.

The Wandering Jew did so well that Farrar was negotiating a transfer to St Martin's Theatre when air raids began in 1940. A warning note to the audience on the play's programme says bracingly, 'In the event of an Air Raid Warning: This Theatre is underground and built of steel and concrete. If the Audience remain the Play will continue, but any who wish to leave will find the Theatre exits easily accessible.'[55]

Soon afterwards the Grafton was bombed, wrecking part of the backstage and dressing rooms. Other West End theatres were again closed; it was impossible to continue, and Farrar went back into acting in films. The Grafton Theatre was finished.

The surviving Dominion, the Grafton and the long-lived Scala were protean institutions, never settling into one cultural groove but forever adapting themselves to changing times and circumstances in order to survive. In this, they were typical of Fitzrovia's people, so many of whom were making new lives in the city and finding opportunities to flourish in the myriad of emerging entertainment enterprises using new media. The dramatic arts are by nature on society's edge, seeking the Other Side of everyday experience; perhaps Fitzrovia's eccentric and oddly located, struggling but versatile entertainment halls best embodied this quality and in so doing were faithful to the historic spirit of Fitzrovia.

Life with the BBC

Meanwhile, home entertainment was being transformed. The radio, starting to be broadcast nationwide from 1922, was 'accepted casually and easily as an unobtrusive element in daily life' in London and other towns and cities by the end of the 1930s.[56] For working-class consumers this momentous change in their home life occurred more slowly than for the middle classes, who could afford the relatively high price of a radio set. But by 1936, 'People's Sets' had come on the market selling for 5 or 6 guineas – still more than a week's wages for many workers – while a booming hire-purchase trade aided those who would otherwise have found the price beyond their pocket. By 1939 more than 9 million wireless licences had been sold, with nearly half going to low-paid customers on incomes of between £2 10s and £4 a week.[57] Since listening was often a communal activity in poorer areas, with neighbours gathering round one family's radio set, broadcasting coverage was widespread across the population by the start of the war.[58]

Fitzrovia had a place in radio and television history even before BBC Broadcasting House was built on its doorstep. Its experimental and innovative character came to the fore again in 1880, when it was the location for early experiments in transmitting radio waves; in fact, it was the scene of the very first UK radio broadcast. The inventor, David Hughes, had moved to 94 Great Portland Street in 1877. From there, he demonstrated the world's first wireless transmission of sound.[59] He sent sound waves from his flat to Langham Place, oddly conjuring up the ghosts of the future by choosing the site of BBC Broadcasting House to receive the transmission. Unfortunately, the Secretary of the Royal Society didn't accept that sound waves had been transmitted, so the Royal Society didn't validate Hughes' experiment. In 1929, over fifty years later, the first BBC television broadcast, using the Baird system, was conducted at 8 Hallam Street, a side street running parallel to Great Portland Street. The BBC chose the Marconi-EMI system in preference to Baird's, however.

BBC Broadcasting House opened in Langham Place in 1932, having moved from Savoy Hill on the Embankment. The BBC had needed to expand its headquarters and, after considering several spots in central London, settled on Langham Place because a suitable site happened to be put on the market for development at the right time, well located close to Oxford Street and with the cultural bonus of having the Queen's Hall almost opposite.

Broadcasting House, its fresh stone exterior standing out among the smoke-grimed older buildings like a white molar in a dingy row of teeth, became a distinctive landmark on Fitzrovia's western border. The BBC was now broadcasting to the nation from Langham Place, with huge and growing numbers listening.

What effect did the presence of the BBC have on the immediate locality? Firstly, the BBC must, at least indirectly, have contributed to the mystique of the Fitzrovia Set. Rubbing shoulders in the Wheatsheaf and the Fitzroy Tavern, the BBC crowd and the Fitzrovia Set overlapped in the 1940s and 1950s, merging into one another around the edges in the Fitzrovia Set's later years. Julian Maclaren-Ross, in *Memoirs of the Forties*, provides evidence that BBC staff in the higher ranks of the organisation were looked to as potential commissioners of work by Maclaren-Ross himself and others, and the organisation helped to sustain some of the group's members. Dylan Thomas was one important beneficiary: his best-known work, *Under Milk Wood*, was produced by the BBC as a radio play in 1954.

Did the BBC also play a role as an employer of local people? Broadcasting House employed hundreds of administrative, technical and managerial staff. However, the BBC had a reputation for recruiting its officers from the establishment, so a local youngster without good social connections might have had a better chance of getting in on the bottom rung, as a junior clerk or a page boy.

According to Mark Hines, in *The Story of Broadcasting House* (2008):

At 8.30 numbers of clerks would arrive to sort the first postal delivery for the various departments ...Young page boys buzzed through the building in smart blue serge suits, black ties and stiff white collars, delivering to in-trays and collecting from out-trays every forty-five minutes ...There were ninety-five boys, who joined the BBC at fourteen years old and had to attend evening school as a condition of employment. The BBC paid two-thirds of their school fees and gave them a dress allowance of half a crown (the equivalent of about £4.50) a week.[60]

Did any of these boys live in Fitzrovia? One hopes so.

Additionally, the BBC's effect on the existing entertainment industry in Fitzrovia was considerable. Some local venues survived, or at least flourished, perhaps only thanks to the BBC. Radio and television broadcasting centres frequently took over performance venues in Fitzrovia.

The history of the Queen's Hall became interwoven with that of BBC radio broadcasting up till the Second World War, when it was destroyed by bombing. The BBC has been credited with saving the Promenade concerts from extinction in 1927 as John Reith himself negotiated with the managing director of the Queen's Hall, succeeding in keeping the Proms going without a break.[61] The BBC Symphony Orchestra, formed in 1930 under Adrian Boult, also frequently performed from Queen's Hall. The lease of St George's Hall (Maskelyne's), next to the Queen's Hall, was acquired by the BBC in 1933, and it was changed into a concert studio; it was destroyed at the same time as the Queen's Hall.[62]

The Dominion Theatre was another broadcast location, while the Grafton Theatre was also taken over by the BBC from 1940 after it had been damaged by bombing.[63] The Paramount Theatre in Tottenham Court Road became a centre for BBC broadcasts at this time as well, with the Paramount Orchestra, conducted by 'Anton' Arthur Sweeting, being broadcast weekly on the BBC Light Programme and Home Service.

The BBC eventually operated from so many centres in Fitzrovia that it must have exerted, and probably continues to exert, its own subtle influence on the locality in ways that it is difficult to fully appreciate. It seems as if nothing in the BBC's publications or archives has as yet addressed the interaction between place and institution. Let's hope that one day this gap will be filled by a local historian or an interested member of the BBC.

'London's Harlem' in Tottenham Court Road: Dancing at the Paramount

The Paramount Ballroom, next to the Paramount Theatre, was transformed in the 1940s, in ways that owed nothing to the BBC but fitted in perfectly with Fitzrovia's reputation as a home for outsiders and a space for experimentation where the usual rules could be waived. The Paramount Ballroom opened in 1936. Its first resident band leaders were Freddie Bretherton and Clive Erard, and it featured musicians like Art Gregory and his band.[64]

By the end of the 1940s, the ballroom had shed any sedateness that the BBC connections of the adjacent Paramount Theatre might have conjured up, becoming one of the few halls where jive music was regularly played. It became one of the rare places where the races regularly mixed socially, with its black and white patrons dancing the jitterbug together in the latest dance craze.

William Sansom writes about jive, in a piece called 'A Public for Jive':

> A 'solid' driving beat is produced that 'sends' the dancers. It seems almost as if an invisible material force is at work, as though the instruments emit successive walls of sound that force the dancers on their way ... The hep-cats are at it, the jive is on, they're in a groove. Swing skirts are circling, zoot-tails flying; smiles are set solid on their lips, eyes glazed in a tremendously concentrated inward scrutiny of the body's motion. They throw each other away, then, magnetised, come together ... legs are kicked in special ways, arms extended, the whole body bent in calculated distortion.[65]

The Paramount provided a lush environment for dancing. According to Sansom:

> It lies underground, the ceiling is low and warmly lit; chocolate and crimson pillars are topped with heavy gilt Corinthian capitals; fans like aeroplane propellers hang motionless from the ceiling. One wall of the immense room

is ornate with heavy rose damask, with mirrors, with curling gold baroquish plaster work.[66]

Sansom's description of the hall's décor gives it and its activities decadent overtones. And jiving and jitterbugging did attract social disapproval, partly for being American inventions that were supposedly degrading British dance culture. Class snobbery played a part, too, since many participants were work-ing-class young people. But the sharpest edge to that disapproval was caused by fear of the social mixing going on between British women and Afro-Caribbean or African American men at these dance sessions. Sansom describes 'a strong *colony* [my italics] of coloured men, mostly in uniform' at the Paramount. The use of 'colony' perhaps indicates Sansom's own racial bias, hinting that these 'coloured men' are lesser men than white dancers. Colonialism's oppressive and demeaning ideology was still strongly in force at this time.

Kevin Guyan's 'Glitter and Glamour: Race and Dance in 1940s London' (2013) describes the Paramount dance hall, in terms we're now familiar with when it comes to Fitzrovia, as a boundary-stretching arena, 'a strong example of a geographical space in which boundaries of race, gender, sex and sexuality could be tested through the interactions of black men and white women … an arena in which identities are constructed, reified, challenged and erased'.[67] Although several clubs in Soho were venues for racial mixing, the Paramount in Fitzrovia attracted special notoriety. Guyan puts his finger on the likely rea-sons for this, 'It could be suggested that the Paramount's location, beyond the borders of Soho; its label as a "dance hall" rather than a "club"; and its inclusion as part of the established Mecca chain were understood as a greater risk for racial mixing that went beyond its permitted confines'.[68]

Once more, it seems that a Fitzrovia location is a sign that an activity is threatening to be beyond boundaries and beyond control – even more so because it seems to be challenging the norms established by the big dance chain, Mecca. Again, the potential for disorder and contamination seems to be enhanced by an address in Tottenham Court Road. Old fears were hard to die.

Guyan shows how the Paramount's management avoided enforcing an open 'colour bar' while still trying indirectly to restrict entry for black men. It made up impromptu entrance requirements like wearing a tie or arriving with a female partner – requirements that the men could often get around with the help of female friends in the hall. According to the *Daily Mirror* of 4 December 1949, the hall was known as 'London's Harlem'. The paper made a point of distinguishing the Paramount 'Harlem' from New York's Harlem, claiming that the real Harlem was 'acutely colour-conscious' and 'finds white company embarrassing' while the races supposedly mixed easily at London's dance hall 'Harlem'. But the piece itself was racially charged and sensational, stating that some could be revolted by the sight of 'dance-fevered' white teenage girls 'nuzzling and clutching the hefty, grinning dancers' and claiming that the accompanying pictures 'scandalised London'.

The police had their eyes on the Paramount. It was one of the main targets of a raid in December 1945, not long after the war had ended, where 100 police and military were searching for deserters from the army and other criminals. There were drug raids, too, and, in 1950, the dancing stopped. Mecca had decided to repurpose it as a banqueting hall, hoping to attract visitors to the forthcoming Festival of Britain held in 1951. The dancers protested. The *Daily Express* reported that a large group of West African students had held a meeting and decided to appeal to the Minister for Commonwealth Relations, but they were unsuccessful and on 16 July 1950 the hall closed for dancing. It now hosts dancing of a different kind – as the lap-dancing club, Spearmint Rhino.

'Innocent Enjoyment': Girls' and Boys' Clubs in Fitzrovia

Some young people in Fitzrovia spent their leisure hours in the thriving local boys' and girls' clubs. The references we've seen in club annual reports to 'healthy' and 'unhealthy' leisure pursuits demonstrate the anxiety of many club organisers about working-class youths who were thought to be at the most risk of criminality and degeneration. Regulating young people's leisure time had, by the 1900s, become seen as essential to the benefit of society, leading to an 'institutionalisation of leisure' at this time.[69] The issue appeared to be as much of a problem in the 1940s as in the 1900s. Young women's leisure, most of all, was perceived as needing intervention to prevent undesirable, even socially destabilising, outcomes.

Fitzrovia's reputation as a moral minefield naturally intensified adult fears about children's welfare. Local children, especially girls, could not be guarded too carefully against the perceived dangers of life on the Other Side of Oxford Street. The Reverend Walters describes Fitzrovia's 'grave and difficult problems', such as 'intemperance, and the infamous traffic in social vice' in the West London Mission's annual report of 1900–01. The journalist Robert Machray, in *The Night Side of London*, details these vices in 'A "Night Club"'. He describes a 'members' establishment 'somewhere off Tottenham Court Road', where a man can join on the night for a guinea on a false name and enjoy music, dancing, (expensive) drinks and meeting young women.[70] These women are 'the lures which draw men to the club', though at the same time they all behave 'with the utmost quietness and propriety', looking 'rather dull and more than a trifle bored', according to Machray.[71] There must have been many places in the vicinity where sex was quietly sold. One of the illustrations in 'A "Night Club"' is supposedly a caricature of the owner showing grossly exaggerated Semitic features: an anti-Jewish, anti-immigrant jab reinforcing Fitzrovia's 'low' reputation.

The Wesleyan West London Mission, based in Cleveland Hall in Cleveland Street, ran girls' and boys' clubs from the late 1880s onwards. These clubs aimed to 'influence those who are growing to womanhood and manhood' and to create 'a home of innocent enjoyment and social life', according to their annual reports for 1900 and 1901. The girls' club's first organiser, Mary Neal, also hoped that the clubs would be 'living schools for working women, who will be instrumental in the near future, in altering the conditions of the class they represent'.[72] Their teenaged members almost all left school at 14 with no more than an elementary education, and the clubs provided much-needed further education as well as recreation. We can see from Neal's words that the clubs were often actively working to supplement, even to replace, working-class young people's domestic influences with those the organisers considered to be more suitable – more orderly, as well as culturally richer. Charles Booth extolled the reach of the West London Mission, saying, 'Its expansion has been astonishing, and its success, at least in West London, triumphant and wonderful'.[73]

The Christian clubs were not the only ones in Fitzrovia. In a building in Fitzroy Street formerly housing a dubious nightclub, as the result of an act of moral regeneration, the West Central Jewish Lads' Club came into being.[74] It was founded in 1898, but by 1900 had outgrown its premises and moved around the corner to 38 Fitzroy Square. This new building was bought for the club's use and granted free of rent by Mrs Nathaniel Montefiore, one of the leading members of a famously philanthropic Jewish family. Girls could attend the West Central Jewish Girls' Club, entirely separately run and headed by Lily Montagu. The girls' club began in 1893 in Dean Street, Soho, but moved to Alfred Place, just east of Tottenham Court Road in Bloomsbury, in 1913.

The Jewish clubs had an additional purpose to the Christian ones: to help Anglicise first- and second-generation Jewish immigrant children and young adults and socialise them into the 'British way of life', by exposing them to national cultural norms and activities, particularly sports in the case of boys.

The Jewish clubs, especially the girls' club, were also outstanding in providing educational activities that would improve young people's general development and job opportunities.

Membership of the Jewish Lads' Club, to begin with, was around eighty boys, growing rapidly during the first decade of the twentieth century to reach about 250 and remaining high during the 1930s and 1940s. The West Central Jewish Girls' Club was just as popular and it was the largest club for Jewish girls to operate prior to the Second World War.

The jazz musician Benny Green, a local boy who joined the Jewish Lads' Club, said when interviewed in 1993, 'The people who ran the boy's club had a profound effect on me – profound'.[75] Alec Flinder called the Jewish Lads' Club the 'great influence of my life', and for Max Minkoff it was 'the greatest joy of my life ... I used to go any minute I could'.[76]

Green, Minkoff and Flinder, in the 1930s and 1940s, were among the second-generation immigrant Jewish cohorts who grew up under the club's influence. Flinder describes a night at the club:

> [Y]ou would pay your subscription which I think was twopence or three-pence for the week ... you would go in and if you felt like a nosh you could get a hot dog, a kosher hot dog, in a roll at the bar, with a cup of lemon tea. Then you would go and play table tennis ... and we were one of the top teams ... Two table tennis rooms on the first floor. In the basement there were two billiard tables ... or you could go to the gym, there would be gymnastics going on, or hand ball. ... On certain evenings there would be small bore shooting going on in the main hall, that was an evening activity. If you were engaged in a particular activity such as drama there would be rehearsals going on, or there would be ... political discussions.[77]

Benny Green, whose secondary education was disrupted by the Second World War, felt that any education he received took place at the Jewish Boys' Club.

> I learnt to speak in public there, I played the saxophone before an audience for the 1st [*sic*] time in my life there. ... I learnt a bit of civic responsibility – you know I took the minutes of the meetings at the Club and I became the editor of the Club Magazine ... [78]

Green makes it clear that the managers of the club, some only in their twenties and often ex-members, 'delegated a huge amount of responsibility to the boys and that was where we learned a great deal'. From early on, boys could be elected members on management committees. They could serve on the Games Committee, then later they were able to join the General Purposes Committee so that they had a say in much of the club's daily running.

With the use of a library of several hundred volumes, plus journals and newspapers, and regular debates, talks and lectures, club members could develop themselves in ways that most of their families could not have imagined. Boys had to leave at the age of 19, but in 1905 the club established a Jewish Men's Club to cater for those who wished to continue with the club experience. Substantial numbers of club members appeared to wish to do so: the annual report for 1910 stated, 'Nearly all members on leaving join the Men's Club, and the healthy influence is continued in the allied Institution'.

Fitzrovia's Wesleyan Mission clubs for girls and boys also manifested a strong educational purpose, revealed in one member's account of a typical week at the Cleveland Hall Girls' Club:

> On Monday evenings we have a deportment class ... We also have a musical drilling class on Tuesday evenings ... Some of the girls go to the University Extension lectures at Craven Hall [in Foubert's Place, off Regent Street] on Thursday evenings ... On Saturday afternoons Miss Brooke is taking four of the girls for six weeks running, to the National Picture Gallery, and Miss Halliday takes some others to the Wallace Collection ... Then we have an art needlework class on Saturday evenings, where Miss Hawley teaches us all sorts of fancy work.[79]

Evidently, far more was being attempted here than simply keeping girls and young women off the streets by occupying their time. This member touchingly says, 'All day long we try to put into practice some of the things we learn at the club', making it clear that, at least for some of the girls, spiritual development and educational development were going hand in hand.[80]

At the Jewish Girls' Club there was an especially strong emphasis on education. It had a semi-formal alliance with local schools, whereby Lily Montagu was informed of recent school leavers so that she and her sister could visit potential club members at home and talk to them and their families.[81] Montagu speaks of a 'syllabus' of classes and activities at her club, spanning domestic science, technical training classes for various trades, art, music and drama classes, literature, languages and public affairs, and university tutorial classes – as well as physical training.[82] The club received support from schoolteachers who came in to deliver this syllabus. It seems that in many respects the club operated like a college of further education. Lily Montagu stresses the importance of her girls being able to receive and appreciate new ideas, evidently valuing the cultivation of independence of thought.

Montagu's own thinking was sometimes well ahead of her time. She championed sex education within the clubs, inviting lecturers to tackle this topic and allowing 'unrestricted questions', as she puts it, afterwards.[83] She regarded this as a moral imperative, stating that she tried to ensure that her lecturers approached the subject from a religious as well as a medical standpoint. As an ideal, she favoured sex instruction given in the home by mothers from a very young age, so that '[t]he child is thus saved from associating with the beginning of life anything sordid or unclean'.[84] It is fairly safe to infer that these lectures did not extend as far as contraception: even though Marie Stopes' work on contraception had begun in the 1920s, knowledge regarding this matter was firmly confined to married women for several decades afterwards. We can see how the club lectures would fit into a wider programme of reducing the social risks associated with young working women's social activities, by providing the guidance believed to be lacking in their homes.

At the Jewish Lads' Club there was little in the way of formal classes. Annual reports often noted the club policy of not trying to replicate the evening classes given by educational institutions in which, they said, many members participated. Instead, emphasis was put on sports and games as a means of development for boys and young men, with cricket and football teams, swimming, gymnastics and drill, boxing and shooting, as well as billiards, table tennis, chess and draughts.

The club regularly took part in competitions run by the Federation of London Working Boys' Clubs, the Jewish Football League and the Jewish Athletics Association. Club teams often did well in cricket and gymnastics. The belief was that, through sports and games above all, the sons of immigrant families could assimilate British values and further the integration of their families into their host culture.

Military training was thought to be another important component of British manliness. The Jewish Lads' Brigade, formed in the 1890s, held weekly drilling sessions at the club and attracted a good number of members. Close by, at Cleveland Hall, the West London Mission ran both boys' and girls' brigades 'where physical drill is taught and a knowledge of ambulance work is given', according to the 1905 Annual Report.

The public school ethos of building character through sport influenced the whole youth movement, with its focus on working-class youth. David Dee says, in his essay on physical recreation and the Jewish Youth Movement, 'The idea that playing sports would help in both the moral improvement of the young boys and girls and in the maintenance of class stability was ubiqui-tous'.[85] The Jewish Lads' Club also adopted the public school house system, on which its internal sports competitions were based, with each of the four houses named after Jewish notables, including, of course, Montefiore. There were club rules specifically banning gambling and the selling of goods on the premises, with immediate expulsion for rule breakers.

The provision of ample sports facilities within the clubs was perhaps also necessary to deter sports-inclined boys from taking up other, less strictly super-vised, activities available in the locality. A stone's throw away from the Jewish Lads' Club, in Fitzroy Street, was the Olympic Gym run by William Klein, specialising in boxing, wrestling and weightlifting and attracting major figures in boxing such as Primo Carnera. A *Picture Post* article by Denzil Batchelor, dated 18 November 1950, trades on Fitzrovia's shady reputation by tying the gym to the adjacent Warren Street used car market, making it an extension of the area's supposed low life. Batchelor's piece is titled 'Straight out of Runyon', evoking the American writer of gangster novels, and Batchelor claims to have been bought lunch by 'Joe the Greek'. The illustrations to the article promi-nently feature black fighters, unsubtly raising similar racial stereotypes to the portrayals of the black male dancers at the Paramount. It's unlikely that boxing at the Jewish Lads' Club had anything to do with the Olympic Gym on its doorstep, given the club organisers' preoccupation with 'respectability'.

Perhaps due to the Anglicising aspect of the Jewish Lads' Club, or simply as a recognition of the spiritual limitations of teenage boys, there was little if any emphasis on the Jewish religion. Neither the annual reports nor the club rules show a religious role for the club, and later attendees such as Flinder and Green testify to the minimal role of religion there. Benny Green does claim that there were brief prayers in English at the end of the evening, though sketchy enough for him to call them 'a farce'. Alec Flinder denies the existence of prayers there altogether, except for a Sabbath service at the boys' annual summer camp.

At the Jewish Girls' Club, faith played a much stronger role. However, ser-vices were unorthodox in focusing on individualised prayers reflecting the girls' own circumstances rather than the formulaic prayers of Orthodox Judaism. Lily Montagu's liberal Judaism was influenced by individualist Protestantism in this respect. Compulsory prayers were held at the end of every evening session, with additional Sabbath services. The club's motto was, 'If I strive not after my own salvation, who shall strive for me, and if not now, when?' Anne Holdorph argues that, at the Jewish Girls' Club, the expression of a liberal Jewish faith allied to Protestant Christian traditions was 'to encourage the members … to adapt to more English behaviours' – part of the overall Anglicisation project, in other words. It differed from the Jewish Lads' Club, in which sports rather than religion was the favoured method of socialisation.[86]

There were collaborations between the Jewish Lads' and Girls' Club members, such as joint dramatic performances, the co-running of the annual Lads' Club Children's Tea Party and, later, dances. This led to some engagements and marriages. Trudie Flinder met Alec Flinder at a club dance, and Alec says, 'There were lots of marriages sprung from the girls club and the boys club'.[87]

Lily Montagu was very much in favour of her girls engaging in mixed activities at the club, as well as their being able to invite parentally vetted young men to join their summer trips away from London. She believed that giving her girls the freedom to meet their young men in a socially sanctioned situation was far preferable to their meeting unknown suitors outside. She must have thought that Fitzrovia, with cafes, cinemas and dance halls on its doorstep, was an ever-present source of 'unsuitable' liberties for young people. Even Lyons' Corner House, respectable though it was, gave youthful customers the freedom to meet each other discreetly. The older Jewish Girls' Club members were much more likely to be thinking of forming engagements than their male counterparts of the same age, so providing a means of meeting suitable Jewish boys seems to have been more of a preoccupation for the girls' club than the lads' club.[88]

The clubs' educational and social integration projects seem to have borne fruit with at least some of their members. Of the interviewees who attended the Jewish clubs, Laura Philips became a dress designer, while Alec Flinder studied architecture. Trudie Flinder credits the girls' club, as well as a supportive headmaster, with arranging the training that enabled her to become a secretary rather than work in her father's tailoring workshop.

For all the good work of the clubs, it must surely have been true that Fitzrovia itself, on the frontier of both Bloomsbury and the West End, was crucial in helping to shape some of these young people's identities and futures. A short walk could lead curious working-class children to a national cultural treasure house of museums, galleries and entertainment halls – and department stores, too, were full of cultural riches. Alec Flinder makes the point that, for those whose Orthodoxy hadn't sealed their cultural horizons, Fitzrovia's proximity to the West End was a formative influence: 'I found that living in the West End cheek and jowl with the British Museum, for example, was a wonderful thing. To be able to go along just to walk into places like that and the Queens Hall …'.[89]

Just by crossing Tottenham Court Road a child like my mother, who lived in Howland Street, could see the British Museum with its vast treasury of artefacts. Hardly anywhere else in London could a working-class child be so close to experiences that might be life changing.

Cultural Crossings in Fitzrovia

The Other Side of Oxford Street at the dawn of the twentieth century was an experimental space for the new entertainment industries. For workers and their children with a few pennies to spend, it offered innovative mechanical entertainments, and the magic of the cinema. Charles Urban made the Scala Theatre the home of new cinematic techniques and spectacle; just one of Fitzrovia's versatile venues that were receptive to constant changes in technology and public taste and accepted these transformations in the same spirit as did Fitzrovia itself. At this time, one can see the synergy between Fitzrovia's immigrants and the new entertainment media, particularly when it came to film exhibition and associated industries.

By the 1930s, there was another social nexus in Tottenham Court Road: the massive Lyons' Corner House that replaced the Oxford Music Hall. This new Fitzrovia hub of social life and leisure opportunities for people of limited means was almost entirely established by Jewish immigrants to London. It was a social change that enriched not just local lives but other lives far beyond Fitzrovia. Lyons' Corner House and its place in the social life of Fitzrovia will be covered in the next and final chapter, on eating out.

The immigrant generations growing up in Fitzrovia in the first half of the twentieth century embodied the transition between being an alien and becoming British. In their separate ways, the young people's clubs and the cinema were both indispensable to making this transition: they both seeded ideas of Britishness in young minds. And, in both these arenas, Fitzrovia's immigrants were often not just the main audience for but also the main purveyors of these messages about Britishness. Just as importantly for Fitzrovia's children, to live on the Other Side of Oxford Street was to be exposed to a world of cultural glories. But even Fitzrovia's spell could only reach so far. Some, perhaps many, in Fitzrovia didn't make that vital cultural crossing. My mother was one of those who did not: she never in her life visited the British Museum.

From Fried Fish to Lyons' Corner House: Eating Out in Fitzrovia

More than anything else, the convivial pubs and cafes on the Other Side of Oxford Street created the idea of 'Fitzrovia'. These local eating and drinking places, from the 1920s onwards, drew writers, artists and socialites looking for 'their' geographical and cultural niche within the city. But how do we square this 'Fitzrovia Set' image with the culinary experience of most of the area's residents and workers? This chapter will try to capture the flavour of eating out on the Other Side of Oxford Street for local working people to whom the Bohemian 'Fitzrovians' were all but invisible.

Even before the 1900s boom in London's restaurant and cafe culture, Fitzrovia's small, local, often family-run restaurants were within the means of at least some working people. The almost exclusively foreign-owned eating places in Charlotte Street began by serving their own communities of workers rather than catering for middle-class English customers as did the West End restaurants. The first and second-generation immigrant owners and cooks running these local businesses influenced the cafe and restaurant dining experience. Fitzrovia's enduring ability to attract and welcome outsiders was central to the vital activity of eating out in London.

There were very few eating places in the grand style in Fitzrovia: wealthy customers visiting central London normally ate in the first-class hotels and restaurants of Mayfair, Piccadilly and the Strand. Many local workers never even used cafes and restaurants. Instead, they bought their lunches and dinners from pubs where they could pick up a sandwich with their beer, or cooked-food shops selling pies and fried fish, or street sellers hawking a range of takeaway items.

For many working people in Fitzrovia, as elsewhere in London, eating out meant eating in the street. And eating out, whether in the street or in cafes and restaurants, was shaped by immigration. This chapter will explore all the different ways in which the ordinary working residents of Fitzrovia habitually ate out, and how this activity – often as basic as buying an ice cream or eating fish and chips in the street – changed during the first half of the twentieth century under the impact of the new arrivals to London.

We'll also investigate one more side of eating out on the Other Side of Oxford Street: the experiences and contributions of its many restaurant and hotel workers. They were mostly foreign workers, coming predominantly from a small group of West European countries. The major nationalities were German, Austrian, Swiss, Italian and French. Catering was a leading occupation in Fitzrovia and its catering workers clustered together closely, since working long and irregular hours meant having to lodge near to where they worked.

The buildings in and around Charlotte Street were full of waiters and chefs. What was these workers' experience of the growing social custom of eating out in this neighbourhood? And how did a largely peripatetic immigrant workforce impact on the local industry?

Fitzrovia's catering workforce would have flowed back and forth over Oxford Street as waiters and chefs circulated around the eating establishments of Soho, and as the Soho workers found cheaper accommodation in Fitzrovia. This circulatory pattern echoed the wider role played by the circulation of catering workers around Europe and into central London. We'll see if this flow between Europe and London and around the West End brought about any changes in eating out that specifically affected the industry in Fitzrovia. But first we'll consider eating out at its cheapest and most essential: the provision and consumption of food bought – and often eaten – on the street.

Street Food

By the turn of the twentieth century, street food was abundant in Fitzrovia, a locale situated next to the shops, meeting places and theatres of the West End. Eating choice had greatly expanded over the previous century or so. Henry Mayhew gives us ample detail of what street food was available to hungry nineteenth-century Londoners in the way of pies, cakes and pastries, sandwiches, fried fish and baked potatoes, confectionary, ice cream, coffee and ginger beer.

Sandwiches were often sold in pubs or outside theatres and concert rooms: Mayhew calculates that 436,800 sandwiches a day were being sold in this way around 1861. Baked potatoes were another popular item, sold warm from a can on four legs, containing a hot water compartment and poised above an iron fire pot. Bakers' shops commonly sold pastries, buns and other snacks which often took the place of a meal for poorer customers. And pies sold in the street were a draw for hungry people – featuring meat, eels or seasonal fruit, they were baked in large batches and distributed to the sellers.

Market stalls sold snacks as well as fruit and vegetables, raw meat, fish and other items for home cooking. Great Titchfield Street was the site of a large and busy market, where resident Winifred Ekpenyon's father worked:

> My father was a costermonger, he had a fruit stall and he had to be at Covent Garden for 3 o'clock in the morning. While he was gone we children got up at 6 o'clock, cleaned the brass for the stall and took it to Great Titchfield Street market before we went to school. He would meet us there and we would help to take the stuff from the cart so that he could sort it out and put it on the stall. Great Titchfield Street market used to be from Langham Street to Oxford Street ... I also used to go on Saturdays and work on the stall to help my father out. I used to put the grass out on the stall and then lay the fruit out and then when the customers came I would serve them. I liked this very much.[1]

By the end of the nineteenth century the press was reporting an increase in the sale of cooked food from small shops and markets like Great Titchfield Street. Some food flavours were foreign: German bakers were already becoming a feature of London life, and big developments in Fitzrovia's German baking and bread-making businesses occurred after 1900.

German bakers were sprinkled about the locality by 1910. Charles Schneider's bakery occupied premises at 33 Tottenham Court Road, and Vandenhaute's was at 33 Charlotte Street. Zoller's bakery was one of two in Cleveland Street at the same time.

Charlotte Street was a home from home for German workers and business owners. According to Panikos Panayi, forty German names were attached to businesses there by 1913. Ten businesses in Charlotte Street were connected with food: 'Two butchers, four restaurants, one baker and three foreign provision dealers'.[2] As well as this, by 1913 there were food manufacturers of German origin, including W. Bedbur of Portland Street, whose businesses were a German mustard factory, delicatessen and wine factory.

Journalists sometimes connected the food bought on the street with a reprehensible decline in home cooking and lowered standards generally. In a trip to one of the poorer working neighbourhoods of London on 20 January 1888, a *Standard* reporter found bountiful and cheap food available in the street markets. However, the reporter disapproved of poorer working people spending comparatively scarce resources on choice cuts of meat and, especially, on prepared food which, he argued, was less nutritious as well as causing housewives to go 'from bad to worse from having less to do'. Mothers, he complained, drawing authority from the opinions of a local law officer, were too lazy to prepare healthy meals for the children, 'An experienced police inspector, with whom we have some talk, tells us that he knows the case of a woman who often gives her children tinned lobster (7½d. the tin) and bread and butter for dinner because she does not care about the bother of cooking'. 'What will the future of the London poor be ... fed on makeshift meals or prepared salted meats, cheap pickles, cheap sweetstuffs, and abominable cakes and pastry?' demanded the reporter, laying the blame where he felt it was due, 'On all sides the story is that "It's all the fault of the mothers and the cooked-food shops only encourage them in their laziness"'.

It was only after this burst of moral indignation that the journalist uncovered a leading cause of this female shiftlessness: the women, rather than having worked in domestic service – as the majority of London working women did in earlier generations – were now choosing to be 'bookbinders, boot closers, label pasters, and such like ... girls who have been used to "their liberty"'. These women presumably wanted and needed the higher wages and greater personal freedom offered by these widened working options. There were many women working in such occupations in Fitzrovia by the end of the nineteenth century, as well as in dressmaking and other clothing trades. These working women, according to the writer, had missed the 'home training' that would have given them cooking and household management skills. Like their social betters, for better or worse, they were exercising choice about how and what to eat.

Adulteration and poor hygiene seem to have been common in many street food trades, as well as in shops and dairies. Ice-cream selling came under scrutiny, with periodic alarms about its hygiene raised in medical reports and the press, often greatly heightened by prejudice against the sellers who were almost always Italians. *The Lancet*, in an October 1879 report on housing conditions in the Italian Quarter of Clerkenwell, reported:

> the milk, the eggs, the cornflour mixtures, etc., used to make the penny ices, are left standing in the foulest dens, where they must absorb the noxious gases that infect the atmosphere, and where they are boiled and mixed in the same saucepans and cauldrons in which the Italians scald and wash their dirty

linen! It is to be hoped that the freezing process may kill the germs of disease
… but the idea is not appetizing, and the prospect somewhat uncertain.[3]

Legislation came from the 1870s with the Sale of Food & Drugs Acts and was
progressively tightened after 1900. The local boroughs became responsible for
enforcing laws on the production, storage and sale of food after the London
Government Act of 1899. They had powers to inspect premises for cleanliness
and to test samples of food and drink for adulteration and contamination. Not
only shops and cafes were inspected but street stalls and markets, cowsheds and
slaughterhouses. Within thirty or forty years the inspectors' increasing powers
had largely eliminated food contamination.

The MOHs of St Pancras and St Marylebone, the authorities covering
Fitzrovia, were active in enforcing the regulations. The St Marylebone MOH
Report of 1910 details the lengths gone to by inspectors in surveying a street
vendor spotted in Foley Street, who was claiming to sell 'pasteurised' milk
when the milk was in fact heavily contaminated. After inspectors followed
the vendor around his beat for several days the milk was tested and seized,
and proceedings were taken against the vendor, who stopped selling milk.
The number of cowsheds in the neighbourhood was small, and declining, but
even in 1930 there was a functioning cowshed in Fitzrovia, with ten cows, at
42a Clipstone Street.

A favoured hot street drink among London's working people was coffee.
At a penny a full mug and a ha'penny a half mug it was always in demand and
with more than 300 coffee vendors in the city it must have been readily available north of Oxford Street. In fact, according to Mayhew, the best pitch in
London was nearby on Oxford Street at the corner with Duke Street.[4] Coffee
stalls also sold snacks, tobacco and cigarettes. Vendors could make 30s in a
morning, and sometimes sold late into the night for those still out on the town
and very early in the mornings for people on their way to work.

However, adulterated coffee was pretty much the rule at coffee stalls, if
Mayhew is to be believed, although the drink was still a welcome refreshment to many customers. The street sellers' coffee was often adulterated with
chicory: a plant of the dandelion family whose root, baked and ground, was
often added to make it go further.

Coffee was one of the products to be brought under the scrutiny of the
borough MOHs. The inspectors' efforts were reported at length by the conscientious MOHs of St Pancras and Marylebone under whose aegis Fitzrovia
came. Their reports during the early decades of the twentieth century show
that dry goods such as sugar and cocoa – and coffee – were frequently adulter-

ated. In 1911, a St Pancras inspector reported that a sugar sample proved to be largely made up of unidentified 'dyed crystals'.

However, milk posed the biggest hygiene risk, along with other dairy products and lard. Unclean storage conditions and adulteration were both a big problem. Milk was often watered down, sometimes with dirty water, and butter and lard might have other fats added to it. Law breakers were sent to court and fined, although the St Pancras reports sometimes expressed frustration at fines being far too low to deter offenders.

Milk hygiene became an even greater concern in these reports after the final report of the Royal Commission on Tuberculosis in 1911. The commission's report found links between the disease in cattle and human beings. Alarmingly, it concluded that 'there can be no doubt that a considerable proportion of the tuberculosis affecting children is of bovine origin' and transmitted through drinking milk.[5] Understandably, from 1911 much of the focus is on milk in the food hygiene sections of the local MOH reports, with copious testing and record-keeping taking place. St Pancras inspectors in both 1911 and 1921 complained of low standards, and small shopkeepers selling milk being heedless of possible health risks and resentful of officials intruding.[6]

Things radically improved after tuberculin-tested and pasteurised milks became available. Acts were passed in 1922 and 1923 introducing a licensing system for milk producers and sellers of these grades of milk. One of these licensed dairies was Richards' Dairy at 161 Whitfield Street selling 'Grade A Tuberculin tested' milk. By 1931 there were dozens of such dairies throughout the Borough of St Pancras. By the time of the 1951 St Pancras MOH report, all dairies had to sell graded milk – and not one milk sample was found to be adulterated.

Coffee Rooms and the Temperance Movement

For working people who couldn't afford to eat at the neighbourhood cafes and small restaurants but wanted something other than street food, the working men's clubs were a handy alternative. Many clubs offered tired working men an evening meal, coffee and somewhere to socialise, and prices were modest. One such place was the local Communist Working Men's Club or *Verein*, which furnished its members with food and drink. Some clubs and agencies for immigrants also provided soup kitchens for those in need, as we saw in Chapter 1, and young working-age people who belonged to boys' and girls' clubs, such as the Jewish Lads' Club in Fitzroy

Square, could satisfy their hunger there on hearty snacks. The Jewish Lads'
Club branched out into kosher hot dogs, although this was probably a later
twentieth-century development.

The spread of coffee rooms for working men (women didn't enter them,
except as waitresses) had started to develop poorer people's options for eating
out. It was an innovation which was clearly visible north of Oxford Street,
where, by the end of the nineteenth century, coffee rooms were compet-
ing with the local pubs. Coffee houses had, of course, existed for centuries,
although coffee drinking of this nature had been associated with much more
affluent and socially powerful classes of customer. Coffee house culture at its
eighteenth-century peak was the creation of those who influenced the intellectual and political developments of their age and those who were in their
orbit. This form of coffee-drinking environment was on its way out during
the nineteenth century.

However, from the mid-nineteenth century onwards, coffee houses offering
plain meals and snacks as well as coffee had opened to cater for working men.
With taxes on coffee decreasing and the drink becoming more affordable,
there were about 1,600–1,800 such establishments in London by 1843, according to the statistician G.R. Porter.[7] The Victorian Temperance Movement had
sensed an opportunity, with the coffee rooms, to take custom away from the
pubs that were still many workers' house of resort. Some coffee rooms offered
newspapers and magazines, a bit like the older-style coffee houses, and some
were regular venues of radical clubs such as the Chartists.

According to one proprietor, quoted by Porter:

> A few years ago it used to be almost a matter of ridicule amongst working
> men to drink coffee; now they hold up to emulate each other. I believe that
> not one-third of my customers ever goes into a public-house at all. I have
> never heard an indecent expression, and, with two exceptions, have never
> seen a drunken man in my house [*The Progress of the Nation* ..., 246–47].[8]

The first Temperance coffee room in London, one of a chain of British
Workman Public Houses, opened in 1873 in Limehouse. Then the People's
Café Company, founded in 1874, opened a branch in Drummond Street near
Euston Station – just across Euston Road from Fitzrovia – to cater for railway
employees. By 1879 there were 100 establishments like these in the city, usually
designed in the familiar public house style.

The impact of the Temperance coffee house movement can clearly be seen
in Fitzrovia, although according to Clayton the movement was already on the

wane by the 1890s. The *Post Office Directory* for 1899 shows five businesses described as coffee rooms in Tottenham Court Road, mostly clustered near the Oxford Street end, near the busiest shopping areas. Charlotte Street possessed, in addition, a Temperance Hotel which was a teetotal version of an inn, providing accommodation and function rooms, as well as refreshment. The hotel in Charlotte Street was one of several Temperance hotels within walking distance: they were also to be found in Cardington Street, St Pancras, conveniently positioned just beside Euston Station, in Guilford Street off Russell Square, and Southampton Row, Holborn. Charlotte Street's Temperance Hotel must have posed a sharp contrast to the more hedonistic places of refreshment that crowded around it. It was, however, short-lived – listed at No. 7 in 1910, by 1920 it had vanished, replaced by a clothier's.

The coffee rooms provided some form of counter-refreshment to Tottenham Court Road's thirteen pubs. Lockhart's Cocoa Rooms at 113 Tottenham Court Road was another such initiative, reflecting the rising popularity of cocoa and its co-option as an instrument of the Temperance Movement. In fact, the main cocoa manufacturers such as Cadbury, Fry and Rowntree were all Quaker reformers and dedicated to temperance. The Cocoa Rooms in Tottenham Court Road, with Lockhart's distinctive white and blue china crockery, was part of a chain set up by Robert Lockhart, who typically opened his premises right next door to a pub. He didn't quite manage to do that in Tottenham Court Road, as the Cocoa Rooms at No. 113 were a few doors down from the Roebuck Public House.

Cocoa was more expensive than coffee at 4*d* a cup, and was also offered at many of the coffee houses. The cocoa rooms also sold meals at just a few pence, eventually resulting in pub owners feeling the need to compete by providing sandwiches, and sometimes also hot food such as sausages and mash, to hungry working men. Charles Booth praised the cocoa rooms in 1903, contrasting them favourably with the coffee rooms, although the heyday of the cocoa rooms, too, was probably already over.

The coffee rooms failed to thrive in the longer term, however benevolent the intentions of their Temperance Movement founders. Too many, it seems, were spartan, dreary places that couldn't continue to attract customers, particularly when other choices of inexpensive eating place were appearing. The journalist George R. Sims, writing in 1921, described the then-vanished coffee shops:

> They were mostly dingy places with high-backed boxes and a slip-shod waiter or an untidy handy girl to attend to your wants.

You might sit in a time-worn, boxed-in compartment, and under a dim gas jet take your cup of tea – it was generally served slopped over into the saucer – and have your hot buttered toast or your muffin, if your means would allow, and glance at a greasy magazine or periodical that had as great a variety of thumb marks as the Scotland Yard collection.

In some of the coffee shops in the mid-day hours you could get a chop and potatoes, but as a rule the menu was limited to eggs and bacon and the humble bloater.[9]

However, some local coffee rooms hung on even into the 1950s. Fulstone Moore's coffee rooms were a solid presence at 103 Cleveland Street throughout the first half of the twentieth century, while numerous other local eating places came and went.

But the glory days of coffee rooms were done. In place of the coffee and cocoa rooms came tea rooms, as public tea drinking gained in popularity. By the 1880s, the Aerated Bread Company (ABC) had opened a chain of tea shops in London. The ABC and other chains, such as Pearce & Plenty, were challenging and ousting the old coffee rooms, with raised standards of provision and service aiding the transition, although the tea shops were aimed more at serving white collar than manual workers. By 1921, George R. Sims, writing for the *Daily Mail*, was evoking the charms of what had then become the national institution of teatime:

To-day the tea habit is common to all classes of the community. It is as popular in the private apartments of palaces as it is in the common kitchen of a licensed lodging-house.

The tea hour is part of the British Constitution. It is a fashionable function. It is an important part of the programme of pleasure. Work is suspended for it and it has its place in the National game. Middlesex may be in danger, Surrey may be at the point of collapse, but in the 5.30 edition of the evening papers you may find in the stop-press news, 'Middlesex 100 for 4. Tea'.[10]

There was a steady move in Fitzrovia, typical of many other parts of London, away from pubs being the most important refreshment places, with the number of pubs showing a significant fall as the century progressed while other refreshment outlets increased. Whether the Temperance Movement alone should be credited for this change is doubtful. Perhaps greater importance should be placed on the growing need to cater for women in a locality where, by 1900, thousands of women were not only going shopping but also working in shops, offices and local industries like the clothing industry. Pubs had been almost exclusively male environments, so catering businesses profited by recognising women's place in the worlds of work and leisure.

The 'Bohemian' Cafe

The options for eating out in Fitzrovia broadened considerably between 1900 and 1930. At the poshest end of the local scale was Pagani's Restaurant in Great Portland Street, which had opened as early as 1871. It earned a top-flight reputation, aided by its tiny Artists' Room upstairs. Special guests were encouraged to put their signatures and messages on the wallpaper: Sarah Bernhardt, Lillie Langtry, Caruso, Tchaikovsky, Puccini and Oscar Wilde did so, to name but a few. Pagani's would have been beyond the pockets of most residents but attracted more affluent customers from across the city, of the kind who also ate at first-class West End restaurants. Panayi notes, 'The menu at Pagani's essentially consisted of Continental haute cuisine, indicated largely by the fact that this restaurant, like other high-class establishments in central London, offered French menus.'[11] The owner of Pagani's was Italian, but the restaurant did not serve Italian food: according to Panayi, there was no distinct Italian cuisine offered to restaurant customers at this time.

For the majority who couldn't afford Pagani's, Charlotte Street was already gaining its reputation as a centre for eating out. Schmidt's, at 33–43 Charlotte Street, opened in 1901 as a sausage shop but soon became a restaurant and gathering place for Fitzrovia's large German community at a time when Charlotte Street was known as *Charlottenstrasse*. Schmidt's lasted until 1975. L'Etoile Restaurant, run by Frank Rossi, opened in 1906 at 30 Charlotte Street, and also lasted for decades.

Bertorelli's Ice Cream Palace opened in 1912, in Charlotte Street, although its specialties were beyond the pockets of many locals. However, local children who couldn't afford to visit Bertorelli's went to other, more affordable places for delicious ice cream. Sam Lomberg, a local child in the 1920s, reminisces:

> I promise you, you'll never ever taste anything as good as Freedman's ice cream. Abie Freedman's shop was … in Cleveland Street, he made the ice cream himself and during the summer months there would always be a queue outside his shop. I don't know when the shop closed, but sorry to say it wasn't there when I came home after the war.[12]

Charlotte Street's cafes and restaurants thrived and increased in number during the 1910s and 1920s. In 1910, the street had six restaurants and a coffee room listed, mostly owned by foreign restaurateurs: Gustav Kleinschmager at No. 31, Charles Rössler at No. 59, John Losenegger at No. 93, Joseph Mauker at No. 12, and Frank Rossi at No. 30, owner of L'Etoile Restaurant. These restaurants tended to be small enterprises whose customers were predominantly from Fitzrovia's large communities of Germans, Austrians, Swiss, French and Italians, and tended to be artisans and manual workers. Thomas Burke summons up the unpretentious atmosphere of these smaller cafes when describing Soho's eating spots in *Nights in Town* (1915) – as we know, at that time 'Soho' was an inclusive label that could cover both sides of Oxford Street:

> The atmosphere of the cheaper places is … distinctly more companionable … in the smaller places, which are supported by a regular clientele of the French clerks, workmen, and warehouse porters who are employed in and about Oxford Street, the sense of camaraderie and naturalness is very strong. These people are not doing anything extraordinary. They are just having dinner, and they are gay and *insouciant* about it, as they are about everything except frivolity. It is not exciting for them to dine on five courses instead of on roast mutton and vegetables and milk-pudding. It is a common-place.[13]

It seems that these places didn't change very much over time. Writing of Schmidt's Restaurant in a later book, *Dinner is Served* (1937), Burke says:

> The German place, Schmidt's, is known to all London Germans, and visited by most German tourists. Schmidt's gives you German family cooking, and family cooking, in most parts of Europe, is pretty good. Its prices are quite modest. Its *hors d'oeuvre* are interesting, and its other general dishes are various *goulasches*; goose, of course; venison; innumerable kinds of sausage; *Sauerkraut*; unusual cheeses; and Viennese pastries.[14]

By 1920, the number of eating places in Charlotte Street had increased to nine, with innovations being a cooked meat shop run by Edith Stern and a coffee bar branded as Café-Bars Conté Ltd – this is an early mention of the 'coffee bar'. Sam Lomberg had fond memories of this cafe:

> One of my very special treats was when my dad took me to the Café Conté on the corner of Charlotte Street and Goodge Street – Café Conté looked just like (and smelled like) a typical French cafe. The owner was French and

so were most of his regular customers. They would sit there sipping a Pernod or drinking coffee and dunking their croissants, while playing dominoes, chess or draughts. Dad loved going there on Sunday mornings – it reminded him of his days in Paris. I have yet to drink coffee or eat croissants, which taste as good as Café Conté's.[15]

Sam Lomberg's recollections again suggest that these small cafes existed to serve the local foreign communities rather than being tourist spots.

A few eating places have gone down in history, permanently connected with the Bohemian crowd of writers and artists who later became labelled the Fitzrovians. The Eiffel Tower Restaurant at 1 Percy Street, one of Fitzrovia's posher dining places, was notably patronised by artists and intellectuals, including the Vorticists, from the time of the First World War. Hugh David stresses the outlandishness of visiting Fitzrovia at this time, 'Despite the almost exotic remoteness of Percy Street and Fitzroy Square ... the more adventurous were already discovering it ... They began sloping off to the Eiffel Tower restaurant ...'[16]

Through the 1920s the Eiffel Tower was a favourite among a set that included the writer Michael Arlen, the artist Nina Hamnett, and the socialite Nancy Cunard, who in 1923 wrote a poem entitled, 'To the Eiffel Tower Restaurant'. Cunard romanticises the Eiffel Tower's foreignness, the 'wits and glamour, strong wines, new foods, fine looks/strange-sounding languages of diverse men ...'.[17] Cunard's words conjure up the sense of adventure that socialites must have felt in crossing the barrier of Oxford Street from Soho into Fitzrovia.

Fish and Chips, Pubs, Sandwich Chains and Tea Shops

Changes in eating out were much more widespread in Fitzrovia than in the cosy restaurants of Charlotte Street and, again, the influence of immigrants was at play, even at the great British institution of teatime. Twentieth-century transformations in eating out were also enlivening Tottenham Court Road, Fitzrovia's main artery. In 1899 Tottenham Court Road had featured nondescript coffee rooms and dining rooms, spiced up with a few Italian or Ticinese-owned restaurants whose menus were hopefully more varied than sausage and mash or lamb chops. However, by 1910 things were noticeably different and some of that change was due to the advance of that growing public favourite, fish and chips.

After 1900, fish and chips probably became the most popular complete takeaway meal for working people. Fish and chips as a combination came into existence in the 1860s, with a Jewish business, Joseph Malin's Fish Shop in Cleveland Street, Poplar, being credited by several sources as the first place to sell it. Fried fish on its own was commonly sold, by both street sellers and shops, considerably before fish and chips evolved. 'Chatchip', or William Loftas, a veteran of the fried fish trade, dated fried fish shops to the mid-nineteenth century when he wrote about the trade's history in the *Fish Trades Gazette* on 12 March 1921. He said that baked potatoes were at that time often sold with the fish, asserting that chips were introduced from France only about thirty-five years before the time he wrote the piece.

Not only were Jews like Joseph Malin probably the first to sell in the UK what became the classic English food combination of fish with chips, but before that they had also brought the fried fish of their food tradition into the British consciousness. Claudia Roden explains this contribution, 'The Jews in London had a very particular way of frying fish in batter and eating it cold which has become a classic of Jewish cooking in Britain. It was a legacy of Portuguese Marranos (crypto-Jews) who came to England in the sixteenth century, many of them via Holland ....'[18]

'Chatchip' called Jewish vendors 'the fathers of the fried fish trade', and Jewish vendors were later instrumental in developing and popularising fish and chips. Samuel Isaacs, originally of Whitechapel, ran a chain of fish restaurants selling the dish, one of which was in Tottenham Court Road.[19]

From the early days of fried fish selling there were complaints about its smell; an odour often connected with working-class districts where the dish was popular. Like the Italian areas, the Jewish neighbourhoods were a special target of complaints about dirtiness and odours associated with their characteristic food. A commentary in *Household Words*, as early as 1851, talks of 'a neighbour of mine, of the Jewish persuasion, who smells fearfully of fried fish'.[20] However, anti-immigrant and anti-Semitic stereotyping notwithstanding, fish and chips evolved into the nation's most favourite dish in the first half of the twentieth century.

Some commentators disapproved of this early form of fast food on health and hygiene grounds. However, others, including of course 'Chatchip', praised fish and chips for its nutritious qualities and its cheapness. 'Chatchip' noted that a whole family could be well fed for 6*d*, claiming that it had traditionally been 'the only hot meal in the day procurable by thousands of poor people in this country'.[21]

Fish and chips must surely be the outstanding example of immigrant influence on British tastes, marrying the fried fish beloved of Jewish immigrants and chipped potatoes French style (or perhaps Irish style – sources disagree here).[22]

It's not surprising that fried fish and fish and chips had caught on early in Fitzrovia. As we know, by the late 1800s sizeable communities of Jews and Jewish-run business enterprises existed on both sides of Oxford Street. And perhaps – just perhaps – Fitzrovia was even the original source of this great national dish. 'Chatchip', in 1922, tantalisingly waved around the idea that fish and chips, rather than originating with Joseph Malin's shop in the East End, came from the Jews of 'Soho', although he gave no details or sources regarding this assertion.[23] With little distinction being made in the early twentieth century between Soho and Fitzrovia, is there a possibility that 'Chatchip's elusive Eden was Fitzrovia? We'll probably never know.

By 1910, the corner block at the junction with Oxford Street contained two Jewish-owned fish shops: Arnand Malzy's Fish Restaurant at No. 1a, formerly a fishmonger's, and the above-mentioned chain, Sam Isaacs' Fish Restaurant. These testaments to the locals' love of fish and chips remained until the 1940s, although by 1930 Sam Isaacs' name had been replaced by Nuthall's.

The locals very often purchased their fish and chips from small takeaway shops in side streets. Sam Lomberg affectionately mentions Solly's Fish and Chip Shop in Cleveland Street, which served the food in the traditional style, wrapped in newspaper. Sam comments, 'While we were in London last September, I tried some fish and chips, not wrapped in a piece of a newspaper – just didn't taste the same.'[24]

Another resident, Nellie Muller, remembers, 'The biggest treat would be going round the chip shop to get fish and chips. There were lovely Jewish fish shops along Cleveland Street.'[25] Nellie was probably talking about shops like Solly's, Solomon Levene's at No. 80 Cleveland Street, or Joseph Foust's at No. 71, both listed as selling fried fish in 1930.

Panikos Panayi says that this period until the 1960s was 'the high point of the history of fish and chips in Britain'.[26] Prices stayed low through the 1910s and 1920s, commonly a penny each for fish and chips, or perhaps only half a penny for chips. By 1935, this had risen to 3*d*, with smaller or bigger portions costing 2*d* or 4*d*.

The growth in eating places can also be seen in Great Titchfield Street, which wasn't a key street in terms of leisure and eating out like Tottenham Court Road or Charlotte Street but was still an important thoroughfare, central to the local clothing trade. In 1900, Great Titchfield Street had no places for refreshment, apart from three pubs. Yet, by 1930, besides the pubs it possessed several cafes and restaurants, dining rooms and a sandwich bar. It was likely to have been local workers who were using the new dining facilities, rather than the visitors or shoppers who might have been patronising the neighbourhood's more well-known thoroughfares.

A 'sandwich bar' listed at 52 Great Titchfield Street in the 1930 *Post Office Directory* is the mark of a new development: the specialist sandwich chain. The Great Titchfield Street sandwich outlet almost certainly catered for workers in the clothing trade shops and workshops that dominated this long street opening into Oxford Street. According to Antony Clayton, the first sandwich chain appeared in the 1920s – Sandy's All-British Sandwich Bar in Oxendon Street, near Piccadilly, offering 'sixty varieties at 4*d* to 6*d*'.[27] The sandwich bars were a sign that a trade previously relying on street sellers had been regularised, probably partly due to increased hygiene regulation.

Public houses were still many people's main places of refreshment, although before the turn of the century not much food was available in pubs for hungry workers. In Tottenham Court Road, there were twelve pubs in 1910, dropping to ten by 1920. By 1950 there would only be six. However, there was an improvement in what these more select houses were offering.

A movement had begun towards the end of the nineteenth century to offer light meals as well as tea, coffee and soft drinks in pubs, and to put in more comfortable seating instead of expecting customers to stand at the bar or sit on wooden benches and stools. This movement was reinforced by encouragement from the government during the First World War when the Central Control Board (Liquor Traffic) urged publicans to provide more in the way of refreshments and social facilities.

Some local pubs played an important part in the community. The Fitzroy Tavern at the corner of Charlotte Street and Windmill Street, reopened and run by Judah Kleinfeld from 1919, had such a welcoming atmosphere that it became wildly popular. It later attracted the Fitzrovia Set of artists, writers and intellectuals as well as regular local customers. Judah Kleinfeld appears to have been an unusually liberal and generous landlord. Sally Fiber, his granddaughter, says, 'In the 1930s, the tailors got paid on Sunday mornings. They put on their high hats and came and had a whiskey and smoked the free cigars handed out by my grandfather.'[28] One early acquisition at the Fitzroy was an electric pianola 'adorned with lights on the front and pale pink shades trimmed with glass beads'.[29]

The Fitzroy Tavern owners also became known for their charitable work for the neighbourhood's children. They used quirky fundraising techniques:

> In a particularly competitive darts game, one customer became very frustrated when he lost, and threw his dart in the air. It lodged in the ceiling.

Pop was in the bar at the time and heard the winner remark, 'That would be a good way to raise money for charity'. It gave Pop a brainwave and that night he wouldn't go to bed until he had perfected the scheme in his mind. He would invite customers to put money into coloured paper darts, which were then twisted up to hold the money and thrown onto the ceiling. From this inspired idea of Pop's the Fitzroy Money Box started, later to become the famous 'Pennies From Heaven'.[30]

Sydney Diamond was a local man who used the Fitzroy Tavern and remembers the pub's tradition of ceiling collections for local children. The Fitzroy Tavern was just one example of a 'local' inspiring affection and loyalty, not just from the notables of the Fitzrovia Set but from Fitzrovia's ordinary residents as well.

Big developments in eating out were on the way, embracing the new cultural scene of women eating out and tea drinking. In the 1920s, cafe life on the Other Side of Oxford Street was transformed by the large-scale expansion into Tottenham Court Road of Joseph Lyons and Co. The UK's first major eating chain, this culture-changing venture was another innovation by entrepreneurs of Jewish immigrant heritage – Joseph Lyons, his brothers-in-law, Isidore and Montague Gluckstein, and Barnett Salmon. Lyons' tea shops would be a dominant decades-long presence in the area, and would become a social and cultural presence as much as a catering phenomenon.

A Lyons' cafe opened at No. 123 Tottenham Court Road early in the century, to be followed, in 1928, by the Oxford Corner House at the junction of Tottenham Court Road and Oxford Street. This Lyons' Corner House was one of three monumental Lyons' eating houses in central London that would become hubs of the city's social life. The Oxford Corner House not only provided low-priced, palatable food to a mass clientele in elegant surroundings but, in so doing, became an intrinsic and much-loved part of Londoners' lives and histories, attracting crowds of people who could not have afforded the West End restaurants. It was built on the site of what had been another popular cultural institution: the old Oxford Music Hall. The Dominion Theatre, opened in 1929, was soon to face the Corner House on the opposite side of Tottenham Court Road.

The importance of the Oxford Corner House was underlined by the attendance of the Duke and Duchess of York, the future King George VI and Queen Elizabeth, at its opening ceremony. Peter Bird gives some idea of the scale and grandeur of the building, and its historic role:

Lyons employed Oliver Bernard to design the interior and he used 550 tons of finest marble imported from the quarries of France, Italy, Greece,

Switzerland and Ireland to create the restaurant's most striking feature – the 20-foot-high pictures decorating the walls. They ran for hundreds of feet around the walls depicting trees, waterfalls, mountains, lakes and cypress trees and prompting the individual restaurants to be named the Niagara and Mountain View Cafés. The exterior of the building was faced in a kind of white terracotta. It claimed to be the largest restaurant in the world.[31]

The Oxford Corner House catered for customers' entertainment by putting on music and dancing, activities happily appropriate to the site's musichall history. Again, this was managed on the grand scale. Joseph Lyons set up a dedicated Band Office, run by Major Montagu Gluckstein, a son of one of the firm's founders, who became 'one of the largest employers of freelance musicians and entertainers in the country'.[32]

Lyons targeted female customers above all, 'with promises of light refreshments and a reassuring atmosphere of comfort, cleanliness, efficiency, and respectability'.[33] Its importance for women was emphasised in a piece written by Lady Angela Forbes, part of a special twenty-five-year anniversary celebration of J. Lyons that was probably paid-for content, in the *Daily Mail* of 5 October 1921:

> Lyons had the foresight to anticipate a demand that was inevitable; others, not only in the catering business but in every branch of public and private service, were quick to follow their example.
>
> Today the Lyons teashop is everywhere. For the business girl ... the nearest teashop is never far away. The girls who crowd the teashops at midday no longer need the protection of a room reserved for their sex alone. They share a table with men as naturally as they take a seat – or a strap – in tram and tube... From every point of view, and most emphatically from a woman's, London has changed for the better during the past 25 years; in that metamorphosis the teashops have played a meritorious part.

As Forbes implies, Lyons' Corner House, ultra-respectable as it was, allowed the freedom for younger customers to meet each other discreetly – and frugally.

Lyons' tea shops were also regular socialising places for Jewish people. As a local Jewish resident, Laura Phillips, explains, 'We had a cup of coffee and a pastry for about sixpence ... There were bands on every floor and entertainment. So, we sat there and boys came along and sat with you.'[34] Perhaps because the chain was founded by Jewish entrepreneurs, Jewish customers seemed to have a special fondness for it. Lyons' tea shops' connection with the Jewish community has been explored by Judith Walkowitz in *Nights Out*.[35]

Eating Out in Wartime

Both world wars had an impact on eating out in Fitzrovia, in different ways. The First World War appears to have temporarily curtailed the growth in eating out, to judge by the number of eating places in Tottenham Court Road. The directory for 1920, soon after the First World War ended, shows a sharply reduced number of eating places – apart from pubs – in Tottenham Court Road, compared with 1910. Restaurants were down from eleven to only seven in number. The two fish restaurants and Lyons' tea shop had survived, as well as four 'dining rooms'. Their owners' names perhaps hint at the reason for this fall: in 1920, the names all appear to be British, whereas before that several establishments had been owned by those with foreign surnames – Fietta Giovanni's dining rooms at No. 106 was gone by 1920, for example. Anti-foreigner sentiment during and after the First World War, along with voluntary departures of restaurateurs to their countries of origin, or even deportations, may have caused the closure of some eating places. It's also possible that some cafes closed because their owners, who may have been naturalised Britons, were away fighting with British forces.

In Charlotte Street it was a somewhat different story during the First World War. Restaurants and cafes didn't close here so much as change ownership, if the *Post Office Directory* is to be believed. It's notable that, in 1910, all the listed owners were men whereas, by 1920, several eating places are being run by women. In one restaurant, Losenegger's, a wife or daughter had clearly taken over, with Catharine Losenegger replacing John Losenegger. Celeste Bertorelli now had refreshment rooms where Alfred Thomas' Coffee Rooms had been in 1910, while Anna Detrische had opened a new cafe at No. 32. Were these women coming to the forefront due to men being in the army? Or were they simply being listed as nominal owners due to a feeling that a cafe with a woman named as owner would be less likely to be attacked in a wartime atmosphere hostile to foreigners? We can only speculate, as many of these small cafes and restaurants have left little permanent trace on the historical record.

Circumstances were different when the Second World War was raging. By 1940, the number of eating places in Tottenham Court Road had grown to fifteen, instead of diminishing in number. With many people in the 1940s doing war work on the home front, working long, irregular hours and having their home life disrupted by heavy bombing in the area, it was now crucial that the population should have ready access to eating places providing cheap meals. Restaurants and cafés had the advantage of being off-ration. For those who could afford it, top West End restaurants like the Ivy, a five-minute walk away from Tottenham Court Road, could carry on serving their clientele first-class menus without being restricted by rationing. For the most affluent Fitzrovia locals and visitors, Percy Street's establishments had the same advantage.[36] For those on a limited budget, Lyons made a virtue of serving inexpensive meals, offering a cup of tea for 3*d* or 4*d*. Lyons' menus declared, 'FOOD is a munition of War Don't Waste it.'[37]

To meet the need for daily meals, hundreds of mass-feeding stations, soon to be called British Restaurants, were set up across London. They had evolved from the London County Council's Londoners' Meal Service, catering for those who'd been bombed out. British Restaurants were open to everyone but tended to attract office and industrial workers. There was a British Restaurant in High Holborn, not far from Fitzrovia, but it seems that private restaurants and cafes may have filled the locals' needs more than the British Restaurants.

During the Second World War, St Pancras Town Hall became the Emergency Food Office for the area, the place where people had to queue for ration books for domestic food consumption. Fish and chips maintained its popularity during the war, with plenty of outlets in Fitzrovia. There's a quirky wartime side note summing up the nation's feelings about fish and chips from the Federation of Fish Friers, 'British soldiers identified each other during the "D" Day landings by calling out "*fish*" and the response or password was "*chips*". Any other response and they would have certainly had their chips.'[38]

The Fitzrovia Flavour: Immigrants and Eating Out

It should be obvious by now that Fitzrovia's immigrant families played a leading role in local catering and hospitality, in the same way as they did in the area's clothing trade, entertainment industry and other key aspects of local life. The catering industries in London relied on mobile and flexible migrant labour more than most other industries, and the concentration of food and catering outlets in Fitzrovia and Soho drew large numbers of outsiders.

Sometimes first- or second-generation immigrants entered traditional areas of the catering trade without necessarily making big changes to them. As we've seen, some Jews became publicans in the neighbourhood, even though Jewish people were, on the whole, light drinkers. Sydney Diamond, a pub-goer who used the Fitzroy Tavern, vouches for Jews' moderation in drink, saying, 'You couldn't see any drunken Jews ... I've never heard or seen any Jewish man drunk, that's the honest truth, never'.[39] According to Gerry Black, by the mid-1930s the local pubs managed by Jewish publicans included the Black Horse and the Blue Posts in Tottenham Court Road, the Bromley Arms and the George in Cleveland Street, the Duke of York in Hanway Street, the Fitzroy Arms in Clipstone Street, the Globe in Maple Street and the Horse & Groom in Great Portland Street – as well, of course, as the Fitzroy Tavern, now run by Charles Allchild, the son-in-law of Judah Kleinfield.

However, Fitzrovia's numerous foreigners did much more than adapt themselves to British ways of eating out. As well as helping to perpetuate British traditions, immigrants' energy and entrepreneurship was responsible for many of the big developments connected with eating out. Their initiatives ranged from the old-style street stalls and roving sellers with trays and baskets to small independent cafes, to the restaurant and snack chains that became part of London's culture and the wider national culture for many decades. Fitzrovia, as in other fields of endeavour, gave local eating out its own individual flavour.

The study of 'culinary transfer', to which the work of Panikos Panayi has made an important contribution, has highlighted three different aspects of migrant influence on patterns of eating out in the UK. These are: migrants importing or making foods from their home countries for consumption by their own communities; migrants selling their foods to British consumers; and migrants changing British tastes as to what is eaten at home.[40] As Fitzrovia's migrants continually moved between and around their Continental countries of origin and the UK, ideas about food and different types of cuisine were more quickly spread, to a wider cross-section of people, in Fitzrovia than in most other parts of London.

Panayi makes an important point about this international flow, which seems to anticipate aspects of the European Union: 'The European-wide nature of this business ... involved people on all levels of this industry moving between European states, almost as part of an apprenticeship system'.[41] Fitzrovia as a centre of German migration, for example, played a vital part in the Europe-wide catering apprenticeship system by giving a home and employment to the German waiters and cooks who thronged Charlotte Street and the surrounding neighbourhood. Concerning immigrants in catering, Panayi stresses:

> Before 1914 the most important group was Germans, although Italians, Swiss and French waiters also had a part to play. The 1901 census suggests a total of 8,634 foreign waiters in the country of whom 3,039 were German.

In 1911 about 10 per cent of waiters and waitresses in restaurant work in London were German ... Twenty-three years later *The New Survey of London Life and Labour* estimated that 122,000 people found employment in the hotel and catering trade in the capital.[42]

During the First World War, hostility to Germans as an enemy people rose to heights that forced many Germans out of business and employment and back to Germany, although numbers rose again in the 1920s. But Germans were far from being the only local group of foreign food workers. Fitzrovia was also packed with Swiss, Austrian, Italian and French workers and small entrepreneurs, all bringing in fresh ideas about food provision. As we've seen, the largely foreign-owned and staffed cafe and small restaurant scene was taking off by 1900 on both sides of Oxford Street, bringing new tastes and new approaches to dining out to English consumers, and only partially being throttled back by the outbreak of the First World War.

Panayi mentions several of the better known and better-class French, Italian and German restaurants on the south side of Oxford Street, like Monico's, Kettner's and the Vienna Café in Oxford Street itself, commenting, 'All of these Victorian and Edwardian Continental eateries remained within central London, suggesting that the only people likely to have used them were the international and, especially, "artistic" bourgeoisie and sections of the higher echelons of British society'.[43]

However, across Oxford Street, in Charlotte Street, Percy Street and elsewhere, it's possible to argue that, with so many potential customers being immigrants of similar social class and background to the food providers, the small restaurateurs and cafe owners would almost certainly have had to keep prices as low as possible, so that they would have been affordable at least to better-off workers, including English customers who were adventurous enough to follow the recommendations of food writer Thomas Burke and try them.

The appeal of these places to the artists and writers who helped to create 'Fitzrovia' was the low prices, as well as the quality of the food and the 'exotic' clientele. The welcoming congeniality of the proprietors played a crucial role also, as at the Eiffel Tower Restaurant, owned and run by Rudolf Stulik, a Viennese Jew who was the soul of the place. Stulik drew his visitors into a romantic intimacy that almost formed their circle for them and that made them, for a while, very loyal to the restaurant.

The Italian-speaking Ticinese of Switzerland were one group who brought a fresh Continental approach to eating out. The Gatti family were leading

Ticinese restaurant owners specialising in ice cream and chocolate who, by the late nineteenth century, ran several businesses in central London, notably at the Adelphi in the Strand. The Ticinese were also early settlers north of Oxford Street, with a strong presence in Fitzrovia. Charles Veglio opened a restaurant at 17 Tottenham Court Road in 1858, after which similar restaurants continued to appear between the 1860s and 1880s. Six Ticinese eating places, including Veglio's, were based in Tottenham Court Road during that period, while another opened in 1877 at 21 Goodge Street, later moving down the road to No. 44. There is a photograph of Menegalli's Restaurant at 87 Tottenham Court Road with the family standing proudly outside its doors. 'C. Menegalli from Gatti's' was painted above the entrance to advertise its celebrated provenance. Its window signs promised 'soups, fish, joints and entrees' with 'always ready chops and steaks from the grill', as well as coffee and the chocolate for which the Ticinese establishments were famous.[44] Good-quality food, varied menus, inviting surroundings and reasonable prices all came together in the Ticinese cafes and restaurants, showing the movement away from the limitations of the old coffee houses and chophouses.

Even assuming that a majority of native-born Fitzrovia residents didn't go to the foreign restaurants, new tastes in food must have reached many of these consumers from the numerous delicatessens and foreign provision shops in the area; and surely almost everyone must have been open to the delights of Italian ice cream, as we've gathered from Sam Lomberg's praise of a local icecream seller.

Furthermore, innovations in eating out weren't solely, or even mainly, confined to the introduction of foreign foods and cuisines. The Jewish Lyons, Salmon and Gluckstein families, who founded J. Lyons and Co. and created the Oxford Corner House, transformed many modestly paid people's experiences of eating outside the home, not through unusual cuisine but through creating an environment and standards of service that ordinary working customers could never have imagined enjoying.

As we saw, Jews in London and elsewhere in Britain were also significant and innovatory presences in the fish and chip trade, followed by significant numbers of Greek Cypriots after 1945. Foreigners had created what became a very British favourite. Panayi writes:

> We might see the fish and chip shop as a place which represents immigrant success and social mobility … At the same time they offer immigrants a way into mainstream British society … The origins of the dish also point to the fish and chip shop as a place of cross-cultural contact.[45]

What of immigrant catering workers' own experiences of Fitzrovia's catering trade? The number of foreign hotel and catering workers in the locality was so large that this was perhaps Fitzrovia's largest group of all workers, possibly even more numerous than in the clothing trade. Writers on eating out could often amuse with their word pictures of waiters and chefs, and these staff were subject to stereotypes according to the kind of establishment they served in. Thomas Burke, in 1915, makes journalistic hay from a night out at a small French restaurant, playing with perceptions of foreign staff as noisy, volatile and 'artistic':

> The large Monsieur, the proprietor, at the counter, bellows down the tube, 'Un POTAGE – Un!' Away in subterranean regions an ear catches it, and a distant voice chants '*Potage!*' And then from the far reaches of the kitchen you hear a smothered tenor, as coming from the throat of one drowned in the soup-kettle, 'Potage!' ... By half-past seven it is no longer a restaurant: it is no longer a dinner that is being served. It is a grand opera that is in progress.[46]

Writers also present the 'model waiter' of the more exclusive and genteelly subdued West End restaurants: discreet, immaculate men murmuring menus in diners' ears and offering well-calibrated suggestions for 'Sir's' evening meal.

But these caricatures tended to minimise the fact that waiting and cheffing were sweated trades subject to very long hours, casual employment and poor pay and conditions. The large percentage of foreign staff in catering tended to make exploitation more likely. This was true into the 1940s and 1950s and many would say it's still true today. Panayi notes that German waiters 'laboured up to 15 hours per day ... Those who intended to return home would accept lower wages to obtain experience'.[47]

The small minority of waiters or chefs who worked in first-class restaurants could do well both in earnings and tips. According to Barbara Drake, who investigated seasonal trades in 1912, a head waiter at a top restaurant could make up to £10 or £12, a huge wage at that time. A head chef could earn between £3 and £6 a week. However, small restaurants like those in Fitzrovia might pay £1 to 30s – if they paid regular earnings at all, it was quite common for immigrant waiters to have no basic pay. Panayi points out, 'In contrast to Englishmen, who demanded a fixed wage, foreigners relied upon tips, from which they could make £2 per week.'[48] 'Tip,' Drake says, stood for 'to improve promptness'.[49]

There were advantages in employing foreign waiters, apart from the cheapness of their labour. In 1892, C.H. D'E. Leppington wrote in *Good Words*, 'The foreigner not only is cheaper but speaks two or three languages to the Englishman's one. A large proportion of hotel and restaurant managers are foreigners, and they prefer to employ their own countrymen. Of the foreigners we probably have the pick …'

It's likely that many workers who worked in Soho lived north of Oxford Street in Fitzrovia, due to the lower rents there. This may partly explain the very high densities of catering workers residing immediately north of Oxford Street, revealed in the 1911 census survey in Chapter 1. I have been informed by someone on the editorial staff of the *Fitzrovia News* that one building in Charlotte Street was used as a rooming house for waiters and chefs until as late as the 1960s.

One major and long-lasting grievance of waiting staff was the 'tronc', or 'trunk', system of pooling and sharing out tips, which was widespread for many decades and still exists in some places. Foreign waiters who were dependent on tips alone had particular reason to resent the routinely unfair sharing out of tips by which head waiters and other senior staff took the lion's share.

The tronc system was the target of campaigns by the National Union of Catering Workers (NUCW), formed during the First World War as a campaigning trade union. The NUCW headquarters was close to Tottenham Court Road in High Street, Bloomsbury. Short-lived unions for catering workers had existed before that, without being very effective. Charlotte Street had been the headquarters, in 1910, of the International Union of Chefs and there had been an Amalgamated Union of Catering Workers a few years before the NUCW was founded, which had broken down. The NUCW aimed to 'obtain a minimum wage (varied according to the grade of worker), shorter hours for all, and substantial concessions regarding holidays'.[50] Its journal, *The Catering Worker*, was written partly in French to reflect the nationality of many of its members; it also appealed specifically to women workers, few of whom were unionised.

The unions were distinct from the societies and associations, often based on nationality, which aimed to help catering workers. One such association, a long-lasting beneficial and social society, was the Unione Ticinese, based at the Schweitzerbund Swiss Club at 74 Charlotte Street. It was a club for Swiss-Italian immigrants, which 'seems to have grown out of a mutual benefit society for Gatti employees founded by Stefano Gatti in 1870 and was extended to include the whole Ticinese colony'.[51] Gatti had chosen the right place for the

Unione Ticinese, since the houses to each side of the Swiss Club were packed to the rafters with waiters and other catering workers. Germans could be looked after by the local *Vereins*. These working men's clubs, besides providing social facilities, might offer help with employment to new arrivals and charitable help for those who had lost their jobs. The 1910 *Post Office Directory* also shows, in Charlotte Street, an International Chefs' and Waiters' Society at No. 84, and a Christian Home for Waiters at No. 48.

Employment agencies also existed specifically for foreign catering staff and Charlotte Street, unsurprisingly, had several. In 1910, A. Albrecht's Employment Agency was listed at 5 Charlotte Street, Andre Heiniger's Employment Agency was at No. 22, Braegger's Foreign Registry Office at No. 41, Marini Guiseppe's Foreign Servants' Registry Office at No. 50, and the Evans & Pickett Employment Agency at No. 98. The London & Provincial Hotel Employees Society was based in Tottenham Court Road.[52] Unfortunately, many agencies gained a bad name with workers because of their high charges. By 1920, only Braegger's and Marini's were still listed in Charlotte Street.

In wartime, with tension high across Europe, migratory workers were viewed with suspicion. Throughout the First World War and the years leading up to it there was strong hostility from much of the public towards foreign workers. They were sometimes accused of being spies and now and again articles would appear in the press on this topic. Waiters came under particular suspicion, presumably because they could regularly get close to those in powerful positions at their dining tables and eavesdrop.

However, the NUCW was strongly internationalist against the highly nationalistic tone of the times. The union remained active after the First World War. In 1925, an NUCW pamphlet, *Sweating in the Catering Trade*, attacked Joseph Lyons and Co. in connection with their treatment of waitresses, called 'Nippies'. The pamphlet revealed another side to Lyons, which had already become much-loved by the general public:

> A short time ago the Press was full of reports about the new dresses which Messrs. Lyons and Co. have issued to their waitresses. 'Nippy looks smart in her new costume,' said the Press. 'We have to pay for them ourselves,' said a member of the Union. A dustman with nearly £4 per week wages is supplied with clothes to wear – free. A messenger in a Government Department, with £3 per week wages, is supplied with two uniforms a year – free. Waitresses are supplied with a uniform by their employers, but they have to pay for them themselves out of anything between 10s and 27s per week!

As this issue reveals, women were grossly underpaid in the catering trade. However, their low pay was characteristic of the other trades typically carried on in Fitzrovia and reflected a universal exploitation of female labour which, sadly, has yet to be eliminated from the world of work. Women working in catering, and foreign male catering staff, were, in fact, among the lowest-paid workers of all. Additionally, hours for men and women were still long, with waiters working twelve to fourteen hours a day and waitresses slightly less. Conditions were sometimes worse than poor, with little ventilation in kitchen areas and nowhere for staff to have meal breaks or change into uniforms. It wasn't unknown for waiters to have to change in the toilets, even in newly 'modernised' premises that, to the customer, looked smart and spacious.

Wages, hours and conditions hardly budged throughout the 1930s. It wasn't until after the Second World War that a Labour Government fixed minimum wages and set a forty-eight-hour week, with longer hours being counted as overtime. From 1948, male workers over 21 whose employer wasn't providing them with food or lodgings received 85–88*s* a week in the City of London. Wages for women in the same circumstances were 72–75*s*.

Milk Bars and Indian Restaurants

By 1950, Tottenham Court Road possessed at least fifteen cafes and restaurants. These eating places included the Restaurant de Montmartre and the Little Vienna Restaurant, Ross's Kosher Restaurant, a couple of Italian or Ticinese cafes, and two milk bars. The eating places were mostly located in the south-western part of Tottenham Court Road, closest to Oxford Street and its shoppers.

In Charlotte Street, restaurants such as La Belle Meuniere became established. In the 1950s, some restaurants there had a mixed reputation, with local underworld figures sharing space with artists and writers:

Tony's was undoubtedly the sleaziest café in Fitzrovia yet also the most popular ... it was known as 91. George, a Maltese gentleman, was the part-time owner, his face disfigured by razor scars. Despite his sinister appearance, he was a kindly, family man. The customers consisted mainly of bohemians, small-time villains and prostitutes with hard faces. They tended to favour the ground floor in the daytime but at night the basement usually filled up.[53]

Old-established eating places in Charlotte Street, like Bertorelli's, Schmidt's and L'Etoile, remained open in 1950. Although it's not possible to retrieve the menus of most of these small restaurants, a look at the names of the owners gives an impression of a highly international environment, even more diverse than before the Second World War.

Newer businesses included O. Bartholdi & Son at No. 6, Z. Panagi at No. 8, the Hungarian Ktori & Benedik at No. 10, Amelia Dolgontchouk at No. 40, Eileen Stais at No. 56, and Georgiou Kyriakos, whose outlets were located at Nos 69 and 91. Cypriot arrivals clearly began to feature as restaurateurs, when Cypriot migration to London increased after the Second World War. The Eiffel Tower's successor, the White Tower, in Percy Street, was owned by Yianni Stasis. Warren Street had two Cypriot-owned restaurants by 1950: Pololi & Constantinou's at No. 45 and Michael Miltiadou's at No. 52. It seems that restaurants were changing hands often just after the Second World War, since, of the *Post Office Directory*'s 1950 list of restaurant businesses, only Amelia Dolgontchouk's name had featured as an owner in 1940.

Indian restaurants were becoming a feature of life in Fitzrovia. The directory for 1940 lists the Khayyam Indian Restaurant at 95 Tottenham Court Road, while Whitfield Street had the Khan Restaurant at No. 137. There's a photograph of the Khan Restaurant, taken in 1945, in Nick Bailey's *Fitzrovia*.[54] The Indian YMCA also served food as well as offering accommodation to Indian students. It had been opened in 1920 in Gower Street, moving several times before settling in 41 Fitzroy Square in 1950.

New eating outlets were coming on the scene to appeal to those who hadn't eaten out before the war. Milk bars started to appear in the 1930s, boosted by a public interest in health and fitness and a campaign to 'Drink More Milk' run by the Milk Marketing Board, established in 1933.

The first chain of milk bars in London was Black & White Milk Bars, opening its first branch in Fleet Street in 1935. They could be viewed in some respects as an updated version of the Edwardian coffee and cocoa shops in that they attracted people away from alcoholic refreshments. However, the milk bars tended to draw a younger crowd who enjoyed the American-style milkshakes and liked the modern chrome and glass décor with high-stool seating at the bar.

From 1935, Charles Forte, the Italian-born restaurant and hotel magnate who dominated the British catering trade in the 1970s and 1980s, managed the Strand Milk Bar, one of another chain, in Upper Regent Street. Tottenham Court Road saw a small outbreak of milk bars by 1940. The Cowboy Milk

Bar – its name reflecting its American origins – appeared at Nos 32–35, along with the Imperial Milk Bar at No. 54, which projected a much more British-sounding image. By 1950, the Imperial's name had changed to the futuristic New Era Milk & Tea Bar.

Forte soon branched out from milk bars with a Forte's restaurant at 1A Tottenham Court Road. Julian Maclaren-Ross says, in his *Memoirs of the Forties*, that the Forte brothers used to block his and other customers' access to the saloon bar entrance of the Wheatsheaf Pub with their milk vans.[55]

The milk bars were replaced after the Second World War by revived and newly trendy coffee bars featuring new Gaggia espresso machines. Public tastes had seemed to run full circle. The new coffee bars drew British youngsters rather than older émigrés and were often associated with the music scene of the 1950s, especially jazz. The Breadbasket, opened in 1955 at 65 Cleveland Street, was 'One of the first coffee bars to host skiffle and early rock 'n' roll', according to Antony Clayton, and hosted jazz names like Alexis Korner.[56]

Spaghetti houses had their moment, too, especially with students and young people who appreciated the novelty and the low prices of the Spaghetti House chain. A branch opened in Goodge Street in 1955.

At the same time, old favourites were losing their edge. After 1945, Lyons, which had become mundanely self-service during the war, couldn't retrieve its old magic. During the 1950s its Oxford Corner House was divided into several themed restaurants in an effort to recapture customers' loyalties. At this time, the company introduced the American inventions of the Wimpy hamburger and Whippsy milkshake into its Corner House and some of its tea shops.

My mother and my two aunts, who could rarely afford to eat out, occasionally took me to a Wimpy Bar in the late 1950s and early 1960s. They were popular throughout the 1960s and 1970s until the advent of McDonald's. Other Lyons' innovations were the Bacon and Egg, Grill and Cheese, Chicken Fayre and Seven Stars.[57] From 1961 Lyons also ran the London Steak Houses. Lyons aimed to succeed with the public once more by concentrating on limited food ranges that were cheap and easy to cook and would appeal to many on limited budgets, but the firm was declining. The Oxford Corner House building was finally sold to Mecca Leisure in 1967. In the 1980s it became a music retailer, the Virgin Megastore, which then briefly called itself Zavvi, before closing in 2009. It was a not unfitting last chapter for a site that had always been associated with musical entertainment.

The Many Sides of Fitzrovia's Food Scene

Fitzrovia contributed to Londoners' widening tastes in food through enterprises of all types and sizes, whose largely foreign ownership played a part in inventing and spreading new ways of eating out. It was the ambience and everyday casualness of eating out here, more than the menus, that was Fitzrovia's gift to London's social scene. The very idea of 'Fitzrovia' arose from this developing scene and 'Fitzrovia' became an element of London's mythology primarily through the social circles created via the medium of certain restaurants and pubs rather than its artistic venues or movements.

The other side of the Fitzrovia of Dylan Thomas and Nina Hamnett was the daily experience of eating outside the home, whether that was fish and chips, a coffee at a stall, a snack in Great Titchfield Street Market, or tea at the Oxford Corner House. And there was another side still: the experiences of the catering workers who served the growing demand for eating out in all its varieties. Food provision, whether at stalls, small shops, markets, cafes or restaurants, was one of Fitzrovia's foremost industries whose workers and entrepreneurs shaped life on the Other Side of Oxford Street. Its peripatetic catering workers, circulating back and forth across Oxford Street, and around central London, the UK and Europe, were a vital part of Fitzrovia's ever-changing social and industrial landscape.

Epilogue

Time hasn't stood still in Fitzrovia. Oxford Street has been calling it closer to the West End, and gentrification has transformed the area, with the ever-increasing pace of building works complicating the lives of its residents and visitors. Old community landmarks are being torn down, with any remaining fragments being incorporated into new luxury apartments and office blocks. The Fitzrovia Neighbourhood Centre is under notice to quit and the Middlesex Hospital, that old heart of Fitzrovia, is gone – although healthcare still has a place there focused on neurology, including the National Hospital for Neurology & Neurosurgery in Cleveland Street.

The abandoned Middlesex Hospital Annexe in Cleveland Street, previously the Strand Union Workhouse known by Dickens, has been sold by UCLH. The old workhouse building where the annexe was based will be incorporated into a residential and commercial complex following protests by residents and historical organisations against its demolition. The Dickens Fellowship has referred to it as 'almost the last workhouse building that survives in central London'.[1] The complex will include, at the last count, forty-six 'affordable' homes, although the housing it will provide is unlikely to be truly affordable to most of London's working families.[2]

One final gift of the Middlesex Hospital remains, recalling the older Fitzrovia: the hospital chapel, renamed the Fitzrovia Chapel. Lavishly restored and jewel-like with its golden mosaics and stained glass, it occupies a central space in Pearson Square on which is yet another upmarket development covering the hospital site. The name Pearson commemorates the chapel's architect, John Loughborough Pearson. There was a local campaign to keep the name 'Middlesex' in this new development, but it was unsuccessful.[3] Open for public viewing on Wednesdays, the Fitzrovia Chapel is otherwise available for hire. Its incongruent presence – as a charity-built chapel for local patients and staff, given over to commerce and gentrification – is an especially poignant echo from the Other Side of Oxford Street.

Bibliography

Ackroyd, Peter, *London: The Biography* (London: Chatto & Windus, 2000).

Adburgham, Alison, 'Give the Customers What They Want', *Architectural Review*, Vol. 161 (May 1977) pp.295–301.

Alexander, Sally, 'Becoming a Woman in London in the 1920s and 1930s' in *Metropolis: London* (ed. David Feldman and Gareth Stedman Jones) (London: Routledge, 1989).

Allen, Michelle, *Cleansing the City: Sanitary Geographies in Victorian London* (Athens, Ohio: Ohio University Press, 2008).

Apparel and Fashion Industry Association (AFIA), *Present Position of the Apparel and Fashion Industry* (London: AFIA, 1950).

Armstrong, David, *Political Anatomy of the Body: Medical Knowledge in Britain in the Twentieth Century* (London: CUP, 1983).

Ash, Maurice, *Guide to the Structure of London* (Bath: Adams & Dart, 1972).

Ashmore, Sonia, et al., '"Mr Bourne's Dilemma": Consumer Culture, Property Speculation and Department Store Demise: The Rise and Fall of Bourne & Hollingsworth on London's Oxford Street', *Journal of Historical Geography* 38 (2012), pp.434–46.

Ashton, Rosemary, *Little Germany: Exile and Asylum in Victorian England* (Oxford: OUP, 1986).

Aston, Mark, *Cinemas of Camden: A Survey and History of the Cinema Buildings of Camden, Past and Present* (London: Camden Leisure and Community, 1997).

Attfield, Judy, '"Then We Were Making Furniture, and No Money": A Case Study of J. Clarke, Wycombe Furniture Makers', *Oral History*, 18.2 (1990) pp.54–57.

Bailey, Nick, *Fitzrovia* (New Barnet, Herts: Historical Publications/Camden History Society, 1981).

Barber, Peter, and Peter Jacomelli, *Continental Taste, Ticinese Emigrants and their Cafe-Restaurants in Britain 1847–1987* (London: Camden History Society Occasional Paper 2, 1997).

Beckman, Morris, *The 43 Group* (2nd ed. London: Centerprise Publications, 1993).

Benton, Tim, 'Up and Down at Heal's: 1929–1935', *Architectural Review*, No. 972 (February 1978) pp.109–16.

Bird, Peter, *The First Food Empire: A History of J. Lyons & Co.* (Chichester: Phillimore & Co., 2000).

Black, Clementina, 'London's Tailoresses', *Economic Journal* 14:56 (December 1904) pp.555–67.

Black, Gerry, *Living Up West: Jewish Life in London's West End* (London: Jewish Museum, 1994).

Bloom, Clive, *Violent London: 2,000 Years of Riots, Rebels and Revolts* (London: Pan Books, 2004).

Breward, Christopher, 'Fashion's Front and Back: "Rag Trade" Cultures and Cultures of Consumption in Post-war London *c.* 1945–70', *London Journal*, 31:1 (June 2006) p.15–40.

Briggs, Asa, *The Golden Age of Wireless: The History of Broadcasting in the United Kingdom*, Vol. 2 (London: OUP, 1965).

British Furniture Trades Joint Committee, *Report to the British Furniture Trades Joint Committee … into Wages and Working Conditions Prevailing in Certain Sections of the Furniture Manufacturing Trade in London During 1938* (London: British Furniture Trades Joint Committee, 1938).

Brown, J. Neill, 'The Industry's Front Page' in *All Our Yesterdays: 90 Years of British Cinema*, ed. Charles Barr (London: BFI, 1986).

Bruce, J. Graeme, and Desmond F. Croome, *The Central Line: An Illustrated History* (2nd ed. Harrow, Middx: The Central Line London Underground Ltd, 2006).

Burke, Thomas, *Dinner is Served* (London: Routledge, 1937).

Burke, Thomas, *Nights in Town* (London: George Allen & Unwin, 1915).

Burnett, John, *England Eats Out: A Social History of Eating Out in England from 1830 to the Present* (Harlow: Pearson Education Ltd, 2004).

Burrows, Jon, 'Penny Pleasures: Film Exhibition in London During the Nickelodeon Era, 1906–1914', *Film History*, Vol. 16 (2004) pp.60–91.

Clayton, Antony, *London's Coffee Houses: A Stimulating Story* (London: Historical Publications, 2003).

Cohen, Deborah, *Household Gods: The British and their Possessions* (New Haven, Conn: Yale University Press, 2006).

Cohen, Max, *What Nobody Told the Foreman* (London: Spalding & Levy Ltd, 1953).

Communist Party of Great Britain, *St Pancras: Homes or Slums?* (London: CPGB, 1945).

Datta, V.N., *Madan Lal Dhingra and the Revolutionary Movement* (New Delhi: Vikas Publishing House PVT Limited, 1978).

David, Hugh, *The Fitzrovians: A Portrait of Bohemian Society 1900–1955* (London: Sceptre, 1989).

Davies, Margaret Llewellyn (ed.), *Maternity: Letters from Working Women Collected by the Women's Co-operative Guild* (London: Virago, 1978).

Dee, David, '"Nothing specifically Jewish in athletics"? Sport, Physical Recreation and the Jewish Youth Movement in London, 1895–1914', *The London Journal*, 34.2 (July 2009) pp.82–101.

Di Paola, Pietro, *Italian Anarchists in London 1870–1914* (London: University of London, 2004).

Dobbs, S.P., *Clothing Workers of Great Britain* (London: Routledge, 1928).

Eastlake, Charles L., *Hints on Household Taste in Furniture, Upholstery and Other Details* (4th ed. London: Longmans, Green, 1878).

Edwards, C., 'Tottenham Court Road: The Changing Fortunes of London's Furniture Street 1850–1950', *London Journal*, 36.2, pp.140–60.

Eyles, Allen, and Keith Skone, *London's West End Cinemas* (Sutton: Keystone Publications, 1991).

Farrar, David, *No Royal Road* (Eastbourne: Mortimer Publications Limited, 1947).

Feldman, David, *Englishmen and Jews: Social Relations and Political Culture 1840–1914* (New Haven, CT: Yale University Press, 1994).

Fiber, Sally, *The Fitzroy: The Autobiography of a London Tavern* (Sussex: Temple House Books, 1995).

Forster, E.M., *Room with a View* (London: Penguin, 1955).

Guyan, Kevin, 'Glitter and Glamour: Race and Dance in 1940s London', https://www.ucl. ac.uk/equianocentre/blackpresenceblog/previous-posts/may-2013

Haldane, Charlotte, *Truth Will Out* (London: Weidenfeld and Nicholson, 1949).

Hall, P.G., *Industries of London since 1861* (London: Hutchinson University Library, 1962).

Handley, R.S. Gordon-Taylor, 'Breast Cancer and the Middlesex Hospital', *Annals of the Royal College of Surgeons of England*, Vol. 49 (September 1971) pp.151–64.

Handley, W. Sampson (ed.), *Cancer Research at the Middlesex Hospital, 1900–1924: Retrospect and Prospect* (London: John Murray, 1924).

Heal, Oliver S., *Sir Ambrose Heal and the Heal Cabinet Factory 1897–1939* (Wetherby, Yorks. (?): Oblong Creative Ltd, 2014).

Hicks, Frances, 'Dressmakers and Tailoresses' in *Workers on their Industries*, ed. F.W. Galton (London: Swan Sonnenschein & Co. Ltd, 1896).

Hines, Mark, *The Story of Broadcasting House, Home of the BBC* (London: Merrell, 2008).

Holdorph, Anne, '"If I strive not after my own salvation, who shall strive for me, and if not now, when?" The Role of Religion in the West Central Jewish Working Girls' Club, 1893–1939', *Women's History Review*, 24, 1 (2015) pp.37–52.

Horne, Mike, *The Last Link: The First 30 Years of the Hampstead Railway* (London: London Underground Ltd [Northern Line] and Nebulous Books, 2007).

Howard, Diana, *London Theatres and Music Halls 1850–1950* (London: Library Association, 1970).

'Indian Film Festival Programme 1955', Asian Film Society (BFI Special Collection, 1955).

Itoh, Keiko, *Japanese Community in Pre-War Britain: From Integration to Disintegration* (Richmond, Surrey: Curzon Press, 2001).

Jacobson, Barb, and Olive Leonard, *Ebb and Flow in Fitzrovia: Interviews with Pensioners in and around Carburton Street, W1* (London: Fitzrovia Neighbourhood Association, 2010).

Jewish Women in London Group, *Generations of Memories: Voices of Jewish Women* (London: The Women's Press, 1989).

Judge, Roy, 'Mary Neal and the Espérance Morris', *Folk Music Journal*, Vol. 5, No. 5 (1989) pp.545–82.

Kershen, Anne J., *Off the Peg: Jewish Mantle Making Trade Unions of London* (London: London Museum of Jewish Life, c. 1988).

Kift, Dagmar, *The Victorian Music Hall: Culture, Class and Conflict* (New York: Cambridge University Press, 1996).

Kirkham, Pat, et al., *Furnishing the World: The East London Furniture Trade 1830–1980* (London: Journeyman Press Ltd, 1987).

Kirkham, Pat, 'Recollections of Furniture Makers: Labour History, Oral History and Furniture Studies', *Furniture History*, Vol. 14 (1978) pp.23–30.

Lewis, Jane, *The Politics of Motherhood: Child and Maternal Welfare in England, 1900–1939* (London: Croom Helm, 1980).

Lipman, V.D., *The Social History of the Jews in England, 1850–1950* (London: Watts & Co., 1954).

List of Car Dealers (6th ed. London: Society of Motor Manufacturers and Traders, 1937–38).

Llewellyn-Smith, Sir Hubert, *New Survey of London Life and Labour*, Vol. 1 (London: P.S. King & Son, 1934).

Machray, Robert, *The Night Side of London* (London: J. McQueen, 1902).

McKernan, Luke, '"Only the Screen was Silent"': Memories of Children's Cinema-Going in London before the First World War', *Film Studies*, Issue 10 (Spring 2007) pp.1–20.

Maclaren-Ross, Julian, *Memoirs of the Forties* (London: Cardinal, 1991).

Mander, Raymond, and Joe Mitchenson, *The Lost Theatres of London* (London: Hart-Davis, 1968).

Mander, Raymond, and Joe Mitchenson, *The Theatres of London* (London: New English Library, 1975).

Marshall, Edward, 'The Dark Alien Executive': Jewish Producers, Emigres and the British Film Industry in the 1930s' in *New Directions in Anglo-Jewish History*, ed. Geoffrey Alderman (Brighton, MA: Academic Studies Press, 2010).

Massil, William I., *Immigrant Furniture Workers in London 1881–1939: and the Jewish Contribution to the Furniture Trade: A Supplement* (London: Jewish Museum, 2000).

Mayhew, Henry, *Mayhew's London*, ed. Peter Quennell (London: Bracken Books, 1984).

Medhurst, Andy, 'Music Hall and British Cinema' in *All our Yesterdays: 90 Years of British Cinema*, ed. Charles Barr (London: BFI, 1986).

Memorandum on the Anti-British Agitation Among Natives of India in England, India Office (1909) IOR/R/2/Box 33/312.

Merrington, W.R., *University College Hospital and its Medical School: A History* (London: Heinemann, 1976).

Montagu, Lily, *My Club and I: The Story of the West Central Jewish Club* (London: Herbert Joseph Limited, 1941).

Morris, Margaret, *The General Strike* (Harmondsworth, Middx: Penguin Books, 1976).

Nasaw, David, *Going Out: The Rise and Fall of Public Amusements* (New York: HarperCollins, 1993).

Newby, Eric, *Something Wholesale* (London: Hodder and Stoughton, 1970).

O'Connell, Sean, *The Car in British Society: Class, Gender and Motoring 1896–1939, Studies in Popular Culture* (Manchester: Manchester University Press, 1938).

Panayi, Panikos, 'Sausages, Waiters and Bakers: German Migrants and Culinary Transfer to Britain *c.* 1850–1914', in S. Manz et al. (eds), *Migration and Transfer from Germany to Britain 1660–1914* (Munchen: Saur, 2007) pp.147–59.

Panayi, Panikos, *Fish and Chips: A History* (London: Reaktion Books, 2014).

Panayi, Panikos, *Spicing Up Britain: The Multicultural History of British Food* (London: Reaktion Books, 2008).

Pankhurst, Sylvia, *The Suffragette Movement: An Intimate Account of Persons and Ideals* (London: Virago Limited, 1977).

Pentelow, Mike, and Marsha Rowe, *Characters of Fitzrovia* (London: Chatto & Windus, 2001).

Petley, Julian, 'Cinema and State' in *All Our Yesterdays: 90 Years of British Cinema*, ed. Charles Barr (London: BFI, 1986).

Pratt, E.L., *The Impasse in the Catering Trade and the 'National Union' Way Out* (London: National Union of Catering Workers, 1915).

Pronay, Nicholas, 'British Newsreels in the 1930s: Audience and Producers' in *Yesterday's News: The British Cinema Newsreel Reader*, ed. Luke McKernan (London: BUFVC, 2002).

Pulling, Christopher, *They Were Singing: And What They Sang About* (London: George C. Harrap and Co., 1952).

Quail, John, *The Slow Burning Fuse: The Lost History of the British Anarchists* (St Albans, Herts: Granada Publishing, 1978).

Ranger, Sir Douglas, *The Middlesex Hospital Medical School 1935–1985* (London: Hutchinson Benham, 1985).

Rawlinson, Carole, *Middlesex Memories* (London: University College London Hospitals Charities, 2007).

Reid, Hew, *Furniture Makers: A History of Trade Unionism in the Furniture Trade 1865–1972* (Oxford: Malthouse Press, 1986).

Rocker, Rudolf, *The London Years* (Nottingham: Five Leaves Press, 2005).

Roden, Claudia, *The Book of Jewish Food: An Odyssey from Samarkand and Vilna to the Present Day* (London: Penguin Books, 1999).

Royal College of Nursing, *Tuppence for the Doctor, Penny for the Nurse: Memories of Public Health Nursing* (2010).

Royal Commission for the Housing of the Working Classes (London: HMSO, 1884–85).

Samuel, Raphael, *The Lost World of British Communism* (London: Verso, 2006).

Sansom, William, 'A Public for Jive' in *The Public's Progress*, ed. A.G. Weidenfeld (London: Contact Publications, 1947) pp.56–62.

Saville, John, *The Labour Movement in Britain: A Commentary* (London: Faber and Faber, 1988).

Schmiechen, James A., *Sweated Industries and Sweated Labour: The London Clothing Trades 1860–1914* (London: Croom Helm, 1984).

Shaw, C.D., and W.R. Winterton, *The Middlesex Hospital: The Names of the Wards and the Story they Tell* (London: Friends of the Middlesex Hospital, 1983).

Smith, F.B., *The People's Health 1830–1910* (London: Croom Helm, 1979).

Sponza, Lucio, *Italian Immigrants in Nineteenth Century Britain: Realities and Images* (Leicester: Leicester University Press, 1988).

Stedman-Jones, Gareth, *Metropolis: Outcast London: A Study in the Relationship Between Classes in Victorian Society* (Oxford: Clarendon Press, 1971).

Summers, Judith, *Soho: A History of London's Most Colourful Neighbourhood* (London: Bloomsbury Publishing, 1989).

Thomas, Edith, *Louise Michel*, trans. Penelope Williams (Montreal: Black Rose, c. 1980).

Tinkler, Penny, 'Cause for Concern: Young Women and Leisure, 1930–50', *Women's History Review*, 12.2 (2003) pp.233–62.

Tonkiss, Fran, *Space, the City and Social Theory: Social Relations and Urban Forms* (Cambridge: Polity Press, 2005).

Visram, Rosina, *Asians in Britain: 400 Years of History* (London: Pluto Press, 2002).

Walkowitz, Judith, *City of Dreadful Delight: Narratives of Sexual Danger in Late-Victorian London* (Chicago: University of Chicago Press, 1992).

Walkowitz, Judith, *Nights Out: Life in Cosmopolitan London* (New Haven: Yale University Press, 2012).

Welsh, David, *Underground Writing: The London Tube from George Gissing to Virginia Woolf* (Liverpool: Liverpool University Press, 2010).

White, Jerry, *London in the Nineteenth Century: 'A Human Awful Wonder of God'* (London: Jonathan Cape, 2007).

White, Jerry, *London in the Twentieth Century: A City and its People* (London: Viking, 2001).

Wise, David Burgess, *History of the British Automobile Industry and of the Society of Motor Manufacturers and Traders* (London: Society of Motor Manufacturers and Traders, 2002).

Wohl, Anthony S., *The Eternal Slum: Housing and Social Policy in Victorian London* (London: Arnold, 1977).

Wray, Margaret, *The Women's Outerwear Industry* (Industrial Innovation Series, London: Gerald Duckworth & Co. Ltd, 1957).

Xeni: Greek-Cypriots in London, Thanis Papathanasiou trans. (London: Ethnic Communities Oral History Project, 1990).

Yoxall, Sir James, *More About Collecting* (London: Stanley Paul, 1921).

Notes

Introduction

1 Fiber, Sally, *The Fitzroy: The Autobiography of a London Tavern* (Sussex: Temple House Books, 1995) p.2.

2 David, Hugh, *The Fitzrovians: A Portrait of Bohemian Society 1900–1955* (London: Sceptre, 1989) p.135.

3 Burke, Thomas, *Nights in Town* (London: George Allen & Unwin, 1915) p.187.

4 David, p.126.

5 David, p.169.

6 David, p.128.

7 David, p.135.

8 David, p.171.

9 David, p.188.

10 Maclaren-Ross, Julian, *Memoirs of the Forties* (London: Cardinal, 1991) p.vii.

11 Maclaren-Ross, pp.138–39.

12 Maclaren-Ross, pp.138–39.

13 See especially http://www.british-history.ac.uk/survey-london/vol21/pt3/pp1-6, the introduction to the survey of Tottenham Court Road area and surrounds.

14 Ackroyd, Peter, *London: The Biography* (London: Chatto & Windus, 2000) p.57.

15 Walkowitz, Judith, *City of Dreadful Delight: Narratives of Sexual Danger in Late-Victorian London* (Chicago: University of Chicago Press, 1992) p.29.

16 Bailey, Nick, *Fitzrovia* (New Barnet, Herts: Historical Publications/Camden History Society, 1981) p.16.

17 Bailey, p.20.

Chapter 1

1 White, Jerry, *London in the Twentieth Century: A City and its People* (London: Viking, 2001) p.103.

2 White, *London in the Twentieth Century*, pp.103–04.

3 'Twenty Years in Soho' quoted in Black, Gerry. *Living Up West: Jewish Life in London's West End* (London: Jewish Museum, London, 1994).

4 White, *London in the Twentieth Century*, p.96.

5   David, pp.84–85.

6   White, *London in the Twentieth Century*, p.104.

7   Lipman, V.D., *The Social History of the Jews in England, 1850–1950* (London: Watts & Co., 1954) p.65.

8   Lipman, p.66.

9   Mayhew, Henry, *Mayhew's London*, ed. Peter Quennell (London: Bracken Books, 1984) pp.285–86.

10   Mayhew, p.286.

11   Black, p.21.

12   Black, p.13.

13   White, Jerry, *London in the Nineteenth Century: 'A Human Awful Wonder of God'* (London: Jonathan Cape, 2007) p.145.

14   Ashton, Rosemary, *Little Germany: Exile and Asylum in Victorian England* (Oxford: OUP, 1986) pp.238–39.

15   White, *London in the Nineteenth Century*, p.143.

16   Sponza, Lucio, *Italian Immigrants in Nineteenth Century Britain: Realities and Images* (Leicester: Leicester University Press, 1988) p.20.

17   Quoted in Sponza, p.106.

18   Visram, Rosina, *Asians in Britain: 400 Years of History* (London: Pluto Press, 2002).

19   Beatrice Potter quoted in Stedman-Jones, Gareth, *Metropolis: Outcast London: A Study in the Relationship Between Classes in Victorian Society* (Oxford: Clarendon Press, 1971) pp.283–84.

20   Allen, Michelle, *Cleansing the City: Sanitary Geographies in Victorian London* (Athens, Ohio: Ohio University Press, 2008) p.134.

21   Machray, Robert, *The Night Side of London* (London: J. McQueen, 1902).

22   House of Commons (HC) debate, 12 November 1912.

23   Feldman, David, *Englishmen and Jews: Social Relations and Political Culture 1840–1914* (New Haven, CT: Yale University Press, 1994) p.78.

24   White, Jerry, *London in the Twentieth Century*, p.112.

25   Jewish Museum Audio, 485.

26   Jewish Museum Audio, 485.

27   Jewish Museum Audio, 299.

28   Jewish Museum Audio, 304.

29   Jewish Museum Audio, 304.

30   Jewish Museum Audio, 304.

31   Jewish Museum Audio, 304.

32   Jewish Museum Audio, 369.

33   Jewish Museum Audio, 369.

34   Jacobson, Barb, and Olive Leonard, *Ebb and Flow in Fitzrovia: Interviews with Pensioners in and around Carburton Street, W1* (London: Fitzrovia Neighbourhood Association, 2010) p15.

35   Jacobsen and Leonard, p.33.

36   Jewish Women in London Group, *Generations of Memories: Voices of Jewish Women* (London: The Women's Press, 1989) p.197.

37   Xeni, trans. Thasis Papathanasiou, *London: Ethnic Communities Oral History Project*, 1990, p.8.

38   Xeni, p.8.

39   Xeni, p.10.

40   Jacobsen and Leonard, p.47.

41   Bailey, p.66.

42   Jacobsen and Leonard, p.15.

43   Summers, Judith, *Soho: A History of London's Most Colourful Neighbourhood* (London: Bloomsbury Publishing, 1989) p.169.

44   Summers, p.169.

Chapter 2

1   Tonkiss, Fran, *Space, the City and Social Theory. Social Relations and Urban Forms* (Cambridge: Polity Press, 2005) p.59.

2   Ash, Maurice, *Guide to the Structure of London* (Bath: Adams & Dart, 1972) p.16.

3   Hansard Online, London County Council (Tramways and Improvements) Bill, Mr James Remnant, 9 June 1904. Complicating things further, transport authority over this area was split between the LCC which controlled transport from Euston Road southwards, and the County of Middlesex which controlled it from Hampstead Road northwards.

4   HC debate, 10 May 1927.

5   Jewish Museum Audio, 485.

6   The first Tube railway line, the City and South London Railway, opened in 1890 running between the City and Stockwell.

7   Bruce, J. Graeme, and Desmond F. Croome, *The Central Line: An Illustrated History* (2nd ed. Harrow, Middx: The Central Line London Underground Ltd, 2006) p.18.

8   Warren Street Station was at first called Euston Road, but was renamed in 1908. Confusingly, Goodge Street Station was called Tottenham Court Road but was renamed in 1908, presumably when Tottenham Court Road Station's original name of Oxford Street Station was changed.

9   Welsh, David, *Underground Writing: The London Tube from George Gissing to Virginia Woolf* (Liverpool: Liverpool University Press, 2010) p.162.

10   Quoted in Welsh, pp.208–09.

11   MOH Report for St Pancras 1906, p.87.

12   MOH Report for St Pancras 1906, p.90.

13   Hansard online, HC Debate, 21 October 1946.

14   Jewish Museum Audio, 306.

15   Jewish Museum Audio, 299.

16   Horne, Mike, *The Last Link: The First 30 Years of the Hampstead Railway* (London: London Underground Ltd [Northern Line] and Nebulous Books, 2007) p.27.

17   Wise, David Burgess, *History of the British Automobile Industry and of the Society of Motor Manufacturers and Traders* (London: Society of Motor Manufacturers and Traders, 2002) pages not numbered.

18   *List of Car Dealers* (6th ed., London: Society of Motor Manufacturers and Traders, 1937–38).

19   Llewellyn-Smith, Sir Hubert, *New Survey of London Life and Labour*, Vol. 1 (London: P.S. King & Son, 1934) p.189.

20   Cabmen's shelters, small green-painted huts, had been built in London since 1875 so that cab drivers could have somewhere to shelter in poor weather and to eat and rest. They often had an attendant who looked after the shelter and cooked food for the men. One of these shelters, since demolished, was in Great Portland Street.

21   Llewellyn-Smith, p.299.

22   See minutes of St Pancras Borough Council dated 29 July 1959.

23   There was already a small pedestrian subway across Euston Road attached to Euston Road Station, created during a station refurbishment between 1929 and 1931.

24   Jacobsen & Leonard, p.30.

25   Jacobsen & Leonard, p.30.
26   The entrance to Friswell's was on Albany Street and nickelinthemachine.com dates Friswell's to as long ago as 1902.
27   O'Connell, Sean, *The Car in British Society: Class, Gender and Motoring 1896–1939, Studies in Popular Culture* (Manchester: Manchester University Press, 1938) p.33.
28   nickelinthemachine.com, accessed 10 December 2015.
29   Tonkiss, p.64
30   Jewish Museum Audio, 319.
31   Jacobsen & Leonard, p.34.
32   Jacobsen & Leonard, p.34.
33   Welsh, p.221.
34   New deep-level shelters were also built at several stations on the Northern Line including at Goodge Street. They were finished by September 1942 but were used for military purposes rather than by the public at first, as the heavy bombing had ceased by then. They were used by the public when raids began again in 1944. Mike Horne records that the still-existing shelters are now used by archive companies as storage space.
35   Many people still had to rely on Anderson shelters in back gardens, indoor Morrison shelters or other types of surface or basement shelter. The Tube played a vital role in the West End, but it was far from being able to protect everyone.

Chapter 3

1   Allen, p.124.
2   Allen, pp.125–26.
3   University College had at first expected its new Faculty of Medicine to be located at the Middlesex, but the Middlesex's governors refused, apparently because a connection with UCLH, the non-sectarian 'Godless institution in Gower Street', risked putting off influential donors. However, a look at histories of UCLH also suggests reluctance among members of University College to make the move to the Middlesex.
4   Armstrong, David, *Political Anatomy of the Body: Medical knowledge in Britain in the Twentieth Century* (London: CUP, 1983) p.8.
5   Jacobsen & Leonard, p.19.
6   MOH Report 1900, p.10.
7   MOH Report 1920, pp.13, 15.
8   Testimony to the Royal Commission on the Housing of the Working Classes, 1884.
9   Allen, pp.125–26.
10   Jewish Museum Audio, 299.
11   Jewish Museum Audio, 319.
12   Jewish Museum Audio, 306.
13   MOH Report 1950, p.4.
14   The Women's Co-operative Guild was the women's branch of the Co-operative Society, whose mainly working-class customers were also Co-op members and shared in their branches' profits.
15   Preface to Davies, Margaret Llewellyn (ed.), *Maternity: Letters from Working Women Collected by the Women's Co-operative Guild* (London: Virago, 1978).
16   Lewis, Jane, *The Politics of Motherhood: Child and Maternal Welfare in England, 1900–1939* (London: Croom Helm, 1980) p.16.
17   Lewis, p.17.
18   Jacobsen & Leonard, p.15.
19   *Nursing Standard*, Vol. 8, Issue 45 (1994) p.42.

20   Rawlinson, Carole, *Middlesex Memories* (London: University College London Hospitals Charities, 2007) p.46.

21   Rawlinson, p.64.

22   Rawlinson, p.46.

23   This is the only set of community health hospital leaflets I saw in the hospital archives, although much has yet to be catalogued and there might be others that have survived.

24   Jacobsen & Leonard, pp.32–33.

25   Jacobsen & Leonard, pp.19.

26   Shaw, C.D., and W.R. Winterton, *The Middlesex Hospital: The Names of the Wards and the Story they Tell* (London: Friends of the Middlesex Hospital, 1983) p.8.

27   Handley, R.S. Gordon-Taylor, 'Breast Cancer and the Middlesex Hospital', *Annals of the Royal College of Surgeons of England*, Vol. 49 (Sept 1971) pp.151–64.

28   Handley, W. Sampson (ed.) *Cancer Research at the Middlesex Hospital, 1900–1924: Retrospect and Prospect* (London: John Murray, 1924) p.43.

29   R.S. Handley, p.13, original italics.

30   Ranger, Sir Douglas, *The Middlesex Hospital Medical School 1935–1985* (London: Hutchinson Benham, 1985) p.109.

31   See http://rcnarchive.rcn.org.uk/data/VOLUME084-1936/page146-volume84-june1936.pdf

32   Royal College of Nursing. *Tuppence for the Doctor, Penny for the Nurse: Memories of Public Health Nursing* (2010) p.5.

33   Davies, p.36.

34   The rate in some industrialised areas outside London such as Liverpool was higher still, even exceeding 200 deaths per 1,000 live births.

35   MOH Report 1910 for St Pancras, p.29.

36   MOH Report 1910 for St Pancras, p.29.

37   Quoted in Lewis, pp.97–98.

38   Lewis, p.98.

39   Smith, F.B., *The People's Health 1830–1910* (Croom Helm Social History Series, London: Croom Helm, 1979) p.124.

40   Wohl, Anthony S., *The Eternal Slum: Housing and Social Policy in Victorian London* (London: Arnold, 1977) p.303.

41   Jewish Museum Audio, 304.

42   Communist Party of Great Britain, *St Pancras: Homes or Slums?* (London: CPGB, 1945).

43   Davies, p.56.

44   Merrington, W.R., *University College Hospital and its Medical School: A History* (London: Heinemann, 1976) p.121.

45   Merrington, p.121.

46   Merrington, p.143.

47   St Pancras MOH Report, p.11.

48   *Middlesex Hospital Journal*, October 1936, Vol. XXXVI, No. 5.

Chapter 4

1   Bailey, p.26.

2   Edwards, C., 'Tottenham Court Road: The Changing Fortunes of London's Furniture Street 1850–1950', *London Journal*, 36.2, pp.140–60.

3   Hall, P.G., *Industries of London since 1861* (London: Hutchinson University Library, 1962) p.72.

4   Hall, p.83.

5   Hall, p.83.

6   Edwards. This shows a decline from 1872, when ten workshops operated in Cleveland Street also, while Charlotte Street had fourteen. By that time workshops had increased north of Euston Road, perhaps due to lack of space around Tottenham Court Road.

7   Heal, Oliver S., *Sir Ambrose Heal and the Heal Cabinet Factory 1897–1939* (Wetherby, Yorks.(?): Oblong Creative Ltd, 2014) p.126.

8   Heal, p.129.

9   Heal, p.129.

10 Benton, Tim, 'Up and Down at Heal's: 1929–1935', *Architectural Review*, No. 972 (February 1978) pp.109–16.

11 Massil, William I., *Immigrant Furniture Workers in London 1881–1939: and the Jewish Contribution to the Furniture Trade; a Supplement* (London: Jewish Museum, 2000) p.vi.

12 British Furniture Trades Joint Committee, *Report to the British Furniture Trades Joint Committee … into Wages and Working Conditions Prevailing in Certain Sections of the Furniture Manufacturing Trade in London during 1938* (London: British Furniture Trades Joint Committee, 1938) p.3.

13 Massil, p.xix.

14 British Furniture Trades Joint Committee Report, p.3.

15 British Furniture Trades Joint Committee Report, p.5.

16 British Furniture Trades Joint Committee Reort, p.4.

17 Kirkham, Pat, et al., *Furnishing the World: The East London Furniture Trade 1830–1980* (London: Journeyman Press Ltd, 1987) p.102.

18 Reid, Hew, *Furniture Makers: A History of Trade Unionism in the Furniture Trade 1865–1972* (Oxford: Malthouse Press, 1986) p.145.

19 Quoted in Reid, p.145.

20 Kirkham et al., p.6.

21 British Furniture Trades Joint Committee Report, p.4.

22 Kirkham et al., p.89.

23 Reid, p.135.

24 Reid, p.138.

25 Edwards, pp.13–14.

26 Attfield, Judy, '"Then we were making furniture, and no money": A Case Study of J. Clarke, Wycombe Furniture Makers', *Oral History*, 18.2 (1990) pp.54–57.

27 Attfield, pp.54–55.

28 Cohen, Max, *What Nobody Told the Foreman* (London: Spalding & Levy Ltd, 1953) p.122.

29 Max Cohen, p.122.

30 Harold Rodgers, cabinetmaker, apprenticed to Waring & Gillows in Lancaster 1905, retired in 1959: quoted in Kirkham, Pat, 'Recollections of Furniture Makers: Labour History, Oral History and Furniture Studies', *Furniture History*, 14 (1978) pp.23–30.

31 Yoxall, Sir James. *More About Collecting* (London: Stanley Paul, 1921) p.73.

32 Forster, E.M., *Room with a View* (London: Penguin, 1955) p.108.

33 Eastlake, Charles L., *Hints on Household Taste in Furniture, Upholstery and Other Details* (4th ed., London: Longmans, Green, 1878) p.63.

34 Cohen, Deborah, *Household Gods: The British and their Possessions* (New Haven, Conn.: Yale University Press, 2006) p.146.

35 Deborah Cohen, p.146.

36 Deborah Cohen, p.155.

37 Adburgham, Alison, 'Give the Customers What They Want', *Architectural Review* Vol. 161 (May 1977) pp.295–301.

38   Deborah Cohen, p.157.
39   Adburgham, p.300.
40   Adburgham, p.296.
41   https://architokyo.wordpress.com/japan-british1910/
42   Itoh, Keiko, *Japanese Community in Pre-War Britain: From Integration to Disintegration* (Richmond, Surrey: Curzon Press, 2001) p.78.
43   Itoh, p.78.
44   Quoted in Itoh, p.80.
45   Quoted in Itoh, p.81.
46   Itoh, p.168.

Chapter 5

1   Quoted in Breward, Christopher, 'Fashion's Front and Back: "Rag Trade" Cultures and Cultures of Consumption in Post-War London *c.* 1945–1970', *London Journal*, 31: 1 (June 2006) pp.15–40, 30.
2   Breward, p.33.
3   Jacobsen & Leonard, p.34.
4   Hall, pp.44–45.
5   Breward, p.17.
6   Breward, p.18.
7   Breward, p.24.
8   Breward, p.25.
9   Quoted in Hall, p.53.
10   Potter's 'peculiar' is more likely to have meant 'distinct' than 'strange'.
11   Dobbs, S.P., *Clothing Workers of Great Britain* (London: Routledge, 1928) pp.24–25.
12   Kershen, Anne J., *Off the Peg: Jewish Mantle Making Trade Unions of London* (London: London Museum of Jewish Life, *c.* 1988) p.15.
13   Black, p.55.
14   Dobbs, p.7.
15   Dobbs, p.178.
16   Dobbs, p.185.
17   Jewish Museum Audio, 485.
18   Wray, Margaret, *The Women's Outerwear Industry* (Industrial Innovation Series, London: Gerald Duckworth & Co. Ltd, 1957) p.58.
19   Apparel and Fashion Industry Association, *Present Position of the Apparel and Fashion Industry* (London: AFIA, 1950) p.44.
20   Quoted in Black, p.58.
21   Quoted in Black, p.58.
22   See Alexander, Sally, 'Becoming a Woman in London in the 1920s and 1930s' in *Metropolis: London* (ed. David Feldman and Gareth Stedman Jones) (London: Routledge, 1989) note 23.
23   Black, Clementina, 'London's Tailoresses', *Economic Journal* 14:56 (December 1904) pp.555–67.
24   Hicks, Frances, 'Dressmakers and Tailoresses' in *Workers on their Industries* (ed. F.W. Galton) (London: Swan Sonnenschein & Co. Ltd, 1896) p.16.
25   Hicks, pp.16–17.
26   Hicks, p.19.
27   Selfridges' archives aren't freely accessible to the public as they are held privately.

28 Wray, p.35.
29 Ashmore, Sonia, et al., '"Mr Bourne's Dilemma": Consumer Culture, Property Speculation and Department Store Demise: the Rise and Fall of Bourne & Hollingsworth on London's Oxford Street', *Journal of Historical Geography* 38 (2012) pp.434–46.
30 Alexander, p.264.
31 Celia Wilmot, quoted in Alexander, p.264.
32 Jacobsen & Leonard, pp.36–37.
33 www.europeana.eu/portal/en
34 www.europeana.eu/portal/en
35 Newby, Eric, *Something Wholesale* (London: Hodder and Stoughton, 1970) p.39.
36 Ashmore, p.439.
37 Breward, p.18.
38 Dobbs, p.7.
39 Schmiechen, James A., *Sweated Industries and Sweated Labour: The London Clothing Trades 1860–1914* (London: Croom Helm, 1984) p.145.
40 Gerry Black, p.56.

Chapter 6

1   David, p.95.
2   Ackroyd, p.474.
3   Ackroyd, p.463.
4   David, p.85.
5   Bloom, Clive, *Violent London: 2,000 Years of Riots, Rebels and Revolts* (London: Pan Books, 2004) p.195.
6   See the UCLH Survey of London, https://blogs.ucl.ac.uk/survey-of-london/tag/hanway-street/
7   David, p.94.
8   Pankhurst, Sylvia, *The Suffragette Movement: An Intimate Account of Persons and Ideals* (London: Virago Limited, 1977) p.90.
9   Pankhurst, pp.90–91.
10 Walkowitz, Judith, *Nights Out: Life in Cosmopolitan London* (New Haven: Yale University Press, 2012) p.23.
11 Sponza, p.19.
12 See sarahjyoung.com/site/2011/01/09/
13 Rocker, Rudolf, *The London Years* (Nottingham: Five Leaves Press, 2005) pp.22–23.
14 Rocker, p.23.
15 Di Paola, Pietro, *Italian Anarchists in London 1870–1914* (London: University of London, 2004) p.123.
16 Thomas, Edith, *Louise Michel* (trans. Penelope Williams) (Montreal: Black Rose, c. 1980, p.318.
17 See Nick Heath, libcom.org/history/a-rose-any-other-name-radical-history-manette-street-london
18 Di Paola, p.47.
19 See alphabetthreat.co.uk/pasttense/communistclub.html
20 Rocker, p.15.
21 Quail, John, *The Slow Burning Fuse: The Lost History of the British Anarchists* (St Albans, Herts: Granada Publishing, 1978) p.164.

22   Quail, p.168. Quail gives a detailed account of the circumstances of the Greenwich Park explosion on pages 162–68.

23   Quail, p.165.

24   Rocker, p.15.

25   Rocker, p.17.

26   Rocker, p.15.

27   Rocker, p.16.

28   Rocker, p.16.

29   Hansard HC debate, 4 April 1881.

30   Rocker, p.17.

31   Rocker, p.17.

32   London Metropolitan Archive (LMA) 070/1 – 5 – LCC Architect's Department: Theatres.

33   Quoted in Di Paola, p.216.

34   LMA 070/1 – 5.

35   Quail, p.216.

36   See Saville, John, *The Labour Movement in Britain: A Commentary* (London: Faber and Faber, 1988) pp.25–26.

37   Quail, p.220.

38   India Office – 'Memorandum on the Anti-British Agitation Among Natives of India in England' (1909) IOR/R/2/Box 33/312, p.5.

39   India Office Memorandum, p.8.

40   Datta, V.N., *Madan Lal Dhingra and the Revolutionary Movement* (New Delhi: Vikas Publishing House PVT Limited, 1978) p.45.

41   India Office Memorandum, p.12.

42   Old Bailey online.

43   *The Guardian*, 29 September 2006.

44   Rocker, pp.120–21.

45   Rocker, pp.108–09.

46   Rocker, p.128.

47   Rocker, pp.130–31.

48   Rocker, pp.130–31.

49   Bloom, p.306.

50   1935 Manifesto, *For Soviet Britain*, quoted in Bloom p.299.

51   libcom.org/history/revolutionary-youth

52   alphabetthreat.co.uk/pasttense/communistclub.html

53   alphabetthreat.co.uk/pasttense/communistclub.html

54   http://libcom.org/history/revolutionary-youth

55   After 1920, branches of the Labour Party continued to work with Communists at local level even though official Labour Party policy was to disassociate itself as much as possible from the CPGB. Battersea Trades Council and Labour Party, for instance, had supported the Communist Party member Sharpurti Saklatvala at the general elections of 1922, 1923 and 1924 when he stood for Battersea North. In 1924, the Labour Party Conference decided that no member of the CPGB could stand for election as a Labour candidate.

56   Morris, Margaret, *The General Strike* (Harmondsworth, Middx: Penguin Books, 1976) p.46.

57   *Camden Journal*, 14 May 1976.

58   Marylebone Council minutes for 20 June 1926.

59   Jewish Museum Audio, 369.

60   Jewish Museum Audio, 369.

61   Haldane, Charlotte, *Truth Will Out* (London: Weidenfeld and Nicholson, 1949) p.182.

62 Haldane, p.183.
63 Haldane, p.185.
64 Samuel, Raphael, *The Lost World of British Communism* (London: Verso, 2006) p.67.
65 See *Radical London in the 1950s* by David Mathieson (2017); also http://www.whatnextjournal.org.uk, issues 7, 8, 10, 14.
66 See nickelinthemachine.com
67 Beckman, Morris, *The 43 Group* (2nd ed., London: Centerprise Publications, 1993) p.200.
68 Beckman, p.16.
69 See news.fitzrovia.org.uk/2012/07/07/ronnie-kasrils-and-anti-apartheid-charlotte-street/

Chapter 7

1 In its earlier days at least, the Oxford was known as a place for prostitutes to gather and in 1871 there were objections to its renewing its licence, although the police had no objections and spoke in support of the management. See Kift, Dagmar, *The Victorian Music Hall: Culture, Class and Conflict* (New York: Cambridge University Press, 1996) pp.137–38.
2 Jacobsen & Leonard, p.14.
3 catsmeatshop.blogspot.co.uk/2010/11, accessed 12 January 2015.
4 Pulling, Christopher, *They Were Singing: And What They Sang About* (London: George C. Harrap and Co., 1952) p.141.
5 *Cassell's Magazine*, 1909, p.507.
6 Mander, Raymond, and Joe Mitchenson, *The Lost Theatres of London* (London: Hart-Davis, 1968) p.447.
7 Jewish Museum Audio, 351.
8 Briggs, Asa, *The Golden Age of Wireless. The History of Broadcasting in the United Kingdom*, Vol. 2 (London: OUP, 1965) p.175.
9 Jewish Museum Audio, 351.
10 Nasaw, David, *Going Out: The Rise and Fall of Public Amusements* (New York: HarperCollins, 1993) p.157.
11 Burrows, Jon, 'Penny Pleasures: Film Exhibition in London During the Nickelodeon Era, 1906–1914', *Film History*, Vol. 16 (2004) pp.60–91, 86.
12 MEPO 2/9172 No. 590446/5.
13 MEPO 2/9172 No. 590446/5.
14 MEPO 2/9172 No. 590446/5.
15 Petley, Julian, 'Cinema and State' in *All Our Yesterdays: 90 Years of British Cinema*, (ed. Charles Barr) (London: BFI, 1986) p.41.
16 Burrows, pp.82, 86.
17 Eyles, Allen, and Keith Skone, *London's West End Cinemas* (Sutton: Keystone Publications, 1991) p.11.
18 The bioscope.net, accessed 7 August 2017.
19 See londonfilm.bbk.ac, accessed 28 January 2015; cinematreasures.org/theaters
20 The Oxford Hall was converted, not into a cinema but a review theatre, in 1917, as review grew in popularity (Kift 25).
21 McKernan, Luke, '"Only the Screen was Silent"...: Memories of Children's Cinema-Going in London before the First World War', *Film Studies*, Issue 10 (Spring 2007) pp.1–20, 2.
22 *Westminster Gazette* dated 5 March 1912.

23   LCC Sunday Cinematograph Entertainments, MEPO 2/9172 No. 590446/35.

24   Medhurst, Andy, 'Music Hall and British Cinema' in *All our Yesterdays: 90 Years of British Cinema* (ed. Charles Barr) (London: BFI, 1986) pp.169–73.

25   Jewish Museum Audio, 351.

26   Aston, Mark, *Cinemas of Camden: A Survey and History of the Cinema Buildings of Camden, Past and Present* (London: Camden Leisure and Community, 1997) pp.13–14.

27   www.dieselpunks.org/profiles/blogs/going-to-the-cinema, accessed 30 January 2015.

28   Brown, J. Neill. 'The Industry's Front Page' in *All Our Yesterdays: 90 Years of British Cinema*, ed. Charles Barr. London: BFI, 1986, 134.

29   Newsreels came out twice a week by the 1930s. See Brown, in *All Our Yesterdays*.

30   Brown, p.135.

31   Brown, p.137.

32   Pronay, Nicholas, 'British Newsreels in the 1930s: Audience and Producers' in *Yesterday's News: The British Cinema Newsreel Reader* (ed. Luke McKernan) (London: BUFVC, 2002) p.142.

33   Brown, p.134.

34   Pronay, p.232.

35   Both houses closed again in 1976 and were demolished, their sites forming part of a large retail and office development in which was the Classic Cinema, opened in July 1981. The Classic was later to become the Odeon Tottenham Court Road, well after the earlier Odeon had closed in 1960. See cinematreasures.org/theatres.

36   Marshall, Edward, '"The Dark Alien Executive": Jewish Producers, Emigres and the British Film Industry in the 1930s' in *New Directions in Anglo-Jewish History* (ed. Geoffrey Alderman) (Brighton, MA: Academic Studies Press, 2010).

37   *The Leader* 17 November 1945, p.19.

38   See Mander, Raymond, and Joe Mitchenson, *The Theatres of London* (London: New English Library, 1975) p.181.

39   Howard, Diana, *London Theatres and Music Halls 1850–1950* (London: Library Association, 1970) p.215.

40   Mander and Mitchenson, *Theatres of London*, pp.182–83.

41   London Metropolitan Archives, GLC/AR/BR/19/0448.

42   Mander and Mitchenson, *Theatres of London*, p.184.

43   Luke McKernan, https://thebioscope.net/2011/12/11/the-delhi-durbar/

44   *Cinema News and Property Gazette*, April 1912, www.arthurlloyd.co.uk/Scala.htm, accessed 3 February 2015.

45   Luke McKernan, unpublished thesis material.

46   www.movinghere.org.uk/stories/story365, accessed 6 February 2015.

47   *The Leader*, 17 November 1945, p.19.

48   'Indian Film Festival Programme 1955', Asian Film Society (BFI Special Collection, 1955).

49   cinematreasures.org/theatres, Accessed 16 February 2015.

50   overthefootlights.co.uk, accessed 16 February 2015.

51   Theatre Collection, University of Bristol.

52   Farrar, David, *No Royal Road* (Eastbourne: Mortimer Publications Limited, 1947) p.49.

53   Farrar, pp.58–59.

54   Farrar, p.61.

55   Bristol Theatre Collection

56   Briggs, p.255.

57   Briggs, pp.253–54.

58   Television, which was broadcast from 1936 but then terminated for the duration of the war, only began to be a mass activity after 1950. The first widely watched transmission was the coronation of Queen Elizabeth II in 1953. It therefore plays little part in this book.

59 For more information about David Hughes see Pentelow, Mike, and Marsha Rowe, *Characters of Fitzrovia* (London: Chatto & Windus, 2001).

60 Hines, Mark, *The Story of Broadcasting House, Home of the BBC* (London: Merrell, 2008) p.114.

61 Briggs, p.172.

62 Mander & Mitchenson, *The Lost Theatres of London*, p.448.

63 See theatrestrust.org.uk

64 nationaljazzarchive.co.uk, accessed 11 August 2017.

65 Sansom, William, 'A Public for Jive' in *The Public's Progress* (ed. A.G. Weidenfeld, London: Contact Publications, 1947) p.58.

66 Sansom, p.56.

67 Guyan, Kevin, 'Glitter and Glamour: Race and Dance in 1940s London', https://www.ucl.ac.uk/equianocentre/blackpresenceblog/previous-posts/may-2013. Accessed 5 May 2017.

68 Guyan.

69 Tinkler, Penny, 'Cause for Concern: Young Women and Leisure, 1930–50', *Women's History Review*, 12.2 (2003) pp.233–22, 234.

70 Machray, p.227.

71 Machray, p.230.

72 Neal quoted in Judge, Roy, 'Mary Neal and the Espérance Morris', *Folk Music Journal*, Vol. 5, No. 5 (1989) pp.545–82, 547.

73 West London Mission Annual Report 1902–03, p.7.

74 Gerry Black, p.219.

75 Jewish Museum Audio, 304.

76 Jewish Museum Audio, 351, 319.

77 Jewish Museum Audio, 351.

78 Jewish Museum Audio, 304.

79 1901 West London Mission Annual Report, pp.42–43.

80 1901 West London Mission Annual Report, pp.42–43.

81 Montagu, Lily, *My Club and I: The Story of the West Central Jewish Club* (London: Herbert Joseph Limited, 1941) p.51.

82 Montagu, pp.52–53.

83 Montagu, p.57.

84 Montagu, p.57.

85 Dee, David, '"Nothing specifically Jewish in athletics"? Sport, Physical recreation and the Jewish Youth Movement in London, 1895–1914', *The London Journal*, 34.2 (July 2009) p.87.

86 Holdorph, Ann, '"If I strive not after my own salvation, who shall strive for me, and if not now, when?" The Role of Religion in the West Central Jewish Working Girls' Club, 1893–1939', *Women's History Review*, 24. 1 (2015) pp.37–52.

87 Jewish Museum Audio, 351.

88 There is some evidence that, although the Jewish Lads' and Girls' Clubs carried out some joint activities, some representatives of the Lads' Club management feared a detrimental Liberal Jewish influence on their own club from Lily Montagu's Girls' Club. At one point at the beginning of the 1930s, a Lad's Club subcommittee proposed starting their own girls' branch to counteract this influence. However, it seems as if nothing came of the suggestion. See Club Subcommittee Minutes dated 7 January 1931.

89 Jewish Museum Audio, 351.

Chapter 8

1   Jacobsen & Leonard, pp.44–45.
2   Panayi, Panikos, 'Sausages, Waiters and Bakers: German Migrants and Culinary Transfer to Britain *c.* 1850–1914', in S. Manz, et al. (eds), *Migration and Transfer from Germany to Britain 1660–1914* (Munchen: Saur, 2007) pp.147–59, 150.
3   Quoted in Sponza, p.228.
4   Mayhew, p.129.
5   MOH Report St Pancras 1911, p.108.
6   MOH Report St Pancras 1911, p.119.
7   Clayton, Antony, *London's Coffee Houses: A Stimulating Story* (London: Historical Publications, 2003) p.124.
8   Quoted in Clayton, p.124.
9   *Daily Mail*, 5 October 1921.
10 *Daily Mail*, 5 October 1921.
11 Panayi, Panikos, *Spicing Up Britain: The Multicultural History of British Food* (London: Reaktion Books, 2008) p.88.
12 news.fitzrovia.org.uk/2011/01/11, accessed 10 June 2016.
13 Burke, Thomas, *Nights in Town*, p.13.
14 Burke, Thomas, *Dinner is Served* (London: Routledge, 1937) pp.52–53.
15 news.fitzrovia.org.uk/2010/09/04, accessed 10 June 2016.
16 David, p.114.
17 Quoted in David, p.126.
18 Roden, Claudia, *The Book of Jewish Food: An Odyssey from Samarkand and Vilna to the Present Day* (London: Penguin Books, 1999) p.100.
19 *Fish Trades Gazette*, 14 Oct 1911.
20 'Down Whitechapel Way', 1 November 1851.
21 *Fish Trades Gazette*, 9 April 1921.
22 Claudia Roden says Irish, but Chatchip, and later Panayi, says French.
23 *Fish Trades Gazette*, 29 July 1922.
24 news.fitzrovia.org.uk/2011/01/11, accessed 12 June 2016.
25 Jacobsen & Leonard, p.33.
26 Panayi, Panikos, *Fish and Chips: A History* (London: Reaktion Books, 2014) p.44.
27 Clayton, p.139.
28 Gerry Black, p.76.
29 Fiber, p.15.
30 Fiber, p.16.
31 Bird, Peter, *The First Food Empire: A History of J. Lyons & Co.* (Chichester: Phillimore & Co., 2000) p.104.
32 Bird, p.103.
33 Walkowitz, *Nights Out*, p.195.
34 Jewish Museum Audio, 306.
35 Walkowitz, *Nights Out*, pp.194–195, 200–202.
36 Maclaren-Ross, p.156
37 www.history.ac.uk/ihr/Focus/War/londonRation.html, accessed 17 July 2016.
38 www.federationoffishfriers.co.uk/pages/history--599.htm, accessed 17 July 2016.
39 Jewish Museum Audio, 305.
40 Panayi, 'Sausages …', p.148.
41 Panayi, *Spicing* …, p79.
42 Panayi, *Spicing* …, p.83.

43 Panayi, *Spicing* ..., p.87.
44 Barber, Peter, and Peter Jacomelli, *Continental Taste, Ticinese Emigrants and their Cafe-Restaurants in Britain 1847–1987* (London: Camden History Society Occasional Paper 2, 1997) p.17.
45 Panayi, *Fish & Chips* ..., p.132.
46 Burke, *Nights in Town*, p.191.
47 Panayi, 'Sausages ...,' p.155.
48 Panayi, 'Sausages ...', p.155.
49 Drake in Smith, F.B., p.101.
50 Pratt, E.L., *The Impasse in the Catering Trade and the 'National Union' Way Out* (London: National Union of Catering Workers, 1915).
51 Barber and Jacomelli, p.10.
52 Panayi, *Spicing* ..., p.85.
53 Clayton, p.146.
54 Bailey, p.66.
55 Maclaren-Ross, p.155.
56 Clayton, p.154.
57 Burnett, John, *England Eats Out: A Social History of Eating Out in England from 1830 to the Present* (Harlow: Pearson Education Ltd, 2004) p.260.

Epilogue

1 http://www.dickensfellowship.org/save-cleveland-street-workhouse, accessed 8 May 2018.
2 http://fitzroviapartnership.com/wp-content/uploads/2017/07/Annex-public-exhibition-boards.pdf, accessed 8 May 2018.
3 news.fitzrovia.org.uk/2013/08/09, accessed 8 May 2018.

Index

Printed in Great Britain
by Amazon

16845287R00174